T0309800

THE SUCCESSFUL TRADER'S GUIDE TO MONEY MANAGEMENT

THE SUCCESSFUL TRADER'S GUIDE TO MONEY MANAGEMENT

Proven Strategies, Applications, and Management Techniques

Andrea Unger

WILEY

This edition first published 2021

© 2021 John Wiley & Sons, Ltd

Registered office
John Wiley & Sons Ltd, The Atrium, Southern Gate, Chichester, West Sussex, PO19 8SQ, United Kingdom

For details of our global editorial offices, for customer services and for information about how to apply for permission to reuse the copyright material in this book please see our website at www .wiley.com.

Library of Congress Cataloging-in-Publication Data is Available

ISBN 978-1-119-79880-4 (hardback)
ISBN 978-1-119-79882-8 (ePub)
ISBN 978-1-119-79881-1 (ePDF)

Cover Design: Wiley
Cover Image: © Andrea Unger

Set in 12/14pt, PerpetuaStd by SPi Global, Chennai, India
Printed and bound by CPI Group (UK) Ltd, Croydon, CR0 4YY

C9781119798804_300321

For the members of my family, who have always stood beside me and offered their support every day, also when taking the most difficult decisions.

CONTENTS

The second millennium began with the explosion of online trading in Europe, as the increase in the amount of available information and advertising of various kinds goes to show, encouraging many to try their luck at trading on the financial markets.

A considerable number of brokers set up shop and offered their services both for trading online and speculation on the markets, and new books are published almost every day, written by expert traders giving a great deal of advice on how to win on the markets. There are dozens of books on scalping, more on speculation in general, and even more on trading systems, not to mention those on technical analysis and even a few on trading psychology. An expert trader following the continuous evolution of these publications can't help but notice that (in Europe) one thing that's missing is a book that explains a subject that's by far the most important for he or she who wants to make trading their profession, in other words: *money management* (hereinafter referred to simply as M.m.).

In this book the author explains all the important points of how to manage your own capital in detail in consideration of the risk and the far-from-remote possibility that you might lose everything before you've even learnt how to place consistently winning trades on the market.

The author has explained the subject in a clear and frank way, making the book suitable for beginners and expert traders alike, and with the obstinacy of someone who's learned their lessons firsthand in the field he repeatedly emphasizes the importance of applying the right money management techniques. It would be a shame not to make the most of all the secrets this book has to offer.

The author's desire to help the reader understand that money management isn't the same as using a stop-loss can be found in every chapter. Also, the various methods discussed throughout the book, which are intrinsic to the strategies that can be applied to manage assets, let the trader prepare a plan of action for their M.m. that's as close as possible to perfect.

Anyone who reads this book will realise that technical analysis, trading systems, and various methods – no matter how valid they may be – are all but worthless without the effective management of your assets, and it would be a real shame if the reader failed to make the effort to apply some of the numerous suggestions they could make on their own after reading the book. The author, however, advises against using a poor strategy with the meticulous application of M.m. even if that can produce acceptable results, and this should perhaps make us reflect on the fact that the correct application of M.m., as well as protecting yourself from the risk of going bankrupt, can also help you obtain spectacular results that would be impossible without correct money management.

I love reading books on trading (I don't think many people have a collection as vast as mine on the subject), and I can truly say this book on money management is a must, and is the first complete and clear book to come out of Italy on how to apply M.m. to financial markets. I was lucky enough to be given the chance to read it first, and made good use of numerous suggestions to manage some futures' trading strategies, so I must compliment the author on the excellent work he's done in creating a book that's a real one of a kind – a book readers would do well to read and read again, always keeping it on hand to use as a point of reference to dispel any doubts on the correct way to manage the method they're adopting.

Domenico Foti

The trading world has changed considerably over the last two decades, and online trading has gradually transformed the sector from specialised to 'DIY', expanding to become so widespread it's now within reach of the investor from the comfort of his or her own home. The 1999 dot.com bubble made investing on the stock exchange more enticing than ever, with people dreaming of getting rich quick in a world that once mostly consisted of Treasury bills and bonds. When the bubble burst in spring 2000, it was, to say the least, painful for most of those who'd ventured into speculating on the stock exchange, and produced a variety of effects, leaving its mark also on those who weren't literally swept away by the crash.

A small number of speculators managed to adapt to the new market, people who'd been trading before the bubble, who'd already survived various ups and downs; and those who managed to turn what had once been a reckless gambler into a professional trader. These survivors, in turn, had an effect on other survivors, leading some to take the same route, revising their trading methods, and encouraging others to try and learn more about the specific sector in order to trade safely and emulate those who'd made their name in trading.

Gradually, more channels were created through which you could obtain trading information, courses were organised, conferences held, and books written promoting a variety of trading techniques.

The motto 'Cut your losses and let your profits run' is on everyone's lips, as is 'First, don't lose too much'. Scalping is the technique favoured by the masses, as all you need is a fast and reliable trading platform, and a marked propensity for interpreting short-term market movements. But many traders, born scalpers, gradually move away from this type of trading to try a less frenetic but perhaps also less enticing approach, and this is where trading systems came in, selling trading signals and courses to construct the same systems.

Those who follow me know I trade almost exclusively with automatic systems, as this is the approach that's best suited to planning your trading in detail.

The year 2008 was bad for the masses, and in time there were other sporadic events – such as the flash crash, the Fukushima meltdown, and the crisis of August 2015, which created more than a few obstacles to those who make a living or are just trying to survive on the stock exchange.

The trading industry opened its doors to the masses, trying to convince people all they needed was just a little time and money to obtain truly unbelievable results. At first the Forex market was promoted, emphasising the notable leverage that could be used, then there was a short-lived attempt to promote trading with options, which paved the way for CFDs, once again emphasising the concept that with little, you could make a lot. Then came binary options, which didn't actually have a lot to do with trading but still promised a road paved with gold, and last but not least cryptocurrencies, which in a way marked the end for binary options, but we're already waiting for the next fad, all riding the wave of greed.

When one mentions money management, though, these words can be interpreted ambiguously and cause confusion. Most people see money management as the rigorous application of a stop-loss, and a set of rules that produce risk/reward rations close to one-third. One classic example of this is a system that aims to make a profit three times the system stop, which is often considered a system with a good approach to money management. Nothing could be further from the truth!

Everything that concerns position management should be considered part of risk management, while money management is used to study what would be the best choice in terms of the percentage of the capital to use for a trade. Explained in such simple terms, it seems quite a banal thing a trader might not consider that important. My hope is to convince you, in the following pages, that this is not the case.

When I got my hands on my first futures' trading system report, it was clear that the monthly profit (or annual profit, depending on how you want to consider it) produced by the single contract analyses wasn't enough to live on or justify abandoning everything else to dedicate my time exclusively to that system. The first thing I thought was: What sort of profits could I make if I used more contracts instead of just one, and in relation to the results, with the same number of contracts, what would change during the negative period of the system in terms of drawdown? If a system made a profit of €10,000/year with one contract, it would certainly be interesting to consider using five contracts to make (or it might be better to say, try to make) €50,000; but the same system could have a maximum drawdown of €2,500, which with five contracts would become a loss of €12,500 at a certain time of the year, and it's therefore important to ask yourself if you could withstand such a loss and continue to follow the signals of the system without qualms.

So, calculating the number of contracts to use becomes much more important than one might think, and is even more so when you see the effect a correct approach to making this choice can have on the results.

Personally, I interpret money management only in terms of the science that tells me 'how much' to use and not how to do so. Some prefer to call this simply 'position sizing' and include risk management also as part of money management, but in my opinion this is a somewhat strained interpretation that does no damage, apart from causing a few misunderstandings.

Everything you'll find in this book can be used to get the best out of the trading system or technique you've decided is best suited to your needs, in order to maximize profits. It won't turn a losing trading system into a winning one, because the basic concept on which the trades are made must be laid on solid foundations.

CHAPTER 1

Martingale and Anti-Martingale

■ 1.1 The Right Stake

As mentioned in the introduction, money management (M.m) aims to establish the best stake to place when opening a trade or, in general, how much of your capital to use in the gamble you are about to embark on.

I think we all tend to adopt quite a simple statistical approach that encourages us to hope in a positive result after one or more negative results, and to fear repeating a success after placing a successful stake. In general, this is why you don't want to continue after a certain number of consecutive winning trades, while after a series of losing trades you'll be sure the next one will be a winner.

This tendency induces us to adopt a sort of risk management that, in general, leads us to increase the stakes after a negative period (betting on the fact that after various losses one should statistically expect a success) and reduce them after a positive period (for exactly the opposite reason).

In this chapter, we'll deal with this question by moving away from the trading environment, to enter a world we're all in any case familiar with: that of the coin toss.

Flipping a coin to see whether it lands heads or tails is a classic statistical example of 50% probability, and analyzing how we manage the stakes, on the basis of one event or another, can produce some surprising results.

This *isn't* trading, and the intention isn't to compare a trading system to betting. The purpose of this first part is simply to demonstrate what might be the best way to manage your available capital, when 'staking' part of it on an event.

If we take 100 people with €100 each, I don't think many would come out winning if they had to bet on a series of 100 or 1,000 coin tosses. In my opinion, most would lose all their capital due to inadequate risk management.

Of the resources to download, at the link https://autc.pro/guide you'll find the Excel file 'HeadOrTail.xls' you can use to run coin-toss simulations. This is the one I used for the various examples we'll be taking a look at.

As I said, let's suppose we have a capital of €100 and we'll use it for a series of 100 and 1,000 coin tosses, 'heads' wins, 'tails' loses. The win/loss ratio will be different for each analysis. In other words, let's imagine we lose €1 on every stake; the amount won, on the other hand, changes as we analyze various examples.

Stake calculation systems are mostly based on two styles that can be grouped together as *Martingale* systems and *anti-Martingale* systems. The first aim to increase exposure in the case of a loss; while the second only increase exposure after a win and decrease it in the case of a loss.

■ 1.2 Martingale

The Martingale system comes from the roulette wheel, and in practice is based on the impossibility of an infinite series of consecutive losses. Therefore, the concept is that the more consecutive losses there are, the greater the probability of a win next time. On this basis, the system involves doubling the stake after every loss. If you bet 1 on the first spin of the wheel, you'll bet 2 on the second if the first bet lost, and if you lose again you'll bet 4, then 8, and so on, and when you get a winning spin of the wheel you'll finally have made a profit. Note that, if you get a win on the second spin, you'd win 2, and after losing 1 on the first spin you'd be 1 up. If you lost also on the second spin, you'd have lost 1 + 2 = 3, so winning 4 on the third spin would again give you a profit of 1. If you lost on the third spin, you'd have lost 1 + 2 + 4 = 7, and winning on the fourth spin would make 8, giving you a profit of 8 − 7 = 1. As this simulation continues, we can see that, when we finally win, we make a profit of 1, just like we would have if we'd won on the first bet.

The above is true if you double the stake, and it's closely related to roulette-betting systems where one bets on red and black or odd and even numbers. In much more general terms, all approaches that simply increase the stake after a loss, and not just ones that double it, are called Martingale approaches; vice versa, these approaches decrease the stake after a win.

I'd like to emphasize that most people probably have a natural inclination to prefer a Martingale-type approach.

Now let's take a look at the simulations. The first is based on the supposition that, a win produces a profit of €1.25 for each €1 bet, while a loss loses the €1 bet. As mentioned above, the probability a coin toss comes down heads is 50%, so out of 1,000 tosses it should, in theory, land 500 times heads and 500 times tails, producing the final result:

$$500 * 1.25 + 500 * (-1) = 625 - 500 = 125$$

€125 at the end for every €1 bet. Obviously, this is pure theory and the situation must be studied more carefully, as must the strategy to adopt.

As we've said, each gambler has €100, so let's analyze the results of 14 gamblers using the Martingale approach, which increases the stake by a factor x after every loss. Each gambler starts with a different risk percentage and, in particular, for the first it's 1%, the second 2%, the third 3%, the fourth 4%, the fifth 5%, the sixth 10%, then 15%, 20%, 25%, 30%, 35%, 40%, 45%, and 50%.

The first gambler with a factor $x = 2$ on the first spin risking 1% bets €1 euro (1% of the €100 capital is €1). If he wins, he'll again bet 1% of the new capital €101.25 (he won €1.25), which is €1.0125. If he lost, however, he'll have €99, and using a factor $x = 2$, he'll double the initial risk to risk 2%, so

$$99 * 2/100 = €1.98$$

If the gambler wins, he'll go back to staking 1%; he would have won in the previous stake

$$1.98 * 1.25 = €2.475$$

and would therefore have a capital of €101.475, of which he'll stake

$$101.475 * 1/100 = €1.01475$$

If he lost, however, he'd have

$$99 - 1.98 = €97.02$$

At this point, he'd stake 4% (double the previous 2%) and bet

$$97.02 * 4/100 = €3.8808$$

and so on.

The second gambler will immediately stake 2% equal to €2 (2% of €100) and then proceed using the same logic; the third would start with €3 (3% of €100) and the last, daring or reckless, would start by betting €50 (50% of €100).

Figure 1.1 shows the results after 100 and 1,000 coin tosses. The simulation produced 53 heads and 47 tails in the first 100 tosses and a total of 467 heads and 533 tails after 1,000 tosses. Note that after 100 tosses, only the gamblers who bet less than 10% still have available funds, while those who started with a greater risk have used up all their capital. The gambler who started with 5% has increased his capital tenfold to €1,051.98. Note that the gamblers' luck was in; in fact, the wins amounted to 53% of the total. Continuing the game, however, after 1,000 tosses, all the gamblers have lost every last penny, perhaps also due to an unfavourable turn of events that brought the percentage of wins in the first 100 tosses down to 46.7%.

multiple = 2

Martingale (increase bet after loss)						
after 100 tosses				**after 1000 tosses**		
heads	53	53%		heads	467	46.7%
tails	47			tails	533	
% risk	ending capital	gain %		% risk	ending capital	gain %
1%	221.99	122%		1%	–	−100%
2%	410.97	311%		2%	–	−100%
3%	649.53	550%		3%	–	−100%
4%	887.26	787%		4%	–	−100%
5%	1,051.98	952%		5%	–	−100%
10%	70.55	−29%		10%	–	−100%
15%	–	−100%		15%	–	−100%
20%	–	−100%		20%	–	−100%
25%	–	−100%		25%	–	−100%
30%	–	−100%		30%	–	−100%
35%	–	−100%		35%	–	−100%
40%	–	−100%		40%	–	−100%
45%	–	−100%		45%	–	−100%
50%	–	−100%		50%	–	−100%

FIGURE 1.1 Loss 1, win 1.25 – double bet after loss. Note how in the first 100 tosses the scenario changes drastically, passing from 5% to 10% as initial risk.

multiple = 1.5

Martingale (increase bet after loss)					
after 100 tosses			after 1000 tosses		
heads	53	53%	heads	467	46.7%
tails	47		tails	533	
% risk	ending capital	gain %	% risk	ending capital	gain %
1%	145.99	46%	1%	23.67	−76%
2%	204.40	104%	2%	−	−100%
3%	274.90	175%	3%	−	−100%
4%	355.54	256%	4%	−	−100%
5%	442.63	343%	5%	−	−100%
10%	759.48	659%	10%	−	−100%
15%	507.48	407%	15%	−	−100%
20%	109.39	9%	20%	−	−100%
25%	2.83	−97%	25%	−	−100%
30%	−	−100%	30%	−	−100%
35%	−	−100%	35%	−	−100%
40%	−	−100%	40%	−	−100%
45%	−	−100%	45%	−	−100%
50%	−	−100%	50%	−	−100%

FIGURE 1.2   Loss 1, win 1.25 – multiply bet by 1.5 after loss. The final result is less 'harsh' than the previous case, but still isn't encouraging.

In Figure 1.2 the same scenario is analyzed in the case in which the gamblers, instead of doubling the percentage after every loss, multiply it by 1.5, a more 'conservative' approach that produces less drastic results.

The entire reasoning behind this is based on the percentages rather than on the resulting figures in euros. One could work on the basis of a hypothesis of starting with €1 and betting €2 in the case of a loss and then €4 after another loss, etc. In practice, this sort of approach would produce results similar to those shown, but with slightly more marked multiplication factors. Note, in fact, the gambler would have bet €2 instead of the €1.98 in the percentage example and €4 instead of €3.8808; note also that a higher multiplication factor causes more damage for the gamblers (the results of Figure 1.2 aren't as bad as those of Figure 1.1), so it's easy to see that the approach based on absolute stakes rather than percentages would have been even worse.

Figure 1.3 shows the Martingale approach, doubling the percentage on a new series of tosses in which, out of the first 100 as many of 57 tosses were wins and, of the 1,000 tosses, the number of wins was just over average at 502 wins, with 498 losses.

multiple = 2						
	Martingale (increase bet after loss)					
after 100 tosses			after 1000 tosses			
heads	57	57%	heads	502	50.2%	
tails	43		tails	498		
% risk	ending capital	gain %	% risk	ending capital	gain %	
1%	193.33	93%	1%	–	−100%	
2%	180.02	80%	2%	–	−100%	
3%	24.67	−75%	3%	–	−100%	
4%	–	−100%	4%	–	−100%	
5%	–	−100%	5%	–	−100%	
10%	–	−100%	10%	–	−100%	
15%	–	−100%	15%	–	−100%	
20%	–	−100%	20%	–	−100%	
25%	–	−100%	25%	–	−100%	
30%	–	−100%	30%	–	−100%	
35%	–	−100%	35%	–	−100%	
40%	–	−100%	40%	–	−100%	
45%	–	−100%	45%	–	−100%	
50%	–	−100%	50%	–	−100%	

FIGURE 1.3 Loss 1, win 1.25 – double stake after loss, a particular favourable situation in the first 100 tosses is in any case advantageous only for those who started betting low. After 1,000 tosses, the results are balanced without any advantages even for the more conservative approaches.

Despite this, the scenario is devastating and the results speak for themselves.

Figure 1.4 shows the same results with the stake multiplied by 1.5 instead of 2. The scenario is certainly less drastic but can hardly be considered encouraging. As the statistics were better than in the first case, how can we explain such a disappointing result?

A brief study of the logic behind the dynamics of increasing the stake sheds some light on this.

Let's suppose we start with 1%. We're in the following risk percentage situation doubling our bets, as in Table 1.1.

Note that after seven consecutive losing tosses, you would have to stake 128% of your remaining capital. This is obviously impossible to do, and you can only stake all you have (100%). After another losing toss, you'll have lost all your capital.

multiple = 1.5

Martingale (increase bet after loss)

	after 100 tosses			after 1000 tosses	
heads	57	57%	heads	502	50.2%
tails	43		tails	498	

% risk	ending capital	gain %	% risk	ending capital	gain %
1%	152.15	52%	1%	319.03	219%
2%	219.30	119%	2%	–	−100%
3%	300.11	200%	3%	–	−100%
4%	390.28	290%	4%	–	−100%
5%	482.03	382%	5%	–	−100%
10%	501.13	401%	10%	–	−100%
15%	–	−100%	15%	–	−100%
20%	–	−100%	20%	–	−100%
25%	–	−100%	25%	–	−100%
30%	–	−100%	30%	–	−100%
35%	–	−100%	35%	–	−100%
40%	–	−100%	40%	–	−100%
45%	–	−100%	45%	–	−100%
50%	–	−100%	50%	–	−100%

FIGURE 1.4   Loss 1, win 1.25 – multiply bet by 1.5 after loss, even increasing the stakes in a more conservative way still doesn't produce results that are anything to write home about.

TABLE 1.1

consecutive losing coin tosses	Percentage risked on next coin toss
0	1%
1	2%
2	4%
3	8%
4	16%
5	32%
6	64%
7	128% ???
8	Capital = zero

Starting with a higher percentage speeds up this process considerably, as Table 1.2, starting at 3%, shows.

Or even starting at 5%, as shown in Table 1.3.

TABLE 1.2

consecutive losing coin tosses	Percentage risked on next coin toss
0	3%
1	6%
2	12%
3	24%
4	48%
5	96%
6	192% -> 100%
7	Capital = zero

TABLE 1.3

consecutive losing coin tosses	Percentage risked on next coin toss
0	5%
1	10%
2	20%
3	40%
4	60%
5	120% -> 100%
6	Capital = zero

The above tables show that, starting with a 1% risk and doubling the percentage risked after every loss, a series of 8 consecutive losses would reduce the capital to zero. Starting on the other hand with 3% all the capital would be lost on the seventh consecutive loss, or the sixth if we start at 5%.

Fans of statistics can calculate the probability that a series of 100 coin tosses comes up 6, 7, or 8 consecutive times tails; they'll see this probability isn't as low as you might think. If they then continue with the analysis to include a series of 1,000 coin tosses the probability increases again. Here, we won't perform an analysis of this kind as it's quite a lengthy process, and in my opinion the results of the simulations provide a sufficiently clear example of the risk taken.

Note that the real problem with this approach is running out of capital, which, when you have to stake 100% you obviously run the risk of losing everything in the case of another loss. The same goes for playing roulette and placing your bet on red or black. Even leaving aside the fact that the ball might land on zero, which makes the odds worse than 50–50, a gambler could bet by doubling their stake each time they lose, but this approach could only be used if you had an infinite capital, with no stake limit. I must ask myself, who, having an infinite capital, would waste their time losing on the stock exchange or at roulette?

In the simulation we're studying, each gambler has an initial limit of €100, and after losing that, he'll be out of the game for good.

We've seen that our gamblers didn't have a lot of luck, and the result should discourage anyone who's considering using this approach in the hope of making money with it. So do you always lose everything, or almost? Not necessarily. Up to now, we've considered gamblers who, using a Martingale approach, increased their exposure in negative periods and decreased it in positive periods. In effect, no matter how logical it might seem from a certain point of view, this approach is totally illogical when we consider that, in practice, he who has less risks more, and he who has more risks less, which puts the approach in an entirely different light.

■ 1.3 Anti-Martingale

So, what can you do? We've mentioned the anti-Martingale system – in other words an approach that decreases exposure after a loss and increases it after a win. In practice, with this approach there's the tendency to increase your exposure as you make profits from winnings, and close defensively in losing periods.

In order to analyze what could have happened with this approach, we'll run the simulation simply using the same investment percentages for each stake. Some might say that in this way we aren't decreasing the stake after a loss and increasing it after a win, but in reality that's exactly what we'll do. In fact, we are not lowering (reducing) the percentage, but the capital to which it is applied will be smaller after a loss, so we will be betting more or less. The gambler who bets 1% of €100, in the case of a loss will have €99 and, placing 1% again on the next bet, will stake €0.99, which is less than the initial €1. Vice versa, in the case of a win of €1.25 on the basis of the above rules, we will have €101.25 and staking 1% we'll place the next bet of €1.0125, which is more than the initial €1 stake. Therefore, using a fixed bet percentage you 'follow' the trend of your capital, with more or less exposure as it increases or decreases.

Now let's go back to the first simulation, the one that after 100 coin tosses produced 53 heads (wining tosses) and 47 tails (losing tosses). This time we'll take 15 gamblers instead of 14, adding one who places 51% of his capital each time. Using the Martingale system this wouldn't make sense, because if the gambler lost and doubled the bet percentage, he'd be immediately in difficulty as he couldn't stake 102%.

As mentioned above, all the gamblers stake the same initial percentage each time. Figure 1.5 shows the results of this approach.

After 100 coin tosses it's immediately clear that the overall situation looks much better than with the Martingale approach. No one has increased their capital tenfold, but a lot more gamblers are making a profit on their initial capital, even those who risked 30% on each bet (with the Martingale approach, gamblers who started with 10% were losing after 100 tosses). Certainly, the profits of the more prudent gamblers are lower than in the previous case, and we can see this by making a direct comparison between Figures 1.5 and 1.1; but this doesn't weigh in favour of the Martingale approach which, as shown above, was devastating as the coin tossing continued. The first 100 tosses in fact were particularly favourable, while

Anti-Martingale					
after 100 tosses			after 1000 tosses		
heads	53	53%	heads	467	46.7%
tails	47		tails	533	
% risk	ending capital	gain %	% risk	ending capital	gain %
1%	120.45	20%	1%	155.97	56%
2%	143.22	43%	2%	214.56	115%
3%	168.13	68%	3%	260.48	160%
4%	194.89	95%	4%	279.24	179%
5%	223.07	123%	5%	264.42	164%
10%	363.48	263%	10%	31.59	−68%
15%	434.78	335%	15%	0.17	−100%
20%	381.47	281%	20%	0.00	−100%
25%	243.86	144%	25%	0.00	−100%
30%	112.11	12%	30%	0.00	−100%
35%	36.32	−64%	35%	0.00	−100%
40%	8.05	−92%	40%	0.00	−100%
45%	1.17	−99%	45%	0.00	−100%
50%	0.11	−100%	50%	0.00	−100%
51%	0.06	−100%	51%	0.00	−100%

FIGURE 1.5 Loss 1, win 1.25 – anti-Martingale system.

the following 900 were distinctly unfavourable and Figure 1.1 shows how all the gamblers lost their capital. The same goes if we make a comparison with Figure 1.2, showing less aggressive Martingale gamblers.

Taking a look at Figure 1.5, what does this show us about the results after 1,000 coin tosses? One can immediately see that, not only various gamblers still have their capital, but they also made a profit. Gamblers who bet 3% to 5% have practically 2.5 times their initial capital. Their Martingale colleagues on the other hand, have lost everything.

This is an unlucky case, but still possible. 1,000 coin tosses are, it must be said, not many for the law of large numbers, and final percentages of heads and tails like those in question are anything but impossible (this data, in fact, was obtained from a real probabilistic simulation done in Excel).

Now let's take a look at the second simulation. In the first 100 coin tosses the success rate was as high as 57% and then, after 1,000 coin tosses there was a much more balanced distribution with 502 wining tosses and 498 losing ones.

Figure 1.3 shows the harsh results of the Martingale approach for this series, proving that with this approach it isn't so much the final result that makes it good or bad (in fact, after 100 coin tosses the situation was theoretically better than that shown in Figures 1.1 and 1.2) but rather the distribution of the coin tosses. (As shown above, it's the number of losing consecutive coin tosses that dictates matters in this case.)

We used the same distribution of coin tosses with the anti-Martingale approach, and Figure 1.6 shows the results. Effectively, these are the figures, after 1,000 coin tosses, the gambler by always placing a 10% stake, instead of the €100 of initial capital, would have €77,863.87 in his pocket! Pure science fiction? No, the potential of mathematics.

The anti-Martingale system doesn't always work, as the various examples in which all capital was lost (*) in Figure 1.6, go to prove. In practice, it's immediately obvious that more conservative approaches make more profit than more aggressive approaches, within certain limits. Gamblers placing large bets won't last long, whatever approach they're using.

(*) N.B.: In reality the capital isn't mathematically lost as it is using the Martingale approach, but we can consider it to be lost when all that remains is less than €0.01. One could actually continue indefinitely staking smaller and smaller amounts if there wasn't a material limit set on said minimum stakes. (You can't stake less than 1 euro cent as this is the smallest denomination of our currency.)

Anti-Martingale					
after 100 tosses			**after 1000 tosses**		
heads	57	57%	heads	502	50.2%
tails	43		tails	498	
% risk	ending capital	gain %	% risk	ending capital	gain %
1%	131.77	32%	1%	342.48	242%
2%	171.39	71%	2%	1,032.68	933%
3%	220.04	120%	3%	2,743.80	2644%
4%	278.90	179%	4%	6,428.39	6328%
5%	319.03	249%	5%	13,288.71	13189%
10%	887.40	787%	10%	77,863.87	77764%
15%	1,656.27	1556%	15%	20,734.87	20635%
20%	2,273.74	2174%	20%	244.14	144%
25%	2,287.15	2187%	25%	0.12	−100%
30%	1,669.05	1569%	30%	0.00	−100%
35%	868.80	769%	35%	0.00	−100%
40%	314.56	215%	40%	0.00	−100%
45%	76.44	−24%	45%	0.00	−100%
50%	11.87	−88%	50%	0.00	−100%
51%	7.70	−92%	51%	0.00	−100%

FIGURE 1.6   Loss 1, win 1.25 – anti-Martingale system, results may appear excessively optimistic but they do reflect reality after 100 coin tosses with particularly favourable results and after 1,000 coin tosses with balanced results.

Figure 1.7 shows the results in the case of a luckier series of coin tosses in which, after 1,000 tosses, the coin came up 512 heads. In this case the final result is even more astounding. The gambler staking 10% would have closed with €725,163.77 compared to the initial €100.

Figure 1.8 shows the results of the Martingale approach for the same simulation.

Figures 1.9 and 1.10 show another comparison in which the result of the final distribution is less 'balanced,' and the coin has come up heads just 486 times.

It's immediately obvious that, while with the Martingale approach the final result is closely tied to the sequence of consecutive coin tosses, with the anti-Martingale approach on the other hand it's the final percentages that have the greatest influence. A simulation with 51.2% of winning tosses, in fact, produces much better results than a simulation with 48.6% wins.

Anti-Martingale					
after 100 tosses			after 1000 tosses		
heads	51	51%	heads	512	51.2%
tails	49		tails	488	
% risk	ending capital	gain %	% risk	ending capital	gain %
1%	115.15	15%	1%	428.78	329%
2%	130.92	31%	2%	1,617.87	1518%
3%	146.96	47%	3%	5,376.71	5277%
4%	162.91	63%	4%	15,750.08	15650%
5%	178.33	78%	5%	40,694.53	40595%
10%	232.63	133%	10%	725,163.77	725064%
15%	222.76	123%	15%	587,284.20	587184%
20%	156.25	56%	20%	21,175.82	21076%
25%	79.63	−20%	25%	31.39	−69%
30%	29.06	−71%	30%	0.00	−100%
35%	7.43	−93%	35%	0.00	−100%
40%	1.29	−99%	40%	0.00	−100%
45%	0.15	−100%	45%	0.00	−100%
50%	0.01	−100%	50%	0.00	−100%
51%	0.01	−100%	51%	0.00	−100%

FIGURE 1.7 Loss 1, win 1.25 – 1,000 coin tosses slightly unbalanced in favour of the gamblers produces very interesting results.

multiple =	1.5				
Martingale (increase bet after loss)					
after 100 tosses			after 1000 tosses		
heads	51	51%	heads	512	51.2%
tails	49		tails	488	
% risk	ending capital	gain %	% risk	ending capital	gain %
1%	135.07	35%	1%	427.89	328%
2%	170.93	71%	2%	–	−100%
3%	203.27	103%	3%	–	−100%
4%	227.41	127%	4%	–	−100%
5%	239.24	139%	5%	–	−100%
10%	94.63	−5%	10%	–	−100%
15%	–	−100%	15%	–	−100%
20%	–	−100%	20%	–	−100%
25%	–	−100%	25%	–	−100%
30%	–	−100%	30%	–	−100%
35%	–	−100%	35%	–	−100%
40%	–	−100%	40%	–	−100%
45%	–	−100%	45%	–	−100%
50%	–	−100%	50%	–	−100%

FIGURE 1.8 Loss 1, win 1.25 – stake multiplied by 1.5 after a loss, with the Martingale approach the final scenario is certainly not encouraging.

	Anti-Martingale					
	after 100 tosses				**after 1000 tosses**	
heads	52	52%		heads	486	48.6%
tails	48			tails	514	
% risk	**ending capital**	**gain %**		**% risk**	**ending capital**	**gain %**
1%	117.77	18%		1%	239.04	139%
2%	136.93	37%		2%	503.50	404%
3%	157.19	57%		3%	935.17	935%
4%	178.18	78%		4%	1,532.54	1433%
5%	199.45	99%		5%	2,217.16	2117%
10%	290.78	191%		10%	2,191.67	2092%
15%	311.21	211%		15%	98.46	−2%
20%	244.14	144%		20%	0.19	−100%
25%	139.35	39%		25%	0.00	−100%
30%	57.08	−43%		30%	0.00	−100%
35%	16.42	−84%		35%	0.00	−100%
40%	3.22	−97%		40%	0.00	−100%
45%	0.41	−100%		45%	0.00	−100%
50%	0.03	−100%		50%	0.00	−100%
51%	0.02	−100%		51%	0.00	−100%

FIGURE 1.9 Loss 1, win 1.25 – anti-Martingale system on the basis of unfavourable results after 1,000 coin tosses. With a bet of up to 10%, there are in any case notable gains.

multiple =	1.5					
	Martingale (increase bet after loss)					
	after 100 tosses				**after 1000 tosses**	
heads	52	52%		heads	486	48.6%
tails	48			tails	514	
% risk	**ending capital**	**gain %**		**% risk**	**ending capital**	**gain %**
1%	147.42	47%		1%	662.55	563%
2%	209.83	110%		2%	1,252.98	1153%
3%	288.68	189%		3%	403.33	303%
4%	384.25	284%		4%	−	−100%
5%	495.24	395%		5%	−	−100%
10%	1,104.60	1005%		10%	−	−100%
15%	1,143.78	1044%		15%	−	−100%
20%	514.05	414%		20%	−	−100%
25%	69.13	−31%		25%	−	−100%
30%	−	−100%		30%	−	−100%
35%	−	−100%		35%	−	−100%
40%	−	−100%		40%	−	−100%
45%	−	−100%		45%	−	−100%
50%	−	−100%		50%	−	−100%

FIGURE 1.10 Loss 1, win 1.25 – stake multiplied by 1.5 after a loss. The same 1,000 coin tosses above produce acceptable results only for gamblers who start betting using a very conservative approach. Starting at over 3% results in the loss of all capital.

■ 1.4 More Examples

In order to demonstrate the power of an anti-Martingale approach, let's take a look at another statistical game. In a bag of 999 balls, 333 of the balls are white, 333 are red, and 333 are black.

We pick a ball at random from the bag and then put it back in (so we don't change the total number of balls or the probability of picking one rather than another). As there are 3 possible picks, we ran this simulation with 99 and 999 cases (instead of 100 and 1,000) to produce figures that can be divided by 3.

The gamblers win €3 for each €1 stake in which a white ball is picked and lose the €1 stake if a red or black ball is picked.

On the basis of the same logic of betting a fixed percentage of your capital (initially equal to €100), Figures 1.11 and 1.12 show the final results with two different simulations.

Anti-Martingale						gain		
after 99 picks			after 999 picks			white = 3		
						red = −1		
white	23	23.23%	white	322	32.23%	black = −1		
red	38	38.38%	red	339	33.93%			
black	38	38.38%	black	338	33.83%	theoretical average gain = 3		
						theoretical average loss = −1		
						theoretical win/loss ratio = 3		
% risk	ending capital	gain %	% risk	ending capital	gain %			
1%	91.03	−9%	1%	1,508.74	1409%	optimal percentage = 11.11%		
2%	80.62	−19%	2%	16,163.74	16064%			
3%	69.54	−30%	3%	124,679.90	124580%			
4%	58.47	−42%	4%	701,177.65	701078%			
5%	47.95	−52%	5%	2,907,939.55	2907840%			
10%	12.51	−87%	10%	51,515,579.09	51515449%			
15%	1.89	−98%	15%	1,503,520.76	1503421%			
20%	0.17	−100%	20%	131.39	31%			
25%	0.01	−100%	25%	0.00	−100%			
30%	0.00	−100%	30%	0.00	−100%			
35%	0.00	−100%	35%	0.00	−100%			
40%	0.00	−100%	40%	0.00	−100%			
45%	0.00	−100%	45%	0.00	−100%			
50%	0.01	−100%	50%	0.00	−100%			
51%	0.00	−100%	51%	0.00	−100%			
optimal %	ending capital	gain %	optimal %	ending capital	gain %			
11.11%	9.68	−90%	11.11%	39,812,137.10	39812037%			

FIGURE 1.11   Loss 1, win 3 – anti-Martingale system. The first 99 picks are unfavourable for the gamblers who have suffered significant losses. The more balanced situation after 999 picks, however, produces astonishing results.

	Anti-Martingale					gain
	after 99 picks			after 999 picks		white = 3
						red = −1
white	41	41.41%	white	356	35.64%	black =
red	26	26.26%	red	317	31.73%	
black	32	32.32%	black	326	32.63%	theoretical average gain = 3
						theoretical average loss = −1
						theoretical win/loss ratio = 3
% risk	ending capital	gain %	% risk	ending capital	gain %	
1%	185.70	86%	1%	5,800.72	5701%	
2%	331.04	231%	2%	232,945.70	232846%	optimal percentage = 11.11%
3%	567.57	468%	3%	6,577,462.79	6577363%	
4%	937.44	837%	4%	132,439,921.61	132439822%	
5%	1,493.84	1394%	5%	1,926,235,429.42	1926235329%	
10%	9,375.31	9275%	10%	13,880,120,010,687.70	13880120010588%	
15%	28,301.19	28201%	15%	115,711,901,369,977.00	115711901369877%	
20%	44,794.89	44895%	20%	2,257,228,168,658.68	2257228168559%	
25%	39,189.93	39090%	25%	153,439,683.21	153439583%	
30%	19,484.17	19384%	30%	43.08	−57%	
35%	5,543.66	5444%	35%	0.00	−100%	
40%	891.77	792%	40%	0.00	−100%	
45%	78.56	−21%	45%	0.00	−100%	
50%	3.59	−96%	50%	0.00	−100%	
51%	1.78	−98%	51%	0.00	−100%	
optimal %	ending capital	gain %	optimal %	ending capital	gain %	
11.11%	14,310.07	14210%	11.11%	38,647,223,516,866.40	38647223514766%	

FIGURE 1.12 Loss 1, win 3 – anti-Martingale system. In this simulation, the first 99 picks were extremely favourable, as the percentage gains clearly show. The situation is rebalanced in the subsequent picks and remains in any case slightly unbalanced in the gamblers' favour, resulting in profits that aren't exactly easy to interpret.

The probability of picking a white ball is obviously one-third, so you have 1 chance in 3 of winning. The payout for a win is however higher than the damage for a loss and correct capital management produces results that are interesting enough to put a smile on your face.

Note that, once again, the simulation for which the results are shown in Figure 1.12 produces much better results than the simulation in Figure 1.11. Figure 1.12 in fact shows statistically unbalanced picks with more white balls, picked 356 times compared to 322 in Figure 1.11. This difference doesn't change the statistics by much, but does change the result considerably, once again going to prove that this management model provides a very positive impulse for the capital.

If we take a closer look at Figure 1.11 we'll see that after 99 picks the scenario wasn't at all encouraging; just 23 white balls compared to the 33 we expected (1/3 of 99), creating significant imbalance in the system. The situation is rebalanced in the following 900 picks, not only recovering all our losses, for those who continued with the original money management model, but also producing surprising results.

Figures 1.11 and 1.12 show also a percentage that's defined 'optimal' calculated theoretically; we'll come back to this point in the next chapter. In any case, you'll see this percentage doesn't always actually produce the best investment results. This is because said percentage is calculated on the basis of the theoretical probabilities that a white ball will be picked, and therefore in consideration of the final scenario with 333 white, 333 red, and 333 black balls (or 33 white, 33 black, and red after 99 picks) while in the real-life scenario the results are slightly different.

■ 1.5 A Miraculous Technique?

The results we've seen until now will certainly have caused a few jaws to drop, and I think very few people could hope to achieve something of the kind without studying the subject in depth. So, we've finally found the answer to all our problems and are now ready to clean out the casino, right?

Unfortunately, I have to dampen your enthusiasm. What we've seen so far is only effective when applied to a winning system. In the coin toss example, a win paid out €1.25 while a loss was just €1. With a 50% probability of winning, the system is advantageous, and therefore whether we manage to increase our available capital (or not) depends only on whether we adopt shrewd risk management.

Let's suppose we have a series of coin tosses in which a win was €1, the same as a loss. Figure 1.13 shows the results that, after seeing the previous figures, might make you turn up your nose.

What's more, these results derive from a situation that's unbalanced in our favour as the coin came up 512 time heads after 1,000 coin tosses. A different situation is shown in Figure 1.14 where the coin came up heads 'only' 495 times, and as you can see this is a losing system.

By way of comparison, Figure 1.15 shows the same series of coin tosses with a win paying €1.25 and a loss of €1, which puts a smile back on your face.

The same is true for balls picked out of a bag. If white pays 3 and you lose 1 for red and black, after 999 picks the situation will be:

$$3 * 333 - 1 * 333 - 1 * 333 = 333$$

The system would produce balanced results if white paid out 2:

$$2 * 333 - 1 * 333 - 1 * 333 = 0$$

Figure 1.16 shows a simulation where, in fact, white pays 2, but we can see that the situation doesn't look good. Figure 1.17, however, shows the

Anti-Martingale					
after 100 tosses			**after 1000 tosses**		
heads	51	51%	heads	512	51.2%
tails	49		tails	488	
% risk	ending capital	gain %	% risk	ending capital	gain %
1%	101.51	2%	1%	120.93	21%
2%	102.02	2%	2%	132.32	32%
3%	101.51	2%	3%	131.00	31%
4%	100.00	0%	4%	117.34	17%
5%	97.52	−2%	5%	95.07	−5%
10%	73.85	−26%	10%	7.30	−93%
15%	43.36	−57%	15%	0.04	−100%
20%	19.48	−81%	20%	0.00	−100%
25%	6.61	−93%	25%	0.00	−100%
30%	1.66	−98%	30%	0.00	−100%
35%	0.30	−100%	35%	0.00	−100%
40%	0.04	−100%	40%	0.00	−100%
45%	0.00	−100%	45%	0.00	−100%
50%	0.00	−100%	50%	0.00	−100%
51%	0.00	−100%	51%	0.00	−100%

FIGURE 1.13 Loss 1, win 1 – anti-Martingale system. Winning the same amount as can be lost there is no longer an advantage for the gambler and there are no interesting results in the final scenario. The less daring gamblers have made some profit after 1,000 tosses, which in any case has more wins than losses (512 compared to 488).

Anti-Martingale					
after 100 tosses			**after 1000 tosses**		
heads	52	52%	heads	495	49.5%
tails	48		tails	505	
% risk	ending capital	gain %	% risk	ending capital	gain %
1%	103.56	4%	1%	86.07	−14%
2%	106.18	6%	2%	67.03	−33%
3%	107.79	8%	3%	47.22	−53%
4%	108.33	8%	4%	30.09	−70%
5%	107.79	8%	5%	17.34	−83%
10%	90.38	−10%	10%	0.24	−100%
15%	58.67	−41%	15%	0.00	−100%
20%	29.22	−71%	20%	0.00	−100%
25%	11.02	−89%	25%	0.00	−100%
30%	3.09	−97%	30%	0.00	−100%
35%	0.63	−99%	35%	0.00	−100%
40%	0.09	−100%	40%	0.00	−100%
45%	0.01	−100%	45%	0.00	−100%
50%	0.00	−100%	50%	0.00	−100%
51%	0.00	−100%	51%	0.00	−100%

FIGURE 1.14 Loss 1, win 1 – anti-Martingale system. In this case, winning the same amount as can be lost, the scenario after 1,000 coin tosses just a little disadvantageous for the gambler (495 wins compared to 505 losses) shows a loss in all cases.

Anti-Martingale					
after 100 tosses			**after 1000 tosses**		
heads	52	52%	heads	495	49.5%
tails	48		tails	505	
% risk	ending capital	gain %	% risk	ending capital	gain %
1%	117.77	18%	1%	292.63	193%
2%	136.93	37%	2%	754.19	654%
3%	157.19	57%	3%	1,713.32	1613%
4%	178.18	78%	4%	3,433.02	3333%
5%	199.45	99%	5%	6,070.79	5971%
10%	290.78	191%	10%	16,329.24	16229%
15%	311.21	211%	15%	1,996.17	1896%
20%	244.14	144%	20%	10.74	−89%
25%	139.35	39%	25%	0.00	−100%
30%	57.08	−43%	30%	0.00	−100%
35%	16.42	−84%	35%	0.00	−100%
40%	3.22	−97%	40%	0.00	−100%
45%	0.41	−100%	45%	0.00	−100%
50%	0.03	−100%	50%	0.00	−100%
51%	0.02	−100%	51%	0.00	−100%

FIGURE 1.15 Loss 1, win 1.25 – anti-Martingale system. The game is once again favourable for the gamblers, paying out more for wins than is lost.

Anti-Martingale						gain		
after 99 picks			**after 999 picks**			white =	2	
						red =	−1	
white	27	27.27%	white	331	33.13%	black =	−1	
red	36	36.36%	red	339	33.93%			
black	36	36.36%	black	329	32.93%	theoretical average gain		2
% risk	ending capital	gain %	% risk	ending capital	gain %	theoretical average loss		−1
1%	81.95	−18%	1%	85.30	−15%	theoretical win/loss ratio =		2
2%	65.98	−34%	2%	59.85	−40%	optimal percentage =		0.00%
3%	52.19	−48%	3%	34.65	−65%			
4%	40.57	−59%	4%	16.61	−83%			
5%	31.00	−69%	5%	6.61	−93%			
10%	6.27	−94%	10%	0.00	−100%			
15%	0.84	−99%	15%	0.00	−100%			
20%	0.07	−100%	20%	0.00	−100%			
25%	0.00	−100%	25%	0.00	−100%			
30%	0.00	−100%	30%	0.00	−100%			
35%	0.00	−100%	35%	0.00	−100%			
40%	0.00	−100%	40%	0.00	−100%			
45%	0.00	−100%	45%	0.00	−100%			
50%	0.00	−100%	50%	0.00	−100%			
51%	0.00	−100%	51%	0.00	−100%			
optimal %	ending capital	gain %	optimal %	ending capital	gain %			
0.00%	100.00	0%	0.00%	100.00	0%			

FIGURE 1.16 Loss 1, win 2 – anti-Martingale system. Also, in this case, a win pays double a loss, but as the probability of losing is twice that of winning (2 balls out of 3 are a loss), the game isn't favourable in a balanced series of picks.

Anti-Martingale						gain
	after 99 picks			after 999 picks		white = 2.5
						red = −1
white	27	27.27%	white	331	33.13%	black = −1
red	36	36.36%	red	339	33.93%	
black	36	36.36%	black	329	32.93%	theoretical average gain = 2.5
% risk	ending capital	gain %	% risk	ending capital	gain %	theoretical average loss = −1
						theoretical win/loss ratio = 2.5
1%	96.52	−6%	1%	430.44	330%	optimal percentage = 6.67%
2%	85.43	−15%	2%	1,421.27	1321%	
3%	76.27	−24%	3%	3,628.44	3528%	
4%	65.59	−33%	4%	7,213.77	7114%	
5%	56.88	−43%	5%	11,242.25	11142%	
10%	18.89	−81%	10%	3,244.97	3145%	
15%	3.82	−96%	15%	4.27	−96%	
20%	0.48	−100%	20%	0.00	−100%	
25%	0.04	−100%	25%	0.00	−100%	
30%	0.00	−100%	30%	0.00	−100%	
35%	0.00	−100%	35%	0.00	−100%	
40%	0.00	−100%	40%	0.00	−100%	
45%	0.00	−100%	45%	0.00	−100%	
50%	0.00	−100%	50%	0.00	−100%	
51%	0.00	−100%	51%	0.00	−100%	
optimal %	ending capital	gain %	optimal %	ending capital	gain %	
6.67%	44.49	−55%	6.67%	13,930.10	13830%	

FIGURE 1.17 Loss 1, win 2.5 – as soon as a win pays out more than the loss, the gamblers start making an interesting profit again.

same simulation in which a win pays just a bit more: White pays 2.5 instead of 2, the game produces balanced results again:

$$2.5 * 333 − 1 * 333 − 1 * 333 = 166.5 > 0$$

and profits are once again seen.

■ 1.6 Conclusions

The above examples make it easy to understand why the anti-Martingale system is the one I choose to apply to money management strategies, and the principle on the basis of which exposure is increased only as capital increases. This is the foundation stone for the concepts illustrated in the following chapters of the book. I hope I've also convinced those of you who had a marked preference for the Martingale system. If this isn't so, do keep reading, as the book contains some good strategies for managing your capital.

CHAPTER 2

The Kelly Formula

■ 2.1 Kelly and Co.

In the last chapter I mentioned an 'optimal' percentage that should, in winning conditions similar to theoretical conditions, maximize profits if used systematically. This percentage is obtained using a theoretical approach based on the Kelly formula.

Kelly worked at Bell Labs and developed his studies to help the phone company AT&T analyze disturbances in long-distance calls. The method was first published in 1956: 'A New Interpretation of Information Rate'. You can find the study online, but I believe only real math buffs will be able to appreciate the subtleties of it. Personally, I just skimmed through it, acutely aware of how little I actually know on this particular subject.

Kelly's study was soon used by professional gamblers to calculate the percentage of the gambler's capital to risk, and maximize profits.

Kelly's criterion considers the distribution of events in the context in which you'll be operating: in consideration of how many times the system is right and how many times it wins on average compared to how many times it loses, it calculates the best percentage to increase your capital.

In practice, Kelly managed to intertwine the statistics of the system, coming up with the best way to exploit them. In his study, he considers the probability of the system winning – in other words, how many times a winning event occurred compared to the total number of events – and then considers how the wins are paid compared to the losses. If a system based on 100 events shows 40 favourable cases and 60 losing ones, the percentage of wins is 40%. If the gambler won 4 for every win, and lost 2 for every loss, the ratio of wins to losses would be $4/2 = 2$. This input data was used by Kelly to calculate the best way to bet on a system of this kind.

In particular, if:

W is the probability of winning

R is the ratio of average wins to average losses

then the optimal fraction of your capital to invest, according to Kelly, is obtained as follows:

$$K\% = W - \frac{1 - W}{R}$$

Or, if you prefer, using the same equation:

$$K\% = \frac{(R + 1) * W - 1}{R}$$

Let's look at a few examples, going back to our coin toss. In this game, we know the theoretical probability of winning is 50%, so $W = 0.5$. The ratio of average wins to average losses depends on the rules of the game, though.

In the previous chapter, we saw that it isn't advantageous to place a bet if the payout for a win isn't higher than the risk of a loss, as there is a 50% probability of winning. Let's see what the Kelly formula has to say in the case of a payout of €1 for a €1 risk. In this case, R is equal to 1; in other words, $R = 1/1$ because the average win is equal to 1, as is the average loss. W is 0.5, as this is intrinsic to the coin toss.

Therefore:

$$K\% = \frac{(1 + 1) * 0.5 - 1}{1} = \frac{2 * 0.5 - 1}{1} = \frac{1 - 1}{1} = 0 \dots$$

In practice, according to Kelly, the best thing to do in the above condition is . . . not risk anything, which is the same conclusion we came to previously.

If we analyze what would be the optimal fraction, according to Kelly, in different conditions such as for example with a €1.25 payout and a €1 risk. With 1.25, therefore:

$$R = 1.25/1 = 1.25$$

$$W = 0.5$$

$$K\% = \frac{(1.25 + 1) * 0.5 - 1}{1.25} = \frac{2.25 * 0.5 - 1}{1.25}$$

$$= \frac{1.125 - 1}{1.25} = \frac{0.125}{1.25} = 0.1, \text{ or } 10\%$$

Therefore, according to Kelly, a game with a 50% probability of winning, an average win of €1.25, and an average loss of €1, is played in the best way (or rather in the most profitable way) using 10% of your capital each time.

Figure 2.1 shows the results of 100 and 1,000 coin tosses with various percentages of capital. Note that after 100 coin tosses, the percentage that made most profit is 30%, closely followed by 25%. The percentage the Kelly formula suggested was best – in other words, 10% didn't produce the expected results.

If we analyze the outcome after 1,000 coin tosses, however, we'll see that in this case Kelly was right; in fact, the capital accumulated betting 10% is the highest of all.

So, why is there this difference?

This is easy to explain: as mentioned above, applied to a coin toss, Kelly refers to a perfect system in which 100 tosses will produce 50 heads and 50 tails. In the example we examined, in reality the scenario in the first 100 coin tosses was very different, coming up heads 60 times. We can check to

AntiMartingale						
after 100 tosses				after 1000 tosses		
heads	60	60%		heads	509	50.9%
tails	40			tails	491	
% risk	ending capital	gain %		% risk	ending capital	gain %
1%	140.96	41%		1%	400.82	301%
2%	196.10	96%		2%	1,414.00	1314%
3%	269.25	169%		3%	4,394.07	4294%
4%	364.93	265%		4%	12,037.29	11937%
5%	488.29	388%		5%	29,088.41	28988%
10%	1,733.21	1633%		10%	3,71,283.85	371184%
15%	4,516.21	4416%		15%	2,15,379.44	215279%
20%	8,673.62	8571%		20%	5,551.12	5451%
25%	12,257.71	12158%		25%	5.86	−94%
30%	12,649.80	12550%		30%	0.00	−100%
35%	9,397.35	9297%		35%	0.00	−100%
40%	4,915.02	4815%		40%	0.00	−100%
45%	1,752.71	1653%		45%	0.00	−100%
50%	407.38	307%		50%	0.00	−100%
51%	287.56	188%		51%	0.00	−100%

FIGURE 2.1 Loss 1, win 1.25 – an extremely favourable situation for the gambler in the first 100 tosses; then the game becomes more balanced while still producing good payouts.

see what Kelly would say if he knew the final percentage of wins before-hand – in other words 60% (so $W = 0.6$):

$$R = 1.25$$
$$W = 0.6$$
$$K\% = \frac{(1.25 + 1) * 0.6 - 1}{1.25} = \frac{2.25 * 0.6 - 1}{1.25}$$
$$= \frac{1.35 - 1}{1.25} = \frac{0.35}{1.25} = 0.28 \text{ or } 28\%$$

The result is that Kelly, for a system with 60% wins that pay out €1.25 with a loss of €1, suggests betting 28% of our capital, and as can be seen in Figure 2.1, stakes of 25 – 30% produced the best results.

I obviously make this digression only for the purpose of mathematical proof. In a heads–tails game, you will always have a 50% possibility of winning (and it's obviously impossible to know beforehand if there will be some series of coin tosses that produces a different result). If we take a look at the evolution of the coin tosses in this simulation, you'll see that after the first 100, the results became more balanced again, with 509 heads and 491 tails after 1,000 tosses.

Let's take the same simulation and have a look at the results of the bets if the payout was €1.5 compared to €1. Figure 2.2 shows the tables of the final result.

In this case Kelly would advise as follows:

$$R = 1.5$$
$$W = 0.5$$
$$K\% = \frac{(1.5 + 1) * 0.5 - 1}{1.5} = \frac{2.5 * 0.5 - 1}{1, .5}$$
$$= \frac{1.25 - 1}{1.5} = \frac{0.25}{1.5} = 0.1667 \text{ or } 16.7\%$$

After 1,000 coin tosses, the gamblers who bet 15% – 20% obtained the best results (also in this case the 16.7% calculated is slightly conservative as the percentage of wins isn't exactly 50%, but 50.9%).

In the first 100 coin tosses, the situation is again biased towards higher percentages due to the extremely lucky series. Out of curiosity, if we run

Anti-Martingale					
after 100 tosses			after 1000 tosses		
heads	60	60%	heads	509	50.9%
tails	40		tails	491	
% risk	ending capital	gain %	% risk	ending capital	gain %
1%	163.44	63%	1%	1,406.36	1306%
2%	262.59	163%	2%	16,832.57	16733%
3%	414.81	315%	3%	1,71,835.69	171736%
4%	644.47	544%	4%	14,99,204.38	1499104%
5%	985.04	885%	5%	1,11,99,496.57	11199397%
10%	6,479.94	6380%	10%	26,80,85,22,213.39	26808522113%
15%	29,169.05	29069%	15%	16,06,79,94,49,613.95	1606799449514%
20%	91,243.22	91143%	20%	25,96,27,04,91,054.93	2596270490955%
25%	1,99,807.79	199708%	25%	1,12,50,03,02,952.46	112500302852%
30%	3,06,197.57	306098%	30%	12,00,74.499.37	120074399%
35%	3,25,630.36	325530%	35%	2,659.55	2560%
40%	2,36,183.18	236086%	40%	0.00	−100%
45%	1,13,604.69	113505%	45%	0.00	−100%
50%	34,760.27	34660%	50%	0.00	−100%
51%	25,853.88	25754%	51%	0.00	−100%

FIGURE 2.2 Loss 1, win 1.5 – a win paid 1.5 times a loss. This really boosts the results of Figure 2.1.

the calculations using $W = 0.6$, the result is:

$$K\% = \frac{(1.5 + 1) * 0.6 - 1}{1.5} = \frac{2.5 * 0.6 - 1}{1.5}$$
$$= \frac{1.5 - 1}{1.5} = \frac{0.5}{1.5} = 0.3333, \text{ or } 33.33\%$$

In fact, percentages of 30% – 35% produce the best results.

We've seen cases in which the actual results were better than the theoretical ones and, as a consequence, a bet placed on the basis of the Kelly criterion could make us kick ourselves for missing the chance to make the most profit.

But, although 1,000 coin tosses seems a lot, it's still not enough to be sure the coin will come up exactly 50% heads and 50% tails (We'd have to toss the coin an infinite number of times.), so there may indeed be situations in which the final result is definitely disadvantageous. Figure 2.3 shows a case like this. As can be seen, after the first 100 coin tosses, and after 1,000, the percentage of wins is less than the expected 50%. This series paid out €1.25

Anti-Martingale						
after 100 tosses				**after 1000 tosses**		
heads	48	48%		heads	477	47.7%
tails	52			tails	523	
% risk	ending capital	gain %		% risk	ending capital	gain %
1%	107.64	8%		1%	195.27	95%
2%	114.42	14%		2%	336.14	236%
3%	120.10	20%		3%	510.44	410%
4%	124.51	25%		4%	684.15	584%
5%	127.47	27%		5%	809.75	710%
10%	119.11	19%		10%	294.16	194%
15%	81.70	−18%		15%	4.86	−95%
20%	40.96	−59%		20%	0.00	−100%
25%	14.86	−85%		25%	0.00	−100%
30%	3.83	−96%		30%	0.00	−100%
35%	0.69	−99%		35%	0.00	−100%
40%	0.08	−100%		40%	0.00	−100%
45%	0.01	−100%		45%	0.00	−100%
50%	0.00	−100%		50%	0.00	−100%
51%	0.00	−100%		51%	0.00	−100%

FIGURE 2.3   Loss 1, win 1.25 – results are below statistical balance (win % below 50%) and the profits aren't interesting.

per win so, according to Kelly, we'd have bet 10% as before. It's immediately obvious that this choice wouldn't have been optimal for this series, though: despite the positive final result, we've made 194% compared to a potential 710% if we staked just 5% of the capital.

This consideration should be an eye-opener and help us see the risks of this kind of approach. While it's true that a better series than expected may mean losing the chance to make more profits, it's also obvious that a less favourable series than expected could cause damage we weren't expecting.

What, for example, can we say about the results in Figure 2.4? Our gambler, armed with his 'new' Kelly formula, goes swaggering off to his friends with a coin to flip to bet on heads or tails. After 100 coin tosses, betting 10% produced the maximum profit possible up to that point, and he's more and more excited about showing off his incredible newfound gambling skills – but after 1,000 coin tosses? I don't think he'd have much swagger left, having just €3 of his initial €100 left. He was unlucky and only 456 of the 1,000 coin tosses were wins, but this can indeed happen and must be taken into consideration.

Anti-Martingale					
after 100 tosses			after 1000 tosses		
heads	50	50%	heads	456	45.6%
tails	50		tails	544	
% risk	ending capital	gain %	% risk	ending capital	gain %
1%	112.59	13%	1%	121.81	22%
2%	125.17	25%	2%	130.94	31%
3%	137.40	37%	3%	124.28	24%
4%	148.95	49%	4%	104.20	4%
5%	159.45	59%	5%	77.20	−23%
10%	186.10	86%	10%	2.71	−91%
15%	159.45	59%	15%	0.00	−100%
20%	100.00	0%	20%	0.00	−100%
25%	45.50	−54%	25%	0.00	−100%
30%	14.79	−85%	30%	0.00	−100%
35%	3.36	−97%	35%	0.00	−100%
40%	0.52	−99%	40%	0.00	−100%
45%	0.05	−100%	45%	0.00	−100%
50%	0.00	−100%	50%	0.00	−100%
51%	0.00	−100%	51%	0.00	−100%

FIGURE 2.4 Loss 1, win 1.25 – the first 100 coin tosses show a balanced result, which, however, doesn't remain so in the following 900 coin tosses, leading to an evident and harmful imbalance after 1,000 tosses.

In order to complete the picture we began outlining in the previous chapter, let's also take a look at what might happen in the ball-picking game if we place bets using the Kelly criterion.

In the ball-picking game, the probability of winning is 1 in 3, as just the white ball wins. Let's suppose a win pays out 3 and a loss costs 1. The Kelly formula would give us the following percentage:

$$R = 3$$
$$W = 0.333$$
$$K\% = \frac{(3+1) * 0.333 - 1}{3} = \frac{4 * 0.333 - 1}{3}$$
$$= \frac{1.333 - 1}{3} = \frac{0.333}{3} = 0.1111 \text{ or } 11.11\%$$

The 11.11% of these results is very similar to what we found was the 'optimal percentage' in some cases in the previous chapter.

Now let's take a look at how the final scenario changes after a series of picks. The results are shown in Figure 2.5.

We can immediately see that after 99 picks, an approach based on the percentage calculated as optimal doesn't produce significant results. In fact, half the capital has been lost. After 999 picks, however, effectively using 11.11% of our available capital to place each bet would have maximised profits.

As in the case of the coin toss, we can immediately see that the first 99 picks were worse that what we hoped for. In a theoretical scenario (and, as mentioned several times, Kelly based his criterion on theory), we should have picked 33 white balls, while we actually picked only 27. This was enough to produce poor results using the percentage calculated theoretically.

Anti-Martingale						gain		
after 99 picks			after 999 picks			white =	3	
						red =	−1	
white	27	27.27%	white	331	33.13%	black =	−1	
red	36	36.36%	red	339	33.93%			
black	36	36.36%	black	329	32.93%	theoretical average gain=	3	
						theoretical average loss=	−1	
						theoretical win/loss ratio =	3	
% risk	ending capital	gain %	% risk	ending capital	gain %			
1%	106.65	7%	1%	2,154.00	2055%			
2%	110.35	10%	2%	32,753.67	32654%	optimal percentage =	11.11%	
3%	110.88	11%	3%	356,196.22	356096%			
4%	108.31	8%	4%	28,07,690.12	2807590%			
5%	102.96	3%	5%	1,62,31,306.92	16231207%			
10%	54.47	−46%	10%	1,41,00,87,033.47	1410086933%			
15%	16.01	−84%	15%	18,39,29,384.24	183929284%			
20%	2.73	−97%	20%	67,270.64	67171%			
25%	0.28	−100%	25%	0.10	−100%			
30%	0.02	−100%	30%	0.00	−100%			
35%	0.00	−100%	35%	0.00	−100%			
40%	0.00	−100%	40%	0.00	−100%			
45%	0.00	−100%	45%	0.00	−100%			
50%	0.00	−100%	50%	0.00	−100%			
51%	0.00	−100%	51%	0.00	−100%			
optimal %	ending capital	gain %	optimal %	ending capital	gain %			
11.11%	49.02	−51%	11.11%	1,53,05,12,294.12	1530512194%			

FIGURE 2.5   Results after 99 unlucky picks and 999 balanced picks. The Kelly percentage maximizes profits if the results of the probabilistic calculations are observed.

Again, out of curiosity, let's have a look at the calculations if we'd known in advance we'd have picked only 27 wins out of 99 – in other words, 27.27%; therefore, $W = 0.2727$:

$$R = 3$$
$$W = 0.2727$$
$$K\% = \frac{(3+1) * 0.2727 - 1}{3} = \frac{4 * 0.2727 - 1}{3}$$
$$= \frac{1.0909 - 1}{3} = \frac{0.0909}{3} = 0.0303 \text{ or } 3.03\%$$

Once again, the mathematical calculations run with hindsight confirm the results of the bets. In fact, the gambler who bet on that series of picks at 3% would be in the best shape after the first unlucky 99 picks.

But the scenario is quite different after 999 picks, in which the white ball was picked as predicted by the probabilistic calculation, producing 331 whites compared to the expected 333. In this case, the percentage calculated using the Kelly formula produces the best increment for the initial capital.

We should emphasize that the 999 picks started with the 99 initial unlucky ones, so after 99 picks the gambler who started staking 11.11% would have just €49.02 remaining; but continuing to stake the same percentage, trusting in the statistics, after 999 picks his capital (hard to read, as it's too large a number) is shown in the second part of the figure.

Figure 2.6 shows another series of picks in which a win paid out €2.5 for every €1 stake (in the previous case the payout was €3). The Kelly formula would therefore be based on $R = 2.5$, while W obviously remains 0.333.

$$R = 2.5$$
$$W = 0.333$$
$$K\% = \frac{(2.5+1) * 0.333 - 1}{2.5} = \frac{3.5 * 0.333 - 1}{2.5}$$
$$= \frac{1.1667 - 1}{2.5} = \frac{0.1667}{2.5} = 0.0667 \text{ or } 6.67\%$$

Note, in this case, that the first 99 picks were luckier than they should have been, in theory; and, in fact, a gambler who started staking a higher risk percentage would have made more than a gambler who stuck to the Kelly percentage. In the scenario after 999 picks however, now quite balanced, the gambler who started and continued staking the percentage calculated using the formula made most profit.

Anti-Martingale						gain		
after 99 picks			after 999 picks			white =	2.5	
white	37	37.37%	white	338	33.83%	red =	−1	
red	33	33.33%	red	333	33.33%	black =	−1	
black	29	29.29%	black	328	32.83%	theoretical average gain =	2.5	
						theoretical average loss =	−1	
						theoretical win/loss ratio =	2.5	
% risk	ending capital	gain %	% risk	ending capital	gain %			
1%	132.37	32%	1%	548.95	449%			
2%	170.31	70%	2%	2,303.66	2204%	optimal percentage =		6.67%
3%	213.17	113%	3%	7,450.36	7350%			
4%	259.79	160%	4%	18,707.37	18607%			
5%	308.48	208%	5%	36,716.03	36616%			
10%	504.60	405%	10%	32,350.66	32251%			
15%	468.37	368%	15%	123.66	24%			
20%	257.07	157%	20%	0.00	−100%			
25%	85.20	−15%	25%	0.00	−100%			
30%	17.12	−83%	30%	0.00	−100%			
35%	2.06	−98%	35%	0.00	−100%			
40%	0.15	−100%	40%	0.00	−100%			
45%	0.01	−100%	45%	0.00	−100%			
50%	0.00	−100%	50%	0.00	−100%			
51%	0.00	−100%	51%	0.00	−100%			
optimal %	ending capital	gain %	optimal %	ending capital	gain %			
6.67%	416.21	316%	6.67%	66,423.88	66324%			

FIGURE 2.6   A balanced scenario after 999 picks confirms the Kelly formula

The same picks are shown in Figure 2.7, in which a win pays out €3 however for a €1 loss, and the Kelly percentage is once again 11.11% as it was calculated previously.

We've seen how a 'mathematical' approach, based on the Kelly formula, can produce notable results; but it can also be less productive if the actual results of the game aren't close to the theoretical ones.

While, on the one hand, the main aim of a gambler is to maximize his profits, it's also obvious that, with any approach, there should be a brake that's applied to make staying in the game more probable.

A gambling approach based on the Kelly formula has, in time, been applied to blackjack and other games based on probability (in fact, the rules of some games have been changed in time also to thwart gamblers using a systematic approach). Interesting studies have been conducted to compare

Anti-Martingale						gain	
after 99 picks			after 999 picks			white =	3
white	37	37.37%	white	338	33.83%	red =	−1
red	33	33.33%	red	333	33.33%	black =	−1
black	29	29.29%	black	328	32.83%	theoretical average gain =	3
						theoretical average loss =	−1
						theoretical win/loss ratio =	3

% risk	ending capital	gain %	% risk	ending capital	gain %		
1%	158.49	58%	1%	2,843.45	2743%		
2%	241.86	142%	2%	56,730.75	56631%	optimal percentage =	11.11%
3%	355.96	256%	3%	8,05,884.22	805784%		
4%	506.00	406%	4%	82,59,936.37	8259836%		
5%	695.68	596%	5%	6,18,26,282.71	61826186%		
10%	2,153.68	2054%	10%	18,49,91,51,926.64	18499151827%		
15%	3,342.02	3242%	15%	7,73,20,49,978.62	7732049879%		
20%	2,799.68	2700%	20%	86,10,642.12	8610542%		
25%	1,322.11	1222%	25%	36.51	−63%		
30%	358.97	259%	30%	0.00	−100%		
35%	56.03	−44%	35%	0.00	−100%		
40%	4.93	−95%	40%	0.00	−100%		
45%	0.24	−100%	45%	0.00	−100%		
50%	0.01	−100%	50%	0.00	−100%		
51%	0.00	−100%	51%	0.00	−100%		

optimal %	ending capital	gain %	optimal %	ending capital	gain %		
11.11%	2,826.88	2727%	11.11%	26,15,02,37,400.28	26150237300%		

FIGURE 2.7 As in the previous case, the first 99 picks make a greater profit for the more aggressive gambler than the Kelly formula, but a more balanced situation after 999 picks makes Kelly a winner.

the probability of making a profit with the safety of the approach used, and the conclusions showed investments made using half the percentage calculated with the Kelly formula were best. What's more, if we consider the results obtained up to now, it's immediately obvious that a more conservative approach is safer.

■ 2.2 Conclusions

Kelly, in his studies, came up with a way to use mathematics to calculate the best risk percentage in a betting game in which the theoretical probability of winning and the payout of said wins are known. The results obtained applying this method are sometimes astonishing, and prove the power of a well-thought-out approach when dealing with random phenomena.

However, theory and practice, as everyone knows, don't always go hand-in-hand, and expectations based on calculated probability aren't always (or it might be better to say aren't ever) precisely as expected. There will be cases in which the results are better than expected, but also, unfortunately, cases in which they are worse. In order to protect ourselves from unfortunate events, it's good practice not to slavishly follow rules dictated by mathematics, but apply limits to risk using the values obtained from theoretical calculations as points of reference.

The above was applied to typical games based strictly on the calculation of probability, but in the world of trading we of course have to operate in the field we know best, and we'll see how the things we've considered to this point can be applied or used to devise a strategy that produces good results.

■ Reference

Kelly, J.L. Jr. 'A New Interpretation of Information Rate.' *Bell System Technical Journal* (July 1956), 917–926. https://archive.org/details/bstj35-4-917.

CHAPTER 3

A Banal Trading System

In order to take the right path, we have to analyze concrete data and try to apply the theories we'll develop to the same. To do so we'll use the results of a trading system that's somewhat banal, but well-suited to our lucubrations.

■ 3.1 Analyzing a System Based on Moving Averages

Here we'll analyze the results of a system based on a crossover of moving averages. This system uses 15-minute bar charts for the euro/dollar exchanged on Forex. The results are in USD. The value of each tick is 12.5 USD, and there is 20 USD of commission and slippage on each trade.

The system uses a faster moving average and a slower moving average and buys when the faster moving average moves higher than the slower moving average, selling when the slower moving average is once again higher than the faster as shown in Figure 3.1 with a 1,250 USD stop-loss per contract.

To limit operations to times not subject to the afternoon frenzy, we decided to consider just the exchange rates from midnight to midday, as if the market were closed in the afternoon.

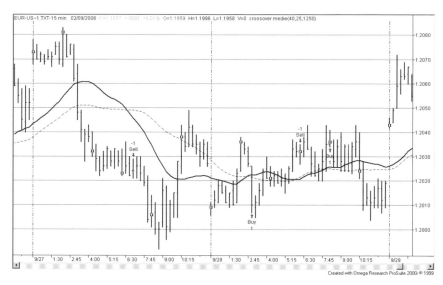

FIGURE 3.1   Example of the dynamics of the system used.

In this sense, the chart was created by eliminating the data after 12.00, as if the stock exchange closed and opened again next morning. This decision was taken deliberately in order to easily obtain some losing trades that were much worse than the max. loss planned. In fact, using a 1,250 USD stop-loss may make you think you're protected within that limit, but deleting half the day's trading, where most of the big movements occur, makes it highly probable that you might open next day with a significant gap.

The instrument used provides good response with 25 periods for the faster moving average and 40 periods for the slower moving average.

In order to further limit the number of system entry points, another filter was used that only allows a long entry if the day's high hasn't exceeded the previous day's high (of course, the high recorded from midnight to midday, as we don't know the prices outside this range). Vice versa, a short entry is only allowed when the day's low is still higher than the previous day's low. The effectiveness of the system is based on the tendencies found in the market in question, if the moving averages cross after previous day's high or previous day's low have already been exceeded the signal is often not very valid. This is why the above filter is used.

For your information, and so you can duplicate the system if you want, here's the EasyLanguage code (remember to use the times 12 a.m.–12 p.m. in the chart settings to exclude afternoon bars):

```
input: slow(40), fast(25),MyLoss(1250);

if average(c,fast) crosses above average(c,slow) and highd(0)<highd(1)
    then buy next bar at market;

if average(c,fast) crosses below average(c,slow) and lowd(0)>lowd(1)
    then sellshort next bar at market;

setstopcontract;

setstoploss(MyLoss);
```

As you can see, the system is extremely banal but, as mentioned above, it suits our purpose well.

The author's database starts from the year 2000 and the system was tested from that date to the end of 2005 for six years.

Some information from the TradeStation report of said system, follows (Figures 3.2–3.5).

As you can see, the strategy pays off, although the results aren't exactly exceptional. The maximum drawdown is in fact about one quarter of the net profit, and for many traders this wouldn't be tenable. Apart from a difficult first year (and perhaps many would have stopped using the strategy), the system paid off in quite a consistent way. Note that, as expected, the maximum loss suffered by the system is much greater than the 1,250 USD stop-loss.

These results are for a single contract, and in a certain sense, might be considered interesting as they are; but our intention is to go further and see what would happen if we applied some of the principles we've studied.

I would like to emphasise that this system wasn't built following the classic precepts, as the decision was taken to eliminate the most frenetic part of the market after midday. The purpose of this strategy is to show the effects of money management on a series of trades, rather than provide specific ideas for trading.

TradeStation Strategy Performance Report

TradeStation Strategy Performance Report - crossover medie EUR-US~1.TXT-15 min. (1/3/2000-12/30/2005)

Performance Summary: All Trades

Total Net Profit	$88.082,5000	Open position P/L	$162,5000
Gross Profit	$406.940,0000	Gross Loss	($318.857,5000)
Total # of trades	964	Percent profitable	49,07%
Number winning trades	473	Number losing trades	491
Largest winning trade	$4.580,0000	Largest losing trade	($2.757,5000)
Average winning trade	$860,3383	Average losing trade	($649,4043)
Ratio avg win/avg loss	1,3248	Avg trade (win & loss)	$91,3719
Max consec. Winners	8	Max consec. losers	7
Avg # bars in winners	82	Avg # bars in losers	47
Max intraday drawdown	($22.602,5000)		
Profit Factor	1,2762	Max # contracts held	1
Account size required	$22.602,5000	Return on account	389,70%

Performance Summary: Long Trades

Total Net Profit	$62.672,5000	Open position P/L	$0,0000
Gross Profit	$216.525,0000	Gross Loss	($153.852,5000)
Total # of trades	482	Percent profitable	49,79%
Number winning trades	240	Number losing trades	242
Largest winning trade	$4.005,0000	Largest losing trade	($2.545,0000)
Average winning trade	$902,1875	Average losing trade	($635,7541)
Ratio avg win/avg loss	1,4191	Avg trade (win & loss)	$130,0259
Max consec. Winners	7	Max consec. losers	9
Avg # bars in winners	86	Avg # bars in losers	52
Max intraday drawdown	($17.690,0000)		
Profit Factor	1,4074	Max # contracts held	1
Account size required	$17.690,0000	Return on account	354,28%

Performance Summary: Short Trades

Total Net Profit	$25.410,0000	Open position P/L	$162,5000
Gross Profit	$190.415,0000	Gross Loss	($165.005,0000)
Total # of trades	482	Percent profitable	48,34%
Number winning trades	233	Number losing trades	249
Largest winning trade	$4.580,0000	Largest losing trade	($2.757,5000)
Average winning trade	$817,2318	Average losing trade	($662,6707)
Ratio avg win/avg loss	1,2332	Avg trade (win & loss)	$52,7178
Max consec. Winners	6	Max consec. losers	7
Avg # bars in winners	78	Avg # bars in losers	42
Max intraday drawdown	($18.270,0000)		
Profit Factor	1,1540	Max # contracts held	1
Account size required	$18.270,0000	Return on account	139,08%

FIGURE 3.2   Strategy report.

TradeStation Strategy Performance Report
Annual Trading Summary

Annual Analysis (Mark-To-Market):

Period	Net Profit	% Gain	Profit Factor	# Trades	% Profitable
YTD	$0,0000	N/A	N/A	0	N/A
12 month	$16.807,5000	9,80%	1,06	155	45,16%
05	$16.750,0000	9,77%	1,05	161	48,45%
04	$10.997,5000	6,85%	1,03	163	41,10%
03	$29.075,0000	22,12%	1,09	166	52,41%
02	$19.057,5000	16,96%	1,07	170	50,59%
01	$22.997,5000	25,73%	1,08	163	56,44%
00	($10.632,5000)	(10,63%)	0,97	147	42,86%

Annual Rolling Period Analysis (Mark-To-Market):

Period	Net Profit	% Gain	Profit Factor	# Trades	% Profitable
05	$16.750,0000	9,77%	1,05	161	48,45%
04-05	$27.747,5000	17,29%	1,04	323	44,89%
03-05	$56.822,5000	43,24%	1,06	488	47,54%
02-05	$75.880,0000	67,53%	1,06	657	48,40%
01-05	$98.877,5000	110,64%	1,06	819	50,06%
00-05	$88.245,0000	88,24%	1,05	965	49,02%

FIGURE 3.3 Annual strategy results.

■ 3.2 Applying the Kelly Formula

In the previous chapter, the Kelly formula gave us an idea of what might be the optimal fraction of our capital to invest. So how can we apply this to a trading system?

The data we have available is shown in Figure 3.2. 'Percent profitable' shows how many trades (as a percentage) were winning, W in the Kelly formula (expressing the value as 0… rather than a percentage).

'Ratio avg win / avg loss' is the ratio of average wins to average losses, R in the Kelly formula.

The Kelly formula:

$$K\% = \frac{(R+1) * W - 1}{R}$$

In which, for the case in question:

$$W = 0.4907\ (49.07\%)$$

$$R = 1.3248$$

Trade #	Date	Time	Type	Cnts	Price	Signal Name	Entry P/L	Cumulative
1	1/6/2000	04:30	Sell	1	1,0316	Sell		
	1/11/2000	07:00	SExit	1	1,0263	Buy	642,5000	642,5000
2	1/11/2000	07:00	Buy	1	1,0263	Buy		
	1/17/2000	00:15	LExit	1	1,0127	Money Mngmt Stop	(1720,0000)	(1077,5000)
3	1/18/2000	10:45	Buy	1	1,0118	Buy		
	1/19/2000	11:30	LExit	1	1,0117	Sell	(32,5000)	(1110,0000)
4	1/19/2000	11:30	Sell	1	1,0117	Sell		
	1/20/2000	10:30	SExit	1	1,0108	Buy	92,5000	(1017,5000)
5	1/20/2000	10:30	Buy	1	1,0108	Buy		
	1/25/2000	11:45	LExit	1	1,0041	Sell	(857,5000)	(1875,0000)
6	1/25/2000	11:45	Sell	1	1,0041	Sell		
	1/26/2000	09:30	SExit	1	1,0001	Buy	480,0000	(1395,0000)
7	1/26/2000	09:30	Buy	1	1,0001	Buy		
	1/28/2000	00:15	LExit	1	,9882	Money Mngmt Stop	(1507,5000)	(2902,5000)
8	1/31/2000	09:45	Buy	1	,9794	Buy		
	2/1/2000	08:30	LExit	1	,9694	Money Mngmt Stop	(1270,0000)	(4172,5000)
9	2/3/2000	08:45	Sell	1	,9726	Sell		
	2/4/2000	00:15	SExit	1	,9897	Money Mngmt Stop	(2157,5000)	(6330,0000)
10	2/4/2000	10:15	Sell	1	,9924	Sell		
	2/15/2000	10:15	SExit	1	,9795	Buy	1592,5000	(4737,5000)
11	2/15/2000	10:15	Buy	1	,9795	Buy		
	2/16/2000	09:45	LExit	1	,9803	Sell	80,0000	(4657,5000)
12	2/16/2000	09:45	Sell	1	,9803	Sell		
	2/17/2000	10:30	SExit	1	,9903	Money Mngmt Stop	(1270,0000)	(5927,5000)
13	2/18/2000	06:00	Sell	1	,9882	Sell		
	2/18/2000	10:00	SExit	1	,9882	Buy	(20,0000)	(5947,5000)
14	2/18/2000	10:00	Buy	1	,9882	Buy		
	2/18/2000	11:15	LExit	1	,9854	Sell	(370,0000)	(6317,5000)
15	2/18/2000	11:15	Sell	1	,9854	Sell		
	2/21/2000	08:00	SExit	1	,9867	Buy	(182,5000)	(6500,0000)
16	2/21/2000	08:00	Buy	1	,9867	Buy		
	2/23/2000	11:30	LExit	1	1,0038	Sell	2117,5000	(4382,5000)
17	2/23/2000	11:30	Sell	1	1,0038	Sell		
	2/29/2000	02:45	SExit	1	,9682	Buy	4430,0000	47,5000

FIGURE 3.4   Some trades with the strategy.

Using the above data, one obtains:

$$K\% = \frac{(1.3248 + 1) * 0.4907 - 1}{1.3248} = 0.106265 \text{ or } 10.6265\%$$

This means that to maximize profits, we should use 10.6265% of our capital for each trade.

This isn't difficult to do when trading stocks: in general, you pay for what you buy. In this case, though, we're trading derivatives, and the value of what you invest is dictated by the margin required for each single derivative.

A BANAL TRADING SYSTEM

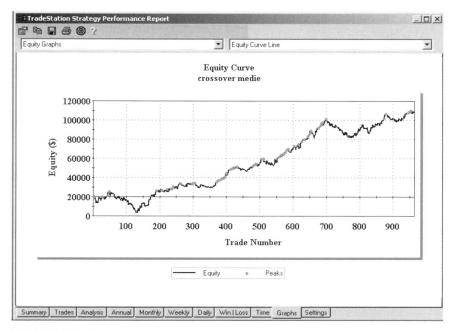

FIGURE 3.5 Strategy equity curve.

To draw an analogy with a euro/dollar contract on CME, let's suppose the margin is 2,500 USD, which means that for every 2,500 dollars available, you could work with one euro/dollar contract.

So, how to proceed? We calculate the amount of our available capital to invest by applying the percentage obtained using the Kelly formula, and then divide this by the margin, to find out how many contracts we can use.

Let's look at a few examples before returning to our data on this specific case.

For example, if we have 100,000 dollars and a Kelly percentage of 25%, the capital to invest would be 25% of 100,000, which is 25,000 USD. If the margin for a contract is 2,500 USD, with 25,000 USD 'investible', we can use 10 contracts (25,000/2,500 = 10).

If the Kelly percentage is 20%, we would have 20,000 USD to invest so, with a 2,500 USD margin we can use 8 contracts (20,000/2,500 = 8).

These calculations are usually rounded down, as a more conservative approach limits risks.

If the Kelly percentage was 17%, the resulting calculation for 100,000 USD would give you 17,000 to invest, which can't be divided by 2,500. In fact $17,000/2,500 = 6.8$ contracts. In this case, even though 6.8 is closer to 7 than 6, we'd trade using 6 contracts (we'll take a look further on at what might happen if we rounded off in a different way).

So, to calculate the number of contracts, we'll use the following formula:

$$\text{contracts} = \text{ENT(capital} * \text{Kelly / margin)}$$

where ENT is the 'entire part of.'

Let's go back to our example, assuming we started with 50,000 USD. For the first trade, therefore, we have:

$$\text{contracts} = \text{ENT}(50{,}000 * 0.106265 / 2{,}500) = \text{ENT}(2.1253) = 2$$

So we'd have used two contracts instead of one.

After every trade, our available capital will have increased in the case of a winning result or decreased in the case of a loss, so we recalculate the number of contracts and apply the result to the next trade.

In our example, the first trade made a 642.5 USD profit, so with two contracts we'd have made 1,285 USD and, starting with 50,000 USD, we would now have 51,285; so the following calculation is:

$$\text{contracts} = \text{ENT}(51{,}285 * 0.106265 / 2{,}500) = \text{ENT}(2.1799) = 2$$

So we'd continue to trade with two contracts, and so on.

Applying this formula to all 964 trades made over the six-year period produces the situation shown as a graph in Figure 3.6.

The thinner line shows the trend of the capital if trading with just one single contract. You start with 50,000 USD and end up with 138,082.5 USD. (In fact, Figure 3.2 shows a profit from the strategy of 88,082.5 USD, which, when added to the initial 50,000, produces this figure.)

The thicker line shows the trend of the capital trading with a number of contracts calculated each time, using the Kelly formula.

As you can see, for quite a long time (around half the length of time for which the strategy was adopted), the performance obtained using the Kelly formula was worse than what you would have made without adopting any particular money management stratagems. Then, suddenly, profits rocket to close with a capital of 433,090 USD six years later.

Why does the Kelly formula produce worse results than a single contract strategy for such a long time?

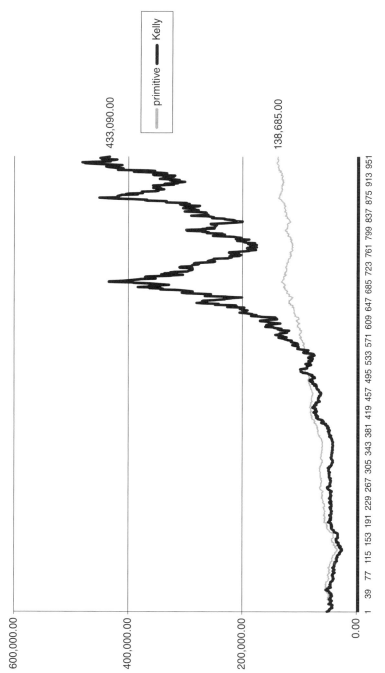

FIGURE 3.6 Comparison between performance with one contract and the Kelly formula.

TABLE 3.1

Trade number	Result	Capital with 1 contract	Contract using Kelly	Capital with Kelly contracts
1	642.5	50,642.50	2	51,285.00
2	−1720	48,922.50	2	47,845.00
3	32.5	48,890.00	2	47,780.00
4	92.5	48,982.50	2	47,965.00
5	−857.5	48,125.00	2	46,250.00
6	480	48,605.00	1	46,730.00
7	−1507.5	47,097.50	1	45,222.50
8	−1270	45,827.50	1	43,952.50
9	−2157.5	43,670.00	1	41,795.00
10	1592.5	45,262.50	1	43,387.50

We can find the answer to this question by simply taking a look at the results of the first trades and what happened in terms of equity, as shown in Table 3.1.

Note that, as may seem obvious, using more contracts amplifies profits in the case of winning trades but also amplifies losses in the case of losing trades; and, in our system, after the second trade the results with the Kelly formula look worse than with just one contract.

The percentage we calculated was for the entire timeline of the system that, sooner or later, would have borne fruit as expected and as shown by the upswing around halfway through the period of the system.

Note also that the line produced by the Kelly percentage is actually a pessimistic representation of the real performance that could have been obtained from the theoretical line. As mentioned above, in fact, the number of contracts is always rounded down, so you're effectively using a lower figure than the Kelly percentage. If we could use fractions of contracts, the scenario would be quite different. Figure 3.7 shows a comparison with a purely theoretical line applying the Kelly formula, without rounding down.

Note that if we could use fractions of contracts we would have made a total of 807,419.77 USD final profit, which is just under double what was obtained in practice.

This result may give you cause to reflect on why you should round the number of contracts down, and encourage you to round the number up, or perhaps round off to the nearest whole number.

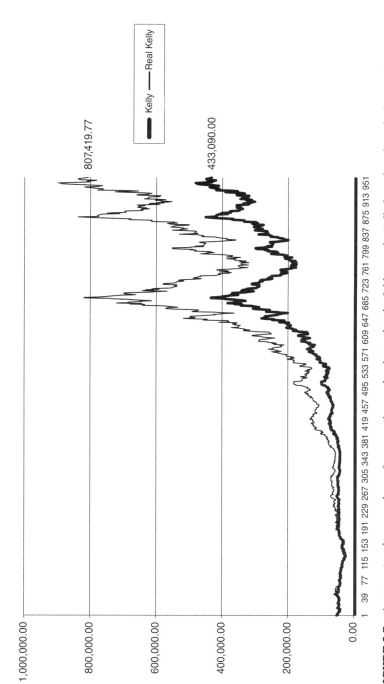

FIGURE 3.7 A comparison between the performance that can be obtained in the field using the Kelly formula and purely theoretical results (thin broken line).

Figure 3.8 provides the answer to this by comparing the exact Kelly line with a rounded-up number of contracts, and the number of contracts rounded off to the nearest whole number (1.7 contracts becomes 2, as does 2.1).

At a glance you won't see much difference between the results of the three methods and, in effect, the final capital doesn't change a lot:

807,419.77 USD without rounding off

798,135 USD rounding up

836,130 USD rounding off to the nearest whole number

It would appear that rounding off to the nearest whole number gives the best results, but this is a purely academic exercise: we'll study this subject in greater depth later and see that it isn't prudent to take this sort of risk.

Applying the Kelly formula to trading proves interesting and the results shown without a doubt encourage us to use it.

There are, however, various considerations to bear in mind in terms of the theoretical results shown.

First, if we compare the chart in Figure 3.5 with any of the lines produced by the Kelly formula, it's easy to see that not only is the capital amplified, but the fluctuations of the same are too.

In Figures 3.6 and 3.7 the line from Figure 3.5 is shown as the 'primitive.' You'll immediately notice this line is definitely flatter and more regular compared to the 'roller coaster' line of the Kelly formula.

If we follow the line produced when we apply the Kelly formula to the letter (therefore rounding down the number of contracts), Figure 3.9 reveals some interesting points.

There is a first significant peak at 434,040 USD followed by a bad period that brought the capital down to 175,172.5 USD. Later, the system produced a new high at 450,957.5 USD, followed by a low of 301,112.5 USD.

Frankly, I have serious doubts that anyone could sit back and watch periods like this without panicking or suffering some kind of emotional consequences. The trader, in fact, doesn't know that, after that low there'll be other highs, and even the greatest faith in a system has its limits.

Finally, Figure 3.10 shows the most significant peak values of the line when the number of contracts obtained using the Kelly formula was rounded off to the nearest whole number.

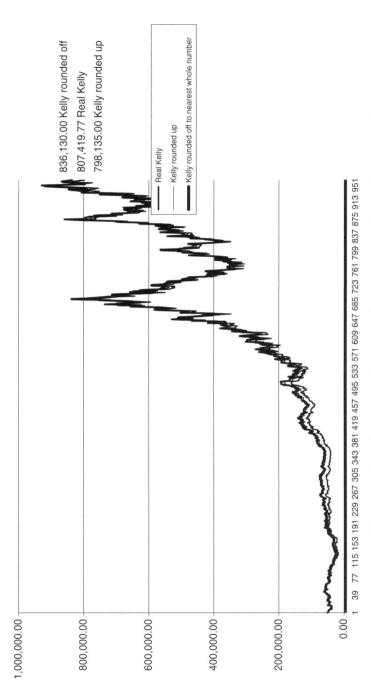

FIGURE 3.8 Comparison of different rounding off methods for the number of contracts calculated using the Kelly formula

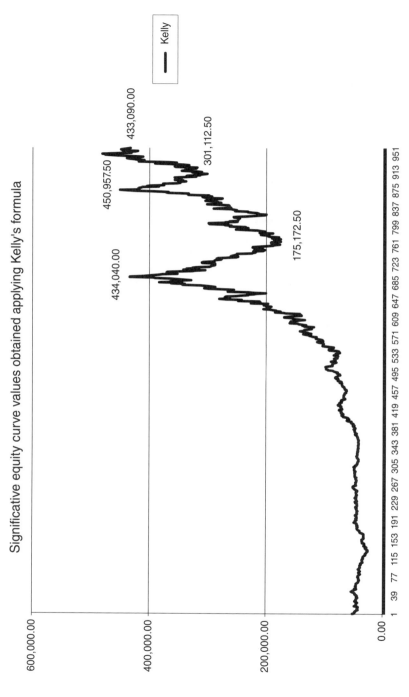

FIGURE 3.9 Peak equity values applying the Kelly formula.

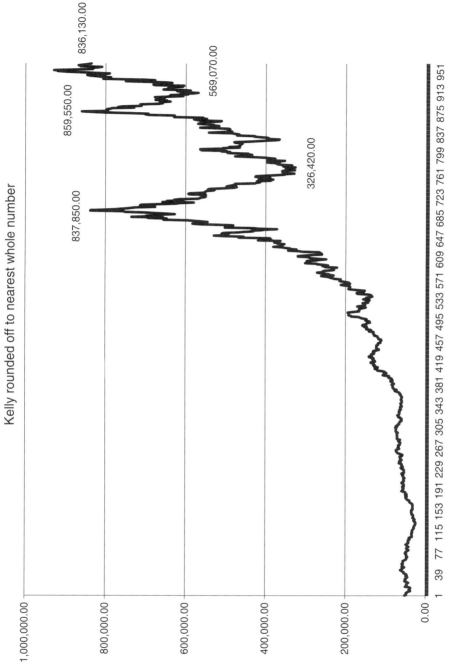

FIGURE 3.10 A half-million-dollar drawdown.

In this case, the final results are, as mentioned above, much more interesting, but there's a significant drawdown too: from over 800,000 dollars the line drops to just over 300,000 dollars. I think many traders might have been discouraged in a case such as this.

We made an absolutely reasonable hypothesis to take the right path using the strategy proposed with an available capital of 50,000 USD, and the results are those shown above.

Now what would have happen if we had just 30,000 USD?

Figure 3.11 shows the resulting equity lines: the primitive again with just one contract (average thickness unbroken line), Kelly (thin broken line) rounding down the number of contracts from the Kelly formula, and the thick broken line obtained by rounding the values of the formula off to the nearest whole number.

The line produced by the simple Kelly method looks strange, and after an all-but-invisible start got bogged down at 23,500 USD, while the equity without money management added the usual 88,082.5 USD to the initial capital (30,000 + 88,082.5 = 118,082.5) and applying the Kelly formula rounded off to the nearest whole number increased the capital from 30,000 to 421,245 USD.

No problem with the primitive, although the flat trend of the Kelly line is perplexing. So, what happened?

The accumulated losses reduced the capital to a value that, using the Kelly formula, produced a number of contracts less than 1 and, after rounding down, this means using 0 contracts.

In particular, with the available data:

$$K\% = 0.106265$$
$$\text{Margin} = 2{,}500$$

So, with the remaining 23,500 USD:

$$\textbf{contracts} = \textbf{ENT(23,500} * \textbf{0.106265 / 2,500)}$$
$$= \textbf{ENT(2,497, 2275 / 2,500)} = \textbf{ENT(0.998891)} = \textbf{0 !\,!}$$

With 0 contracts, obviously the system won't be trading.

As we can see from the chart, rounding off to the nearest whole number, which in this case would be 1, produces very different results, and the system continues trading with 1 contract.

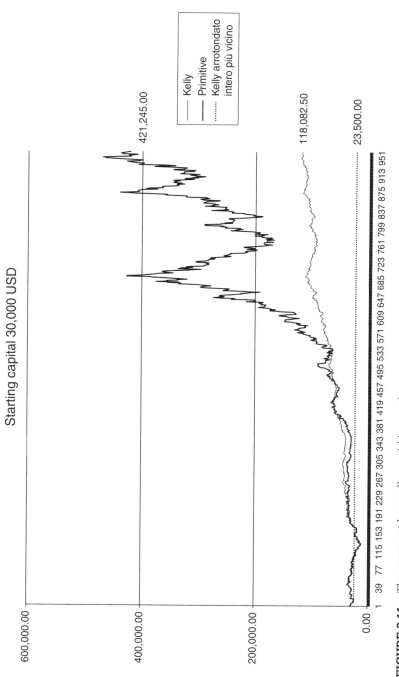

FIGURE 3.11 The system with a smaller available capital.

So, is rounded off to the nearest whole number the best approach? Not at all; also in this case, you might find the number to round off is less than 0.5, which would give you 0.

In particular, with initial capital of 25,000 USD compared to the 30,000 USD in the previous example, we'd obtain the following equity line (Figure 3.12).

Just a little less capital blocks the thin line at a value that's quite close to that of the previous case, but the concept remains valid, and this time we apply also (and more painfully) the principle of rounding off to the nearest whole number. An unlucky start reduces the capital from 25,000 USD to 11,205 USD, and as a consequence:

$$\textbf{Contracts} = \textbf{Rounded off}(11,205 * 0.106265 / 2,500)$$
$$= \textbf{Rounded off}(1,190.6993 / 2,500)$$
$$= \textbf{Rounded off}(0.47628) = 0$$

Simply because we can't apply the Kelly formula in a strictly mathematical way, but have to round off to use a whole number of contracts, we found ourselves in evident difficulty, and had to stop using a system that would eventually have made a profit.

This isn't the biggest problem, though. It's well known that the famous American trader Larry Williams used the Kelly formula in the World Cup Trading championship in which he increased his available capital from 10,000 USD to over 1 million USD in one year. It was an extraordinary result, but Larry Williams soon stopped using this method after a number of crushing defeats.

The main reason is that the formula is based on the past history of the system and calculates the percentage with reference to trades from a certain period.

Future trades may be better than those of the past, but also worse, and putting your trust in an estimate of how a system works can be extremely hazardous.

Let's not forget that in trading the maximum possible loss is never defined, and in this example the trading was done deliberately in a way to make the stop-loss uncertain, so we cannot measure a decent average loss used in the Kelly formula calculations. In our system, for example, we set a stop-loss of 1,250 USD, but in Figure 3.4 there are various trades that lose more. Why? If you take a closer look at the figure, you'll note that these trades all closed at 00.15 – in other words, on the first bar of the day. Evidently, the market opened with a gap so that the stop-loss wasn't triggered at the

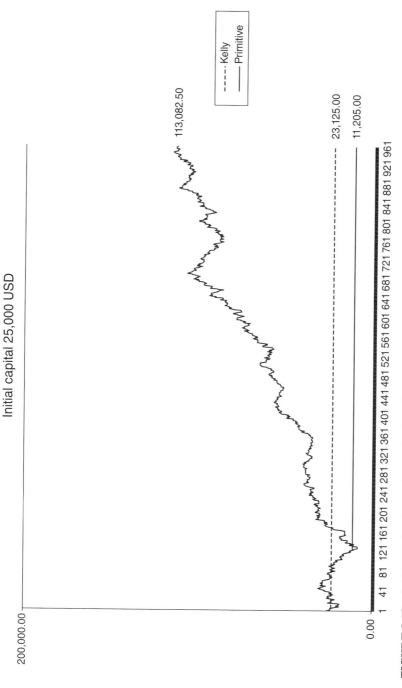

FIGURE 3.12 5,000 USD less is enough to make the technique that produced a result of over 400,000 USD, fail.

desired level. Cases of this kind are considered to be quite normal in this line of work, and you can never put blind faith in a maximum theoretical loss. Even leaving aside the possibility of opening with a gap, and using just intraday techniques, there's always the risk of losing more than you planned as the technology used to send the orders to the market can cause delays or even be unexpectedly blocked.

■ 3.3 Conclusions

In the previous chapter we saw how the Kelly percentage maximizes profits, which are therefore worse if you use higher percentages. So, Kelly represents a case of limit risk, and trading at your limit when you don't fully comprehend the conditions you are trading in is never recommendable.

What's more, it's important to emphasise that, when you start using a system, you don't know its characteristics. Now, after recording data for six years, we could start to use this approach and apply the Kelly formula with the data obtained from the report. This, however, wouldn't have been possible six years ago, and in this case we would have expected a certain number of trades (around 20) and, on the basis of the statistics of these, we would have calculated the first Kelly formula. Then, as we went, we would have adjusted the values by adding new information from the new trades. It's obvious that this approach loses a lot in terms of precision and is detrimental to the basic idea.

For those who, on the other hand, consider the Kelly percentage to be too aggressive, some have suggested one could use fractions of the Kelly percentage; but at this point it's better to study other methods to quantify the most suitable number of contracts to trade with. In the next chapter we'll take a look at some of the most widely used methods and consider the pros and cons of the same, obviously also on the basis of what difference they might make when applied to our system.

CHAPTER 4

Money Management Models

In this chapter I'll illustrate some of the most popular money management methods. The approach we've studied up to now using the Kelly formula attempts to adapt to the characteristics of the system, adjusting the amounts of the bets on the basis of purely statistical data on the same. We've already discussed the limits of this method and the possible negative repercussions. When studying different approaches, the tendency is to concentrate on what the consequences of what we decide to do might be. The methods we'll take a look at are based on concepts the aim of which is to consider negative cases and limit their impact. Kelly tried to maximize profits, without worrying about individual transitory events (in fact he focused on how these combined, analyzing the final statistics). Many methods have, however, been developed to attempt to consider the possible effect of every choice made, step-by-step. So now there's more focus on the effects of losses and the impact these can have both in terms of global equity, but also psychologically.

Some of the methods we'll take a look at start with the most negative case possible, when the system suffers the worst loss, and on the basis of said data, attempt to adjust the amounts used to enter trades and limit possible negative impact.

These methods have been refined and initiated to consider also combinations of negative events, which generally occur in periods of marked drawdowns. Therefore, considering what might be a difficult period to get through for many traders, methods have been devised that attempt to get you out of said period in the best possible way.

We'll start by presenting the systems that aim to adjust the size of the trade to limit loss of capital to a certain value. We'll look at several variations that, over the years, have been proposed by people who've studied these techniques, and other methods that aim to limit fluctuations in the capital by, within certain limits, regulating appreciation and, above all, depreciation.

■ 4.1 The Fixed Fractional Method

The fixed fractional method or fixed fraction or %*f* is by far the most widely used money management method in the world of trading. There may be different facets, but it's always based on the same principle.

In practice, the system bases its calculations on establishing what percentage of your capital to risk on each trade. This percentage is referred to in fact as a fraction or %*f* or simply *f*.

The method doesn't consider the parameters of the trading system, as is the case with the Kelly formula; but attempts to focus on the investor's psychology, with the investor choosing how much they are willing to lose.

The basic method considers the system stop-loss as the loss on a single contract. Once the available capital is known, you establish the fraction *f* you intend to risk, to define the total amount of money you are willing to lose, then this figure is divided by the stop-loss in order to calculate how many contracts you can use.

An example is the best way to explain this principle.

Let's suppose you have capital of €100,000 and are willing to risk 5% of it.

Our system, for example, has a €1,250 stop-loss. Risking 5% of €100,000 means you're willing to lose a total of €5,000. If, in theory, you could lose €1,250 on each contract, you could use four contracts (5,000/1,250 = 4).

If, on the other hand, you want to limit the risk to 4% of the capital, that means a potential loss of €4,000, so, you'd only be able to use three contracts after rounding down the result of the division (4,000/1,250 = 3.2).

TABLE 4.1

Trade no.	Result
1	−500
2	1300
3	700
4	−1250
5	−1000
6	2500
7	5350
8	−1250
9	600
10	350

With this method you recalculate the number of contracts after every trade, and proceed as before.

Let's suppose we have the series of trades shown in Table 4.1.

Now, suppose you want to limit your risk to 5%. Referring to Table 4.2, you'll see the various steps for building the equity with an initial capital of €100,000 and a €1,250 stop-loss.

Figure 4.1 shows various scenarios for different risk percentages.

Note how the results are quite different after the tenth trade, and also how increasing the risk percentage doesn't necessarily increase the final result; at least not in all cases, as can be seen from the result with a 50% risk, which is lower than the result with a 25% risk.

After the seventh trade, a 50% risk made more than any of the others, but on the eighth trade this was drastically put back into perspective after, in fact, 50% of the capital was lost. A €1,250 stop-loss, which was considered the worst hypothesis, had in fact been triggered, and in this case the trader was willing to risk half his capital.

The fact that increasing the risk doesn't always increase profits, appears after all to be quite obvious if we consider that, for a trader willing to risk 100%, it would only take one losing trade at the maximum level to lose all his capital and, therefore, be unable to continue trading.

It must be emphasized that the drawdown is not directly linked to the percentage risked, but this, in fact, depends on the sequences of trades. The only certainty is that by risking a percentage f, your percentage drawdown

TABLE 4.2

Trade No.	Capital	Amount risked	Contracts	Total result
1	100000	5,000 (5% of 100,000)	4 (5,000/1,250)	−2,000 (4 contracts with €500 loss each)
2	98,000 (€100,000 − 2,000 lost in 1st trade)	4,900 (5% of 98,000)	3 (4,900/1,250 = 3.92 to be rounded down)	3,900 (3 contracts with €1,300 gain each)
3	101,900 (€98,000 + 3,900 profit)	5,095 (5% of 101,900)	4 (5,095/1,250 = 4.076 to be rounded down)	2,800 (4 contracts with €700 gain each)
4	104,700 (€101,900 + 2,800 profit)	5,235 (5% of 104,700)	4 (5,235/1,250 = 4.188 to be rounded down)	−5,000 (4 contracts with €1,250 loss each)
5	99,700 (€104,700 + 5,000 lost)	4,985 (5% of 99,700)	3 (4,985/1,250 = 3.998 to be rounded down)	−3,000 (3 contracts with €1,000 loss each)
6	96,700 (€99,700 + 3,000 lost)	4,835 (5% of 96,700)	3 (4,835/1,250 = 3.868 to be rounded down)	7,500 (3 contracts with €2,500 gain each)
7	104,200 (€96,700 + 7,500 just made)	5,210 (5% of 104,200)	4 (5,210/1,250 = 4.168 to be rounded down)	21,400 (4 contracts with €5,350 gain)
8	125,600 (€104,200 + 21,400 just made)	6,280 (5% of 125,600)	5 (6,280/1,250 = 5.024 to be rounded down)	−6,250 (5 contracts with €1,250 loss each)
9	119,350 (€125,600 + 6,250 lost)	5,967.5 (5% of 119,350)	4 (5,967.5/1,250 = 4.774 to be rounded down)	2,400 (4 contracts with €600 gain each)
10	121,750 (€119,350 + 2,400 just made)	6,087.5 (5% of 121,750)	4 (6,087.5/1,250 = 4.87 to be rounded down)	1,400 (4 contracts with €350 gain each)

trade no.	Result	trend with various risk % starting with €100,000 using a €1,250 stop-loss							
		2.50%		5%		7.50%		10%	
		contracts	equity	contracts	equity	contracts	equity	contracts	equity
1	−500	2	99000	4	98000	6	97000	8	96000
2	1300	1	100300	3	101900	5	103500	7	105100
3	700	2	101700	4	104700	6	107700	8	110700
4	−1250	2	99200	4	99700	6	100200	8	100700
5	−1000	1	98200	3	96700	6	94200	8	92700
6	2500	1	100700	3	104200	5	106700	7	110200
7	5350	2	111400	4	125600	6	138800	8	153000
8	−1250	2	108900	5	119350	8	128800	12	138000
9	600	2	110100	4	121750	7	133000	11	144600
10	350	2	110800	4	123150	7	135450	11	148450

trade no.	Result	15%		20%		25%		50%	
		contracts	equity	contracts	equity	contracts	equity	contracts	equity
1	−500	12	94000	16	92000	20	90000	40	80000
2	1300	11	108300	14	110200	18	113400	32	121600
3	700	12	116700	17	122100	22	128800	48	155200
4	−1250	14	99200	19	98350	25	97550	62	77700
5	−1000	11	88200	15	83350	19	78550	31	46700
6	2500	10	113200	13	115850	15	116050	18	91700
7	5350	13	182750	18	212150	23	239100	36	284300
8	−1250	21	156500	33	170900	47	180350	113	143050
9	600	18	167300	27	187100	36	201950	57	177250
10	350	20	174300	29	197250	40	215950	70	201750

FIGURE 4.1 Equity trend for different risk percentages.

will be at least f. Actually, even this isn't an absolute certainty; in fact a percentage f is lost if the trade loses exactly the amount you decided on when setting the stop-loss. But there may also be the fortunate hypothesis in which none of the trades is stopped out, and the only losing trades are trades with a slight loss, the trade being reversed.

If, for example, you are long with an open loss of €500 and there is a short signal, you would close the trade long with a loss of €500, less than the €1,250 set as the max. loss in the system.

While on one hand a losing trade can certainly be considered to be a measure of the psychological stress involved in constantly following the rules of the system, the percentage drawdown is probably even more so; in other words, in percentage terms how much your equity has dropped after reaching the relevant level.

In the above example, the situation of the drawdowns on the basis of the risk is quite different, and it's worth analyzing it, always bearing in mind that you never know how an investment choice will end (if we did know everyone would choose to risk 25%, which after the 10 trades shown produced the best result).

Figure 4.2 shows the drawdown level (shown as DD) for each calculated equity, and the relevant percentage (DD%) for each trade.

For a better understanding of the figure, let's analyze the first equity figure, with a 2.5% risk percentage.

As mentioned above, the first trade lost €1,000, so after starting with €100,000 we now have €99,000 with a drawdown of €1,000. In percentage terms, this is exactly 1% of €100,000.

The following trade brought the equity up to €100,300, the high reached to that point. As this is a new high, the drawdown is reset: it will be recalculated on the basis of this level.

Then, a new winning trade further increases the level of the equity to €101,700, which is again an absolute high and a new starting point for calculating the drawdown.

MONEY MANAGEMENT MODELS

equity f = 2.5%	DD	DD%	equity f = 5%	DD	DD%	equity f = 7.5%	DD	DD%	equity f = 10%	DD	DD%
99000	1000	1.00%	98000	2000	2.00%	97000	3000	3.00%	96000	4000	4.00%
100300	0	0.00%	101900	0	0.00%	103500	0	0.00%	105100	0	0.00%
101700	0	0.00%	104700	0	0.00%	107700	0	0.00%	110700	0	0.00%
99200	2500	2.46%	99700	5000	4.78%	100200	7500	6.96%	100700	10000	9.03%
98200	3500	*3.44%*	96700	8000	*7.64%*	94200	13500	*12.53%*	92700	18000	*16.26%*
100700	1000	0.98%	104200	500	0.48%	106700	1000	0.93%	110200	500	0.45%
111400	0	0.00%	125600	0	0.00%	138800	0	0.00%	153000	0	0.00%
108900	2500	2.24%	119350	6250	4.98%	128800	10000	7.20%	138000	15000	9.80%
110100	1300	1.17%	121750	3850	3.07%	133000	5800	4.18%	144600	8400	5.49%
110800	600	0.54%	123150	2450	1.95%	135450	3350	2.41%	148450	4550	2.97%

equity f = 15%	DD	DD%	equity f = 20%	DD	DD%	equity f = 25%	DD	DD%	equity f = 50%	DD	DD%
94000	6000	6.00%	92000	8000	8.00%	90000	10000	10.00%	80000	20000	20.00%
108300	3100	2.78%	110200	15400	12.26%	113400	25400	18.30%	121600	31400	20.52%
116700	0	0.00%	122100	3500	2.79%	128800	10000	7.20%	155200	0	0.00%
99200	17500	15.00%	98350	27250	21.70%	97550	41250	29.72%	77700	77500	49.94%
88200	28500	*24.42%*	83350	42250	*33.64%*	78550	60250	*43.41%*	46700	108500	*69.91%*
113200	3500	3.00%	115850	9750	7.76%	116050	22750	16.39%	91700	63500	40.91%
182750	0	0.00%	212150	0	0.00%	239100	0	0.00%	284300	0	0.00%
156500	26250	14.36%	170900	41250	19.44%	180350	58750	24.57%	143050	141250	49.68%
167300	15450	8.45%	187100	25050	11.81%	201950	37150	15.54%	177250	107050	37.65%
174300	8450	4.62%	197250	14900	7.02%	215950	23150	9.68%	201750	82550	29.04%

FIGURE 4.2 Equities and the relevant drawdown levels.

The following trade, however, reduces the capital by €2,500 from the high reached to that point of €101,700 to €99,200. The drawdown in this case is, in fact, the difference between the maximum equity and the current level, in other words:

$$101,700 - 99,200 = 2,500.$$

In percentage terms, 2,500 of 101,700 is 2.46%.

Another losing trade decreases the equity again to €98,200. This value differs €3,500 from the high of €101,700 and in percentage terms €3,500 of 101,700 is 3.44%.

A winning trade will increase the equity again to €100,700, but this value isn't a new high and remains exactly €1,000 (0.98% of €101,700) below the best high, up to this point.

Another winning trade increases the equity to €111,400, which is the highest value it has yet reached, so a new starting point for the drawdown values.

Immediately, a losing trade decreases the capital to €108,900, €2,500 less than the previous high it just reached. The drawdown at this moment is exactly €2,500, which, as a percentage of €111,400 (we must now use this new high as a reference), is 2.24%.

Finally, two winning trades increase the equity first to €110,100 and then to €110,800. Neither of these values is a new high, and for each, the difference from the absolute maximum is calculated as, respectively, €1,300 and €600, 1.17% and 0.54% of the maximum level of the equity.

It's evident that, in percentage terms, the worst situation was reached with a 3.44% loss on the high and this value is therefore highlighted.

The same logic was applied to all the other scenarios, and the value at the moment of the greatest loss in percentage terms on the high was highlighted for all.

Note that the maximum percentage drawdown doesn't necessarily coincide with the maximum absolute drawdown. In particular, this can be seen in the last table in which the dreadful drawdown in percentage terms of 69.91% corresponds to an absolute value of €108,500 while, subsequently, there is a drop of as much as €141,250; which at that time, however, was just 49.68% of the maximum equity reached up to that point.

In general, the percentage values are considered, assuming resistance to losses will increase as the capital increases. In other words, losing €1,000 if you have €10,000 isn't the same thing, in psychological terms, as losing

€1,000 if your capital is €100,000. The same amount in the first cases is 10% of the capital, while in the second case it's just 1%, so is considered much more tolerable.

It's evident that greater exposure will produce very different trends, both in terms of profit and loss. The table shows that choosing a 25% risk percentage would have produced the most capital after 10 trades, but one might ask how many speculators would have been able to withstand a 43.41% drawdown, momentarily finding themselves (but, not knowing the future, they certainly couldn't imagine the subsequent recovery) with €78,550 of the initial €100,000.

There's no one percentage that's better than others because each leads to subjective considerations that should always be made honestly. Personally, I don't think I'd be happy in any of the cases with a DD% of over 25%, regardless of the large profits I was hoping for.

In any case, the fixed fractional method is one of the methods I prefer and use to trade. I'll go into this later on in the book to develop other examples and considerations.

■ **4.2 Optimal *f***

At this point, it's worth taking a look at optimal *f*, which you may have already heard of. I'll try to explain it, both in theoretical and practical terms, to clear up any doubts.

The concept was developed and explained by the mathematician Ralph Vince, and his friend Larry Williams. Vince thought it was insane to trade without trying to maximize profits and tried to come up with a system to do just that. He stopped Larry Williams using the Kelly formula, considering it unsuitable for diversified systems like those used in trading where the concept of gain/loss is characterised by various facets.

To calculate optimal *f*, Vince considered the trades the system had made, and of these the worst loss, then parametrised all the trades in relation to the result. Therefore, if the worst loss of a system was €1,200, another loss of €600 is 0.5 (half the max. loss), while a gain of €1,800 is 1.5 (1.5 times the max. loss, with a minus sign as the cash flow is going in the opposite direction).

Ralph Vince presented his theory in the book *Portfolio Management Formula: Mathematical Trading Methods for the Futures, Options and Stock Markets*. As he's a professor of mathematics who learned to trade in the field, the terms he uses can seem confusing and be somewhat difficult to interpret. Let's take a look at the formula he proposes and see how to use it.

These are the terms used by Vince:

P_n – the profit of the nth trade

HPR_n (holding period return of n) – the capital multiplier associated with the nth trade

WCS (worst-case scenario) – the maximum loss in the analyzed period

TWR (terminal wealth relative) – the initial capital multiplier after a series of trades

f – the fraction of the capital risked on each trade

The following formulas are used:

$$HPR_n = 1 - f * (P_n/WCS)$$
$$TWR = HPR_1 * HPR_2 * HPR_3 * \dots HPR_n$$

Optimal f is the value of f that produces max. TWR.

In my opinion, considering it in the above way just creates confusion, so let's take a detailed look at a few examples.

First and foremost, let me explain what a capital multiplier is: let's suppose that in a trade you lose 10% of your capital – you'll be left with 90%. That trade reduced the capital by 10%, leaving 90%, so the capital multiplier is 0.9.

Vice versa, a trade that produced a 5% gain would increase the capital by 5 percentage points and the equivalent would be a capital multiplier of 1.05.

HPR is therefore a number which, when multiplied by the capital, produces the capital after the trade of reference.

If the first trade loses 10% and the second makes a 5% profit on the remaining capital, the final capital is obtained by multiplying the initial capital first by 0.9 and then by 1.05.

The same result is obtained if the winning trade came before the losing one, multiplying first by 1.05 and then by 0.9 to obtain the same result.

trade no.	Result	capital before trade	trade %	trade HPR
1	−500	100000	−0.50%	0.9950
2	1300	99500	1.31%	1.0131
3	700	100800	0.69%	1.0069
4	−1250	101500	−1.23%	0.9877
5	−1000	100250	−1.00%	0.9900
6	2500	99250	2.52%	1.0252
7	5350	101750	5.26%	1.0526
8	−1250	107100	−1.17%	0.9883
9	600	105850	0.57%	1.0057
10	350	106450	0.33%	1.0033
final capital		106800	TWR =	1.0680

FIGURE 4.3 HPR and TWR for the series of 10 trades with just one contract.

The product of all these number gives you the final capital.

Let's take a numerical example and have a look at the 10 trades we used in the previous examples.

At the moment, we'll limit the study to the results that would be obtained using just one contract. The first trade produced a €500 loss, which is 0.5% of the initial €100,000, and as a consequence, the HPR is 0.9950 $(1 - 0.5/100)$. The second trade produced a €1,300 profit, which is 1.31% of the remaining capital of €99,500 and the HPR is 1.0131. The following trade made a €700 profit on the available €100,800 (99,500 + the 1,300 profit), which is 0.69% and the HPR $= 1.0069$ and so on up to the tenth trade that made a €350 profit on the available capital of €106,450, which is 0.33% and the HPR $= 1.0033$.

The final capital is €106,800. Multiplying all the values in the HPR column produces the number referred to as TWR (1.0680), which one can see is the multiplier of the initial €100,000, to obtain the final €106,800.

Applying money management principles, the result of the various trades changes as the number of contracts used changes.

So, let's see how we can explain Vince's HPR_n formula. In the equation, WCS is our −1,250, as this is the worst trade of the series. With this trade the loss is equal, in percentage terms, to the value of f chosen for our method. This is true by definition as we decided that, in the case of a €1,250 loss (our stop-loss) we didn't want to lose more than f% of our capital.

So in this case the HPR is $(1 - f)$. In the hypothesis that f is equal to 0.1, or chosen because we don't want to lose more than 10% of our capital if the

€1,250 stop-loss per contract is triggered, the HPR would be 0.9 with an available capital of 90% remaining.

If the loss was half of €1,250, obviously we would have lost half also in percentage terms, in other words $f/2$, and the HPR would therefore be $(1 - f/2)$. In the case of a winning trade, for example equal to €1,250, it's easy to see that, instead of losing a fraction f of our capital, we gain it, and the HPR is $(1 + f)$.

The meaning of the following formula is clear in consideration of the above:

$$\text{HPR}_n = 1 - f * (P_n/\text{WCS})$$

where P_n/WCS represents the ratio of the result of the trade to the worst trade. If P_n is half the WCS this would be 0.5 and $\text{HPR} = 1 - f*0.5$. If we make a €1,250 profit instead of the same loss, the result of trade P_n would be $-\text{WCS}$ (the opposite of the worst loss) and the P_n/WCS ratio would be $-\text{WCS}/\text{WCS} = -1$ so $\text{HPR} = 1 - f*(-1) = 1 + f$, which is the same result we obtained above using logic.

So, let's calculate the various HPR and TWR for each risk percentage in the same series of 10 trades.

An attentive observer will note that the TWR values obtained, when multiplied by the initial €100,000, do not produce exactly the capital in the examples in Figure 4.2. In the case of the 50% risk, the total was €201,750, while the TWR 2.0726 in Figure 4.4 would produce a final capital of €207,260. The same is true, if we take another example, for the 2.5% risk for which Figure 4.2 shows a final capital of €110,800, while the TWR of 1.1366 in Figure 4.4 would produce a final capital of €113,660. If you've been following closely from the start, you might have already come up with an explanation for this difference. In practice, the TWR results calculated in Figure 4.4 are purely mathematical, while the capital obtained in the calculations in Figure 4.2 reflect the real-world limits and are subject to adjustments due to rounding off the number of contracts to a lower whole number, as fractions of contracts obviously can't be used on the markets. If the real-world profit is more than the theoretical application, this is merely because in a losing trade there were fewer contracts than the theoretical number.

The table in Figure 4.4 represents the process used by Ralph Vince. In practice, once you've done the calculations he proposes, you need a lot of patience, or a suitably programmed calculator, to calculate the TWR for f

trade no.	Result	Pn/WCS	HPR for %f = 2.50%	5.00%	7.50%	10.00%	15.00%	20.00%	25.00%	50.00%
1	−500	0.4	0.99	0.98	0.97	0.96	0.94	0.92	0.9	0.8
2	1300	−1.04	1.026	1.052	1.078	1.104	1.156	1.208	1.26	1.52
3	700	−0.56	1.014	1.028	1.042	1.056	1.084	1.112	1.14	1.28
4	−1250	1	0.975	0.95	0.925	0.9	0.85	0.8	0.75	0.5
5	−1000	0.8	0.98	0.96	0.94	0.92	0.88	0.84	0.8	0.6
6	2500	−2	1.05	1.1	1.15	1.2	1.3	1.4	1.5	2
7	5350	−4.28	1.107	1.214	1.321	1.428	1.642	1.856	2.07	3.14
8	−1250	1	0.975	0.95	0.925	0.9	0.85	0.8	0.75	0.5
9	600	−0.48	1.012	1.024	1.036	1.048	1.072	1.096	1.12	1.24
10	350	−0.28	1.007	1.014	1.021	1.028	1.042	1.056	1.07	1.14
WCS = −1250		TWR	1.1366	1.2732	1.4082	1.5397	1.7857	1.9980	2.1647	2.0726

FIGURE 4.4 HPR values for each trade and TWR for each chosen f.

that changes from 0.01 to 0.99 increasing by 0.01 (or even by 0.001). Of all those TWRs there will be one that's highest, and Ralph Vince called the value of f that produced that TWR, Optimal f.

As long as we're dealing with just a few trades, as in our example, you can do the calculation using a simple Excel table, and Figure 4.5 shows the results of the TWR trend for different f values. Note that the highest value is obtained risking 37% of the capital.

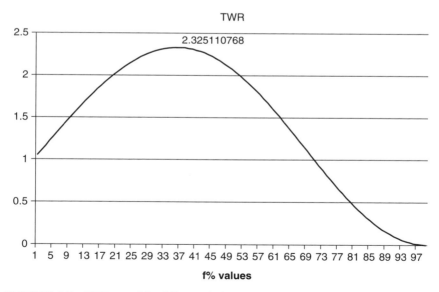

FIGURE 4.5 TWR trend for different f values.

trade no.	Result	37% contracts	equity
1	−500	29	85,500
2	1,300	25	118,000
3	700	34	141,800
4	−1,250	41	90,550
5	−1,000	26	64,550
6	2,500	19	112,050
7	5,350	33	288,600
8	−1,250	85	182,350
9	600	53	214,150
10	350	63	236,200

FIGURE 4.6   Results with $f = 37\%$.

At this point, it's important to field test an f of 37% to see how our 10 trades would have done. Figure 4.6 shows the results.

Everything in this section should be considered for purely educational purposes, and I stress that it's highly inadvisable for anyone to invest on the markets using risk percentages close to *optimal f*. I must also say that the above examples may be distorted by another parameter that hasn't been considered in this section: the margin of each single contract. The limit of the number of contracts obviously depends on the margin required. For example, if the margin was €2,500, the figures would probably hold true anyway (we won't run precise checks as this isn't the purpose of this chapter), but in cases of greater requirements it would have been impossible to make many trades with the specified number of contracts.

◼ 4.3 Secure *f*

The objections raised after analyzing the equity trends as the risk changes, mainly concern the drawdown when taken as an indication of how much the trader is suffering. Towards the end of the 1990s, Zamansky introduced the concept of secure f as an alternative to optimal f.

In practice, this concept re-proposes the investor's psychology as the cornerstone on the basis of which market position choices are made; while optimal f is based exclusively on recorded system data, with secure f the trader takes a decision on the basis of the maximum historical drawdown.

So, of all the possible fractions, you choose the one that maximizes profits, on the condition that the drawdown shown is below a certain percentage chosen by the trader.

If we refer to Figure 4.2, a trader who didn't want to find himself in situations with a worse DD% than 25% would certainly choose an *f* of 15% as his secure *f*. Another trader, more inclined to gambling, might be happy with a DD% of 45% and as a consequence would choose a secure *f* of 25%. On the other hand, if you didn't want a DD% of over 4%, you'd choose a percentage of around 2.5%.

Obviously, secure *f* will never be greater than optimal *f*, as the latter is the value that maximizes system gains to the greatest extent.

If you've been following this chapter closely, you'll see that there aren't considerable conceptual differences between the fixed fractional, optimal *f*, and secure *f* methods, as they're all based on the same principle of limiting the risk of losing to a certain percentage of your capital. The optimal *f* and secure *f* methods try to maximize profits in a way that's compatible with the system, in the first case, and with the investor's psychology, in the second. The fixed fractional method leaves you greater freedom, but its mathematical construction is very similar to the other two.

With the fixed fractional method, I mentioned using the presumed value of the loss to establish the number of contracts; in the examples shown the theoretical system stop-loss was used. As mentioned in the previous chapter, this is not always the best choice, as often the actual loss is worse than what was expected due to market gaps, slippage caused by a fast-market or technical problems with orders. Also referring to what Ralph Vince used, Larry Williams proposed an application of the fixed fractional method as a solution; this time, though, using the system's maximum historical loss. In his first works he even mentioned doubling said loss for the calculations, although later he didn't use this multiplication factor; but it's merely a quasi-philosophical question, as eventually the choice of the percentage to risk is down to the trader, and using double the loss rather than the actual loss could encourage the use of higher percentages, while it would be more conservative to use just the actual loss.

In practice, using the fixed fractional method in a purely theoretical sense, with a system that has a €1,000 stop-loss and a capital of €100,000, a trader who wanted to risk 5% on each trade would start as follows:

$$5\% \text{ of } €100,000 = \text{risk } €5,000.$$

So, €1,000 loss on each contract for the first trade with five contracts (in the worst-case scenario you'll lose €5,000).

Williams, however, would have read the system report and found the maximum historical loss, as he held that value to be more reliable than the theoretical stop-loss value (this is a very valid reasoning, although you should always bear in mind that it won't protect you completely, as you might have a worse trade than that in the future) and then he would have used that in the calculation.

If, for example, the maximum historical loss was €1,200, without prejudice to the 5% risk of the available €100,000, the calculation would be

$$\text{Contracts} = 5,000/1,200 = 4.167:$$

in other words, 4 rather than the 5 someone who took their decision based on theory alone would have used.

As mentioned above, this approach is more prudent and it's advisable to use it even though it's simply just a conceptual modification of the fixed fractional method.

On the subject, Williams said: If you want to stay in the game, use a conservative approach and don't risk a lot; if you want to win trading championships, use Kelly or optimal f.

According to some traders, who've survived various market ups and downs, the concept of optimal f is useful to understand the absolute limit beyond which you should never go if you want to avoid the risk of going bankrupt, the point of no return called the cliff of death.

There are various facets to the fixed fractional method, the approach described in this book is often called the *percent risk model* as you make trades with a fixed risk percentage.

Another, much more banal, method used with futures, is to have one contract for every €10,000 of available capital. The simplicity of this method is obvious, and it's also very simple to calculate the number of contracts. This is exactly the same model as above, in which the risk percentage is:

$$\%f = -\left(\frac{\text{max } loss}{10,000}\right) * 100.$$

In fact, you can lose the maximum loss on each contract and, using this with the capital of reference for that contract (€10,000 by definition for the method), you obtain the percentage to risk (multiply by 100 to obtain the percentage).

The banality of the method is as obvious as its riskiness; a maximum (theoretical or real) system loss of €1,000 is the equivalent of a 10% risk percentage, which can certainly be considered harsh.

■ 4.4 Fixed Ratio

Ryan Jones, in his work *The Trading Game: Playing by the Numbers to Make Millions,* proposes an interesting alternative to the fixed fractional method with his fixed ratio method.

According to Jones, the fixed fractional method reaches a point where the increase in the number of contracts occurs too quickly and results in drawdown levels that are unacceptable for any trader.

His work attempts to give each contract used the same weight, to maintain its effect unchanged as equity increases.

He is quite damning of the fixed fractional method as, in his opinion, it is too slow when increasing the number of contracts initially, and too fast once capital has been accumulated, he says ironically after 10 years.

His reasoning goes more or less as follows:

Let's suppose you have capital of €100,000, a %*f* of 10%, and a max. loss of €5,000.

Said parameters would initially cause you to risk €10,000 (10% of 100,000) so you could use two contracts. In order to use three contracts, you would need to reach €150,000; in fact 10% of 150,000 is €15,000, which would let you use three contracts.

The next step would be €200,000, at which point you'd have four contracts (10% of 200,000 is 20,000, which is four times the max. loss of €5,000).

Note that the incremental single contract steps could be calculated as follows:

$$\text{step} = \text{max. loss}/\%f$$
$$\text{in fact: step} = 5,000/0.1 = 50,000.$$

With every 50,000 of profit you can increase your number of contracts by 1.

Ryan Jones argues (and does so quite logically) that's it's not the same thing to increase your capital by €50,000 using just two contracts, as at the beginning, as it is to do so once you've reached €1,000,000 and are therefore using 20 contracts. In fact, in the first case, assuming you make a profit of €2,500 per trade per contract, you'd need 10 trades

$(2*2,500*10 = 50,000)$; while, in the second case, you'd just need one trade $(20*2,500 = 50,000)$.

Jones criticizes the slow, difficult start and then considers the increase frenetic once you've built up a significant amount of capital. Again, according to Jones, too sharp an increase at a certain point in the life of the system can result in horrendous drawdowns.

Jones proposes a solution that increments the number of contracts: in other words a ratio set between the gain per contract and the increase in the number of contracts. A ratio of 1:5,000 means increasing by one contract when every contract being used in the system has made €5,000 of profit. The value of the increase per contract is commonly called delta.

Having set a value for delta, Jones increases the number of contracts by one when the capital has increased by the value of delta for every contract used.

An example is the best way to explain this concept:

Let's take the previous case, with an initial capital of €100,000 and a max. loss of €5,000. Jones doesn't set a risk percentage, but rather a value for delta that could be anything but which, for example, we'll set as the same as the max. loss; in other words €5,000.

As there is no initial rule, Jones starts trading with the system using just one contract (note that in the %*f* example we started with two contracts due to the characteristics of the system and the chosen risk profile).

In practice, with one contract it's enough for the capital to reach €105,000 to start using two contracts; in fact every contract used (just one in this case) will have made a profit of €5,000.

At this point you have two contracts and, according to the rule, to add a third, each of the two contracts used must make a €5,000 profit, which makes a total of €10,000.

So, from the €105,000 you reached you now have to reach €115,000 in order to start using three contracts.

With three contracts you have to make a €15,000 profit (5,000 each contract) in order to start using a fourth, so when you've past the €130,000 mark you can start using four up to €150,000 where, having made the necessary €20,000 profit (four contracts times the €5,000 delta each) you can add a fifth contract.

You'll immediately note that, although you started with just one contract, after the €150,000 mark you are already using five contracts, whereas with

capital	%f-10%	Fixed Ratio-delta 5,000
100,000	2	1
105,000	2	2
115,000	2	3
130,000	2	4
150,000	3	5
175,000	3	6
205,000	4	7
240,000	4	8
280,000	5	9
325,000	6	10
375,000	7	11
430,000	8	12
490,000	9	13
555,000	11	14
625,000	12	15
700,000	14	16
780,000	15	17
865,000	17	18
955,000	19	19
1,050,000	21	20

FIGURE 4.7 Different capital levels and numbers of contracts used on the basis of the money management method chosen.

the fixed fractional method you started with two but after the €150,000 mark you only had three contracts.

Figure 4.7 shows the trend in the number of contracts using one method compared to the other. Note that, in the initial phase the fixed ratio method increases the number of contracts much faster, and is then passed by the fixed fractional method.

It's clear that a lower delta accelerates the increment in the number of contracts even more, and this is therefore the variable the trader can use to make the method more, or less, aggressive.

As a general guideline, Jones proposes using a delta equal to half the system's maximum historical drawdown, but leaves the trader free to choose his own level of risk.

Note that using this method lets you trade in conditions in which other methods have to limit exposure by ceasing trading. In fact, there isn't a minimum limit at which you should cease trading (unless you have no liquidity to cover the margins set by your broker). In the above case, a 10% fixed fractional method would be reduced to one contract if the capital dropped below €100,000 and you would have had to cease trading if the capital dropped to below €50,000. In fact, 50,000 * 0.1 = 5,000, which is equal to the max. loss, and if less than this value (and it would be if the capital was less than €50,000) you couldn't trade with a max. risk of 10%.

With the fixed ratio method, on the other hand, there is only a level for the first increment, but no stop level and theoretically you could continue to use one contract for as long as margins allow. On the one hand, this is certainly an advantage, but on the other, it might lead to some unpleasant consequences if you can't put a brake on your enthusiasm.

So, is there a formula for calculating the number of contracts for the fixed ratio method, as there is for the fixed fractional method?

The answer is yes. I won't go into detail about how they came up with the formula, but I will show you how to use it:

If the capital < initial capital then contracts = 1

If the capital > initial capital then:

N.B.: In the following equations INT = ENT (entire part of)

contracts = ENT((1 + SQRT(1+8*(capital – initial capital)/delta)))/2)

or:

$$contracts = INT\left(\frac{1 + \sqrt{1 + 8 * \dfrac{(C - Ci)}{delta}}}{2}\right)$$

Let's take a look at a few examples to see how the equation works. We'll consider an initial capital of €50,000 and a delta of €2,500:

$$Ci = 50,000$$
$$delta = 2,500.$$

Starting with one contract, as mentioned above, once this contract made a profit equal to delta we could start using the second contract. So in this case we need to reach 52,500 to start using two contracts. Let's see if that's the case:

$$\text{contracts} = INT \left(\frac{1 + \sqrt{1 + 8 * \dfrac{(52,500 - 50,000)}{2,500}}}{2} \right)$$

$$= INT \left(\frac{1 + \sqrt{1 + 8 * \dfrac{2,500}{2,500}}}{2} \right)$$

$$= INT \left(\frac{1 + \sqrt{1 + 8}}{2} \right)$$

$$= INT \left(\frac{1 + \sqrt{9}}{2} \right) = INT \left(\frac{1 + 3}{2} \right) = INT(2) = 2.$$

From here on, each of the two contracts should make a €2,500 profit in order to start using the third contract. This means we have to add another €5,000 to our capital (2,500 for each contract used). So let's check with the equation:

$$\text{contracts} = INT \left(\frac{1 + \sqrt{1 + 8 * \dfrac{(57,500 - 50,000)}{2,500}}}{2} \right)$$

$$= INT \left(\frac{1 + \sqrt{1 + 8 * \dfrac{7,500}{2,500}}}{2} \right)$$

$$= INT \left(\frac{1 + \sqrt{1 + 24}}{2} \right) = INT \left(\frac{1 + \sqrt{25}}{2} \right)$$

$$= INT \left(\frac{1 + 5}{2} \right) = INT(3) = 3.$$

The equation works, but the reader is free to run further checks to practice using the formula.

The average trade is the average trade of the system; on average, a contract makes a profit on each trade equal to the average trade. If you divide the value of delta by the average trade you get the average number of trades necessary to increase the number of contracts used by 1. With the fixed ratio method, in fact, you always add one contract when each of the contracts used has gained delta.

Increasing the number of contracts at averagely constant intervals of trades greatly increases the stability of the system, without producing sudden fluctuations that could be difficult for the trader to withstand.

So which method is best? As usual, a lot depends on how much feeling the trader has for the market. In certain cases, the choice of one method over another is closely related to starting conditions. A very limited capital in fact won't let you effectively apply the fixed fractional method unless you use very high risk percentages.

Let's compare the fixed fractional and fixed ratio formulas used to calculate the number of contracts:

$$\textit{ff contracts} = INT \left(\frac{(C * f)}{Maxloss} \right)$$

$$\textit{FR contracts} = INT \left(\frac{1 + \sqrt{1 + 8 * \dfrac{(C - C_i)}{delta}}}{2} \right).$$

Note that, with the fixed fractional method, the number of contracts is directly proportional to the capital (C in the equation), while with the fixed ratio method, this number is calculated by taking the square root of the capital.

This means that the increase in the number of contracts is more marked in the first case, except at low capital values. As mentioned above, the number of contracts increases faster in the initial phases of the system using the fixed ratio method, to later be passed by the fixed fractional method.

This can be interpreted in two diametrically opposed ways.

The first school of thought condemns the behaviour of the fixed ratio method, as it risks more when you have less, and risks less when you have accumulated significant capital.

On the other hand, those who defend the fixed ratio method say this behaviour is more than simply the only one you can use with a reduced capital; it also produces a much more stable equity line once the capital has reached higher values.

Let's take another look at our euro/dollar system, with various scenarios resulting from the application of one method or the other, and the limits of first one, then the other.

Figure 4.8 shows the equity produced by applying the fixed fractional method with a 5% risk percentage and an initial capital of €50,000 (for practical reasons from here on we'll stick to euros instead of dollars, even though the currency is really USD; this doesn't change the results in conceptual terms).

Many might think a 5% risk percentage isn't very aggressive, but with an available capital of €50,000, this means risking €2,500, which can be considered acceptable. In actual fact, it's not a single loss that's the psychological problem for a trader; it's a sequence of negative trades. The equity shown has the same initial flat period, then increases rapidly, as we saw in the examples in which we applied the Kelly formula.

The final result is notable, with a capital of €654,917.5, but the maximum drawdown of €350,000 from 639,920 to 275,317.5 is also considerable!

Figure 4.9 shows how a trader would have done, again starting with €50,000, if he risked 10% of his capital on each trade.

The result is impressive to say the least: the upswing reaches incredible highs, but the subsequent crash from €3,173,825 to just €476,732.5 is also incredible (and, in my opinion, intolerable).

FIGURE 4.8 Applying a 5% fixed risk percentage.

FIGURE 4.9 10% risk on each trade.

It looks like we've found another goose that lays golden eggs. What would happen if we used 11% instead of 10%, just 1% more?

The results are shown in Figure 4.10.

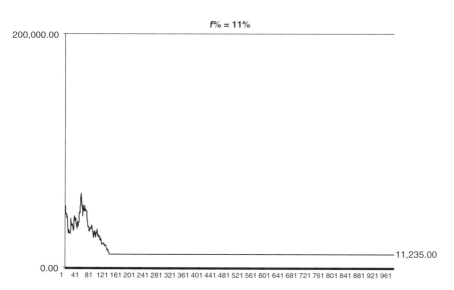

FIGURE 4.10 A risk percentage that's just one point higher blocks the system.

The same thing we saw before (with the Kelly formula) occurs. The residual capital can only be used in theory, but not in practice.

With the fixed fractional method we set a hypothetical max. loss of €1,250, and calculated the number of contracts on this basis.

At €11,235, the calculation is:

$$\text{contracts} = \text{ENT}\frac{(11,235 * 0.11)}{1,250} = \text{ENT}\left(\frac{1,235.85}{1,250}\right) = 0.$$

This may seem slightly puzzling to some who may make the following consideration: if with 11% I can only risk €1,235.85 and then have to cease trading, what could I do with 10%, which is even less? The answer is very simple, risking 10% of the capital from the start you would have reached the same point in the system with more residual funds. In particular, the trade that, with 11%, reduced the capital to €11.235 was trade number 129. For that same trade, starting with a 10% risk, the available capital was still 13,547.5, and the result would be:

$$\text{contracts} = \text{ENT}\frac{(13,547.5 * 0.10)}{1,250} = \text{ENT}\left(\frac{1,354.75}{1,250}\right) = 1.$$

Just a small change makes a big difference in the end.

Note that for this system optimal f would be 23.4%, but you obviously wouldn't be able to continue using this system with such a high percentage; calculated at a purely theoretical level, the only difference being the remaining capital when you threw in the towel, even less than with $f = 11\%$, as shown in Figure 4.11.

So, just as percentages that are too high end in a sort of bankruptcy, percentages that are too low could also prevent you from continuing, or even starting, to use the system.

With an available capital of €50,000 and a max. possible loss of €1,250, obviously the fraction risked must be greater than €1,250 in order to start trading. €1,250 of 50,000 is 2.5%, so this is the minimum possible percentage you could use for this system, at least to start trading. In actual fact, already after the second trade, which reduces the equity to less than €50,000, you will have to cease trading.

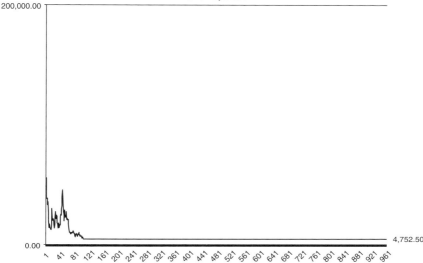

FIGURE 4.11 An attempt using optimal *f*.

With a little trial and error, we can establish that the minimum percentage necessary to continue trading to the end is 3.75%, and this risk would produce the equity in Figure 4.12.

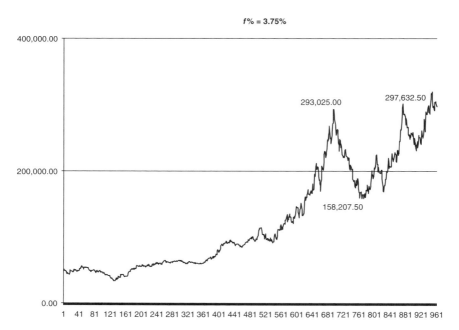

FIGURE 4.12 Minimum risk percentage to keep trading.

Obviously, this percentage depends on the initial capital in the same way as the initial capital depended on the result of the approach when using the Kelly formula.

Note that, even with the minimum possible percentage, the drawdown is still significant. We should remember, however, that this system wasn't considered to be good in the original report (Figure 3.2) and we're only using it in these examples to show the effect of applying money management strategies.

Now let's take a look at the results we would have obtained using the fixed ratio method.

In this case, it's the choice of delta that acts as an amplifier for the number of contracts. The smaller delta is, the faster more contracts can be used as equity increases.

For the first test, let's try a delta that's approximately 50% of the max. system historical drawdown. As shown in Figure 3.2, this drawdown is approximately €22,000, so we'll start with a delta of €11,000. This means we'll add a contract every time each of the contracts used has made €11,000 of profit for the system.

Figure 4.13 shows the results obtained.

The results look quite promising, and there are some similarities to the fixed fractional method line using a minimum risk.

Considering a delta of €11,000 to be rather high, let's take a look at the results with a delta of €5,000 and €2,500, the first acceptable the second very aggressive (these figures weren't chosen at random and are respectively four times and double the maximum theoretical loss).

As you can see in Figure 4.15, the results are better than those obtained using the fixed fractional method with $f = 5\%$ (Figure 4.8), but the drawdown is about the same. Actually, the trend of the drawdown with this system doesn't look good for the fixed ratio method either and, if there's an advantage to be found using this method rather than the fixed fractional method, it lies in the lack of lower risk limits. While in fact, using the fixed fractional method you can't go below certain levels, with the fixed ratio method there are no limits below which the system can't be used.

In the same way, using the fixed ratio method you can push things beyond the higher risk levels, as there's the theoretical possibility of trading with a single contract for as long as margins allow.

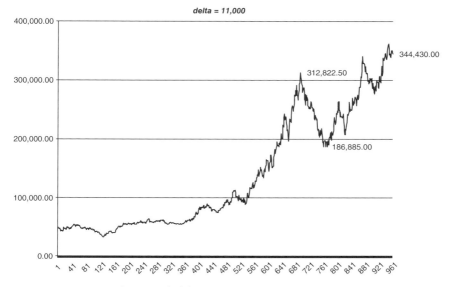

FIGURE 4.13 Fixed ratio with delta = €11,000.

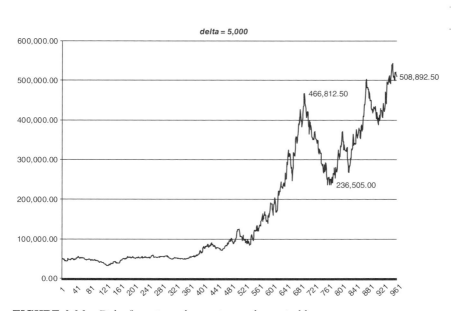

FIGURE 4.14 Delta four times the maximum theoretical loss.

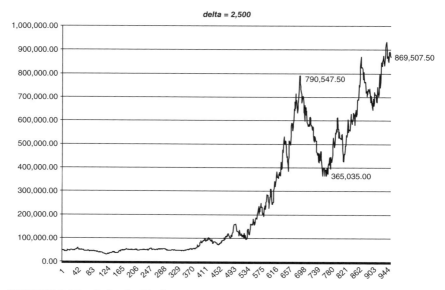

FIGURE 4.15   Delta double the maximum theoretical loss.

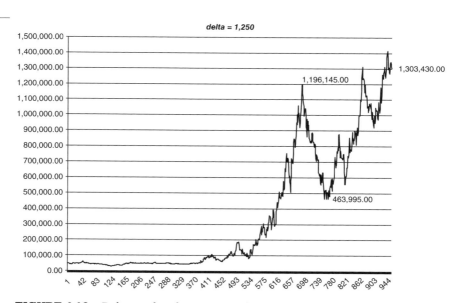

FIGURE 4.16   Delta equal to the maximum theoretical loss.

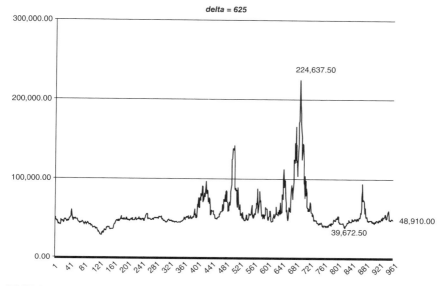

FIGURE 4.17 A delta equal to half the maximum theoretical loss is too aggressive.

An aggressive strategy that pays off (in this specific case) is the one that uses a delta equal to the maximum theoretical loss – in other words, €1,250. The results are shown in Figure 4.16.

You can see some interesting results, with the trend of the drawdown on a par with previous cases, rather than the unsustainable behaviour (compared to the other risk percentages) seen in Figure 4.9.

Finally, here's a limit case, in which the risk becomes excessive and the system fails, as shown in Figure 4.17.

Note that, in this case, the equity never really takes off – except at the system's best moment, when the capital is increased fourfold (max. 224,637.50). But then, the excessive risk reduces the equity to below the initial levels, where it stays to the end.

Note that, in this case, a particularly benevolent future phase of the market wasn't excluded, and this gives the equity a considerable boost, while with the fixed fractional method the system is brought to a halt for good.

■ 4.5 Percent Volatility Model

This method is more difficult to apply in terms of constructing the equation used to calculate the number of contracts.

The idea behind it, as clearly described by Van K. Tharp in *Trade Your Way to Financial Freedom*, is based on market fluctuations and the maximum fluctuation you wish to withstand with your capital.

To measure the fluctuations of the instrument you intend to trade with, a measure of the volatility of the same is used; the daily range from max. to min. is measured, and an average is calculated after a certain number of days. In general, a few days are considered for systems that don't have a long-term open position, and more days are considered for more long-term systems. Let's say it's reasonable to use an average of four to five days for quite fast systems (positions open from two days to one week) and 20 days for systems that follow a trend for longer (positions open from 10 days to one month). The average described is the average of the ranges in the above period. In actual fact, it's more convenient to consider the average true range (ATR) in order to include a possible gap in the opening prices.

In order to understand what the ATR is, we should hypothetically consider a daily futures' bar on the SPMIB index (previously called FIB), the range of which goes from 32,100 to 32,450. The range of this bar is 350 points, or €1,650, as the value of each point is €5. If said bar showed a gap up 50 points on the close of the previous day and the close was 32,050, the true range would allow for this gap and would measure 350 + 50 = 400 points, or €2,000. What's more, as the position will be open for several days, it's only right to consider cases in which the bars were all above or below the close of the previous day.

Figures 4.18 and 4.19 show the two cases in which the bar shows gaps above or below the close.

Now, going back to our model, let's calculate the average of the last five true ranges and take said value as the period volatility. For example, the value may be 300 points, or €1,500.

Supposing we have an available capital of €100,000 and want to set a maximum fluctuation of 2%. The allowed fluctuation would therefore be €2,000. Considering the average volatility of the future calculated as €1,500, the number of contracts is calculated as follows:

$$\text{contracts} = \text{ENT}\left(\frac{2,000}{1,500}\right) = 1.$$

If V_p is the value of the single instrument point (in our example, V_p = 5) and *Vol%* is the allowable fluctuation percentage (in our example,

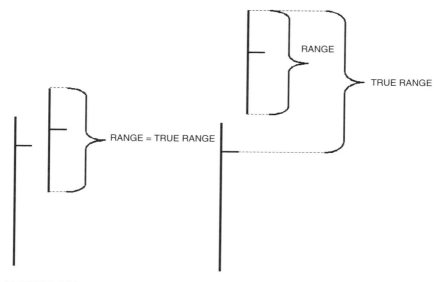

FIGURE 4.18 True range in case of low above previous day's close.

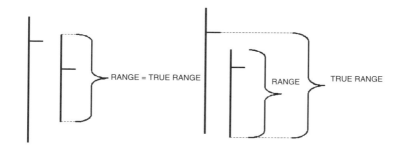

FIGURE 4.19 True range in case of high below previous day's close.

Vol% = 2%), the number of contracts would be:

$$\text{contracts} = \text{ENT}\left(\frac{Vol\% * capital}{ATR(period) * Vp}\right).$$

It's immediately obvious that the construction of this method is more sophisticated as you need to know the true ranges of a certain number of days before the entry point. This value can be calculated when making the trade, but this makes back-testing the system more difficult unless you export a larger amount of data to Excel, or enter the equation for calculating the number of contracts directly in the EasyLanguage code.

The method is of a certain interest as it's not linked, in its own particular way, to the worst loss suffered, although it comes to a halt in conditions considered excessive. Note that, unlike what occurred with the fixed fractional system, which came to a definitive halt once you arrived at an insufficient capital for the maximum allowed loss, this method can be put on standby for periods of time and then start following the signals again in the right volatility conditions. A decrease in market volatility in fact increases the number of contracts calculated by the equation (the volatility is the denominator of the equation, which is a fraction; therefore, the smaller it is, the higher the result) and, at low volatility levels, there may be conditions for following a trade even with very little capital.

Note that this is perfectly logical, if volatility is low you risk less and with less risk you can also trade with less capital.

By way of example, we calculated the results of the euro/dollar system also applying the % volatility method.

Here are the results.

Let's start with 5%, which means you don't want your capital to be affected by volatility over 5%.

Figure 4.20 shows the resulting equity.

MONEY MANAGEMENT MODELS

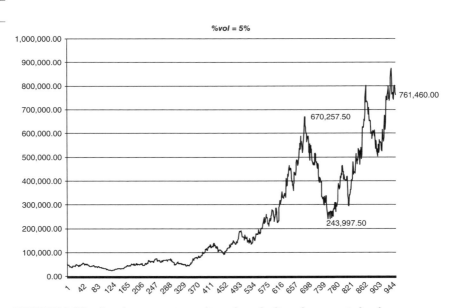

FIGURE 4.20   Results attempting to limit the volatility of your capital to less than 5%.

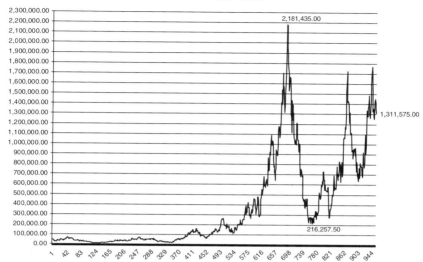

FIGURE 4.21 Results attempting to limit the volatility of your capital to less than 10%.

Figure 4.21, on the other hand, shows the results of limiting volatility to 10%.

As this is conceptually similar to the fixed fractional method, we should of course compare these results with that method and the risk percentages used for the same.

A 5% *f%* produced the results in Figure 4.8, a final equity of €654,917.5 and a drawdown from €639,920 to €275,317.5. Note that with a *%Vol* of 5% the drawdown is very similar to that in Figure 4.8, while the final result is approximately €130,000 higher. Therefore, for the same sufferance the *%Vol* method is best in this case.

At higher percentages such as 10% the *%f* gives better results, with the equity reaching almost 2 million euros (Figure 4.9), but the drawdown is also incredible, from almost 3 million euros to just under half a million.

Using *%Vol* the final result is €1,311,575 but with a lower drawdown, if you can call a drop of almost 2 million euros low.

Remember how more aggressive traders were already brought to a halt by the fixed fractional method risking 11% of their capital on each trade (Figure 4.10)? Using *%Vol,* on the other hand, in this case, you can go much further, as the results in Figure 4.22 show, although I doubt anyone would want to take this as an example for their own trading.

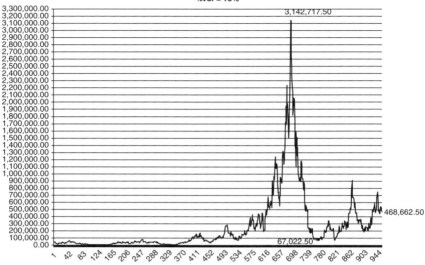

FIGURE 4.22   %Vol allows the use of more aggressive, although not exactly recommendable, percentages.

It's only with even higher percentages that the system goes bankrupt, and in this case, *bankrupt* is exactly the right word as the residual capital with a *%Vol* of 20% would be that shown in Figure 4.23.

With the fixed fractional method, we saw that, depending on the initial capital, not all the risk percentages let you trade. Too low a risk often left insufficient capital, and Figure 4.12 showed how 3.75% was the minimum possible percentage you could use without being brought to a halt.

With *%Vol,* however, the limits are lower simply because there will always be periods in which the market is less volatile, when you can trade also with less capital. Figure 4.24 shows the results, with a percentage that's near the minimum that could be used.

In order to better comprehend how some trades are missed, let's take a look at the table of trades in Figure 4.25, using an allowed volatility of 2%.

After the first trade, possible because the market volatility measured with a five-day ATR was €924.99, if you are willing to risk 2% of the initial €50,000, in other words €1,000, the number of contracts is:

$$\text{Contracts} = \text{ENT}\left(\frac{1,000}{942.99}\right) = 1$$

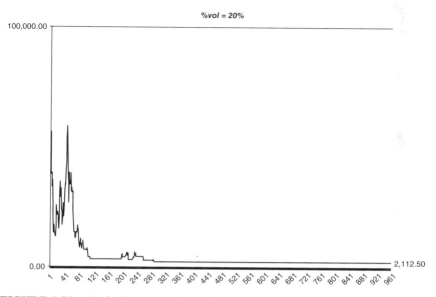

FIGURE 4.23 Too high a risk quickly reduces the capital to a minimum.

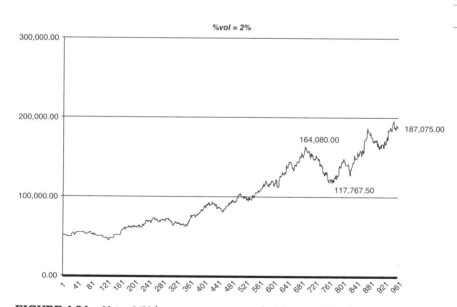

FIGURE 4.24 Using %Vol you can even proceed with just a 2% risk.

trade	volatility	%vol contracts	%vol cumulative	2% of equity
64,250	92,499	1	5,064,250	101,285
−172,000	105,500	0	5,064,250	101,285
−3,250	109,000	0	5,064,250	101,285
9,250	111,250	0	5,064,250	101,285
−85,750	110,750	0	5,064,250	101,285
48,000	109,000	0	5,064,250	101,285
−150,750	103,000	0	5,064,250	101,285
−127,000	105,000	0	5,064,250	101,285
−215,750	130,000	0	5,064,250	101,285
159,250	138,500	0	5,064,250	101,285
8,000	104,750	0	5,064,250	101,285
−127,000	93,250	1	4,937,250	98,745
−2,000	118,750	0	4,937,250	98,745

FIGURE 4.25   First trades using an allowed volatility of 2%.

from this point on, the volatility is always above the level of the maximum range which, recalculated for the level of equity after the first trade of €50,642.5, is €1,012.85. You can only enter the market with a contract when the volatility drops to 932.498. Unfortunately, this is a losing trade and the volatility increases once again, immediately bringing the system to a halt once more.

After running a few tests, there were six cases in which, three pairs showed a similar performance in terms of percentage returns. Of these, the maximum percentage drawdown was measured to see which of them caused the most difficulty to the trader who chose them.

Figure 4.26 shows a table with a summary of these results.

As expected, the fixed ratio method is the one which, for the same returns, has a lower drawdown percentage. It's also interesting to note how apparently the % volatility method produces better results with less risk exposure.

MONEY MANAGEMENT MODELS

fixed fractional	final equity	equity %	max DD%
4%	315,070	530%	46.50%
7%	1,256,233	2412%	71.30%
FIXED RATIO			
12,500	316,003	532%	38.70%
1,260	1,254,973	2410%	62.00%
% volatility			
3.15%	319,855	540%	44.10%
5.60%	1,262,135	2424%	68.90%

FIGURE 4.26   Similar returns using different approaches.

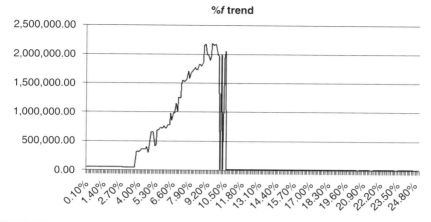

FIGURE 4.27   Final equity trend as the risk percentage changes.

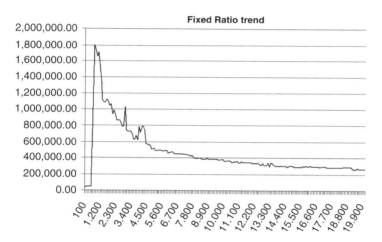

FIGURE 4.28   Trend of the equity as delta changes.

For the system being used, it may be a good idea to create charts of the final equity results, each time, for the percent *f*, fixed ratio, and percent volatility methods.

Figure 4.27 shows the end result for the fixed fractional method as *f* increases. Figure 4.28 shows the trend as delta increases using the fixed ratio method. Figure 4.29 shows the equity trend as the maximum percentage changes using the percent volatility method.

Note the evident differences in the construction of the lines.

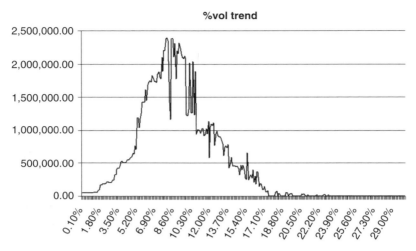

FIGURE 4.29 Trend of the equity as the maximum allowed percent volatility changes.

The line in Figure 4.27 starts flat, and considering the low risk adopted, it's practically impossible to start using the system. Then there is a notable increment as the risk increases until quite an irregular high area. Note that around 10%, there are percentages that produce the highest profits and percentages that lead to bankruptcy. If we take another look at Figure 4.5, the line is very clean with a very regular curvature. Figure 4.27, on the other hand, looks nothing like it, despite being the same method. The difference, once again, is due to the application of a theoretical method in the real world. Figure 4.5 was created without considering market limits, while Figure 4.27 considers everything, from the necessary rounding off of the calculations, to the use of a whole number of contracts, to the limits imposed by margins. In Figure 4.5, the optimal value for maximising profits is 23.4%. In actual fact, you can't use more than 10% because you can't use a fraction of one contract to continue following the signals of the system when the capital is reduced after the first losses (the possibility of using mini futures or something similar isn't considered as it lies outside this context).

The line shown in Figure 4.28, however, shows what happens to the final result using the fixed ratio method. There's an almost vertical upswing immediately (as mentioned above, the lower the delta the more aggressive the system), just over the values that made the system go haywire (see the test with a delta of 625). Then there's a slow but gradual decline with a few ups and downs caused by rounding off to whole numbers of contracts.

Those who wish to avoid sudden fluctuations in returns can use this method, taking care in the initial period or in any period in which the equity drops below the initial capital, with a system that lets you continue in any case with just one contract, as long as the margins allow.

Note that the highest profit that can be obtained using this method is less than the other two cases, although not a lot less.

Figure 4.29 shows the line produced by the limit imposed on the fluctuations in the equity on the basis of market volatility, taken as the average of the last five true ranges.

This line is also quite erratic around the peak percentages. Unlike the line produced by the fixed fractional method, however, there is a much less marked drop, which produces a line similar to the classic 'Gaussian' line. In practical terms, this could mean a brighter future for the trader who, willingly or by mistake, went too far with the percentages (note that, using the fixed fractional method, beyond a certain point there's nothing more that can be done). Obviously, with both the fixed fractional method and the percent volatility method, there are percentages above which there are only losses. The charts in fact don't go as far as 100%, and show a lot less than half that. Also, the fixed ratio method has its limits at much lower delta values, but in a much narrower band than the other methods.

■ 4.6 Levels for Changing the Number of Contracts

The formulas used in the book to calculate a suitable number of contracts for the chosen risk profile can obviously be used for trading; but, in principle, one could also calculate the various threshold levels at which to increase or decrease the number of contracts being used.

Let's take the fixed fractional method, for example, with a maximum theoretical loss of €1,250 and a 5% risk, it's immediately evident that with this method you'll use one contract for every €25,000. The equation is:

$$ff \text{ contracts} = INT\left(\frac{(C * f)}{Maxloss}\right).$$

If we use Contracts $= 1$ we obtain the inverse formula:

$$C = \frac{Maxloss}{f} = \frac{1,250}{0.05} = 25,000.$$

In practice, one contract is added, every €25,000.

TABLE 4.3

Capital	Contracts
< 25,000	System stopped
>=25,000 and < 50,000	1 contract
>=50,000 and < 75,000	2 contracts
>=75,000 and < 100,000	3 contracts
>=100,000 and < 125,000	4 contracts
...	...
>=500,000 and < 525,000	20 contracts

TABLE 4.4

Capital	Contracts
< 55,000	1 contract
>=55,000 and < 65,000	2 contracts
>=65,000 and < 80,000	3 contracts
>=80,000 and < 100,000	4 contracts
>=100,000 and < 125,000	5 contracts

It's simple, one can trade on the basis of Table 4.3.

In the same way you can calculate the fixed ratio levels for a known delta value. With a delta of €5,000 and one contract to start trading with €50,000, by definition, you'd add the second contract at €55,000, the third at €65,000, and so on. So, as shown in Table 4.4.

In this case, the following threshold is again calculated by adding the value of delta for the number of existing contracts.

It can be a good idea to create a table like this so you can quickly see the number of contracts to use for the trade you're opening.

■ 4.7 Conclusions

We've considered various approaches that can be used to manage the number of contracts, some of which are based on the maximum theoretical loss or real past loss of the system, and on this basis you can try to limit future losses to a percentage of your available capital. These methods are based on a risk percentage; in other words how much of your capital you're willing to lose in the trade you're about to place. Another system attempts to increase exposure more gradually once the initial capital has increased, and by considering all existing contracts to be equally important, in practice invests the profits made on the market equally. Finally, the last approach considered assesses recent market behaviour, and assuming the same levels of volatility may be maintained in the short term, aims to limit fluctuations in the equity, limiting the rise or fall of percentage values.

Note that in all the proposed methods, an aggressive approach only pays off up to a certain point. When there is a considerable increase in the percentage drawdown values as risk increases, you reach a failure point at which you lose most of your capital after the initial exponential gains.

■ References

Jones, Ryan. *The Trading Game: Playing by the Numbers to Make Millions*. New York: John Wiley & Sons, 1999.

Tharp, Van K. *Trade Your Way to Financial Freedom*. New York: McGraw-Hill, 2007.

Vince, Ralph. *Portfolio Management Formulas. Mathematical Trading Methods for the Futures, Options, and Stock Markets*. New York: John Wiley & Sons, 1990.

CHAPTER 5

Refining the Techniques

■ 5.1 The Importance of the Trader's Temperament

Once you've familiarised yourself with the techniques described in the previous chapter, with due consideration you can go beyond the basics and study the variations that are best suited to your character.

As we've seen, there are different schools of thought on the exposure to risk, depending on the capital you've accumulated. Ryan Jones with his fixed ratio method prefers a more noticeable risk at first, then a subsequent reduction when you've accumulated significant capital. Everything is relative; a trader who starts with €10,000 could tolerate a €500 loss, which would be 5% of his capital, but he'll probably consider a €5,000 loss hair-raising. If the same trader used the fixed fractional method, and everything went as planned, at a certain point he might have increased his capital to €100,000. At that point risking the same 5% would mean risking the same €5,000, but now it would probably worry him less. What we're doing is analyzing things from the point of view of the person's temperament. If the trader had made that €100,000 over a period of five years, he'd have gradually got used to larger and larger cash flows, and would be naturally ready to face a potential loss of €5,000. If the increment was unexpected, however, and the lucky trader found himself with €100,000 in just six months, I sincerely doubt that, no matter how euphoric he was, he'd be psychologically prepared for the 'new' situation and €5,000 would still seem like a lot.

My intention, with this example, is to get you to reflect on the different positions someone who chooses one or the other route will be in. He who sets a constant *%f* won't worry about how much available capital he has and how long it takes the situation to change, continuing unruffled to mechanically apply the chosen method. He who thinks along the same lines as Jones, on the other hand, will consider it wiser to reduce the risks at a certain point to avoid heavy losses.

The choice between the fractional *f* or fixed ratio method (leaving percent volatility aside for a moment) isn't the only way to match the trader's temperament, though.

■ 5.2 Reduced *f*

If, for example, we decided to trade with a *%f* of 10% until our capital doubled, then reduced it to 7.5% until it was three times the initial capital, and then set the risk percentage to 5% until it was four times as much, to 2.5% up to eight times the initial capital and then 1.25% for every higher value, we'd be trading more aggressively at the start, then reducing our exposure more or less gradually (the steps were chosen merely by way of example).

Table 5.1 shows a summary of the chosen steps.

To check the validity of this approach, we'll compare it with the equity that produces more or less the same result, adopting the fixed ratio money management method.

TABLE 5.1

equity	%f
<= 2 x initial capital	10%
>2 and <= 3 x initial capital	7.5%
>3 and <= 4 x initial capital	5%
>4 <= 8 x initial capital	2.5%
> 8 x initial capital	1.25%

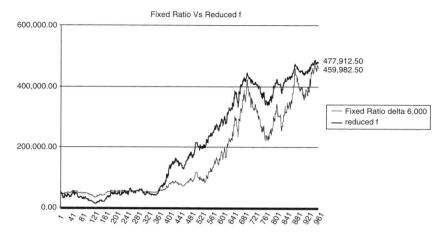

FIGURE 5.1   The final results are almost the same but with different trends.

Figure 5.1 shows a direct comparison with the line produced using a delta of €6,000.

The bold line shows the line produced by the reduced percentage method, while the thin line shows the line produced using the classic fixed ratio method. The idea of the approach to risk is the same in both cases. In fact, both gradually reduce how aggressive the method is as the capital increases. Note, though, how the reduced f method (as I've arbitrarily named it) has a 'softer' trend and the drawdown suffered around halfway is that of the fixed ratio line.

Note also that in the initial period, the reduced f line dropped below the fixed ratio line. In fact, this is the period in which it adopted an aggressive approach with a 10% risk, which accentuates negative periods.

Many variables can be used when choosing steps to build a risk model that's well-suited to any trader.

Let's look at another example, with more aggressive percentages, in Table 5.2.

As well as the final higher percentage, 'stronger' percentages are used throughout this example.

This choice produces a final capital of €623,827.5. To obtain a comparable result using the fixed ratio method, you'd have to adopt a delta of €3,500. Figure 5.2 shows a comparison of the lines.

TABLE 5.2	
equity	%f
<= 2 x initial capital	10%
>2 and <= 3 x initial capital	9%
>3 and <= 4 x initial capital	7.5%
>4 <= 6 x initial capital	5%
> 6 x initial capital	2.5%

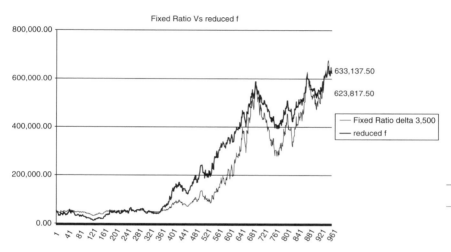

FIGURE 5.2 Another comparison confirms the fluctuations in the equity line with the reduced *f* method are less harsh.

Also in this case we can see that, while both lines show a more pronounced dip in the drawdown period, the reduced *f* method loses 'just' around €200,000 compared to 300,000 with the fixed ratio method.

■ 5.3 Aggressive Ratio

Obviously, we could apply the same principle, inverted, to the fixed ratio method to make it more aggressive after accumulating sufficient funds.

But what we're doing is trying to limit the drawdown and make the capital growth line as tolerable as possible; applying a strategy that decreases delta as the capital increases would be a move in the opposite direction.

Merely by way of example, let's see how a fixed ratio strategy would behave. In this case, we'll call aggressive ratio that reduces delta by 10% every time a profit equal to the initial capital is made. In any case, we'll limit the minimum delta used to a quarter of the initial delta. The values chosen are absolutely arbitrary and the purpose of the same is merely to show the trend of the resulting line.

Table 5.3 shows a summary of the delta used, starting from 5,000, with an initial capital of €50,000.

Figure 5.3 shows the equity compared with an equity that produces a similar final result obtained applying the fixed fractional method (with a risk of 5%).

You'll immediately see that an aggressive ratio strategy doesn't produce any advantages as the equity line looks just like the %f one. The drawdown in the aggressive ratio version is slightly worse than that of the corresponding fixed risk line, so there's no point in looking for special algorithms to vary delta to make the method more aggressive when equity is high.

TABLE 5.3

Equity	Delta
From 50,000 to 100,000	5,000
From 100,000 to 150,000	$5,000 * 0.9 = 4,500$
From 150,000 to 200,000	$5,000 * 0.8 = 4,000$
From 200,000 to 250,000	3,500
From 250,000 to 300,000	3,000
From 300,000 to 350,000	2,500
From 350,000 to 400,000	2,000
From 400,000 to 450,000	1,500
From 450,000 to 500,000	1,250
From 500,000 up	1,250

FIGURE 5.3 A comparison between a classic %*f* line and a Fixed Ratio line with a decreasing delta (aggressive ratio).

■ 5.4 Asymmetric Ratio

In his paper, Jones proposes a variation of his method called *asymmetric ratio*. In this version he studies the possibility of changing the levels at which a contract is added or subtracted as equity increases or decreases. His first consideration is to decrease the number of contracts more quickly when equity decreases to limit the possibility of a drawdown.

This is certainly a good idea, in order to limit damage while still obtaining good results, but it is complicated to implement. Every method someone comes up with needs to be tested, and there's nothing to say that what works well on one system will work well on others.

In order to better understand Jones's idea let's take a delta of 5,000 and an initial capital of €50,000. At €55,000, you'd start using two contracts, and three at 65,000. With a symmetrical method, below 65,000 you'd go back to two contracts and below 55,000 to a single contract. Adopting an asymmetrical method on the other hand you could decide to go back to one contract halfway, or go from two to one at 60,000 instead of 55,000 (60,000 is halfway between 55,000 and 65,000). A test run on our system shows this doesn't produce real benefits, though. The drawdowns, in fact, remain more or less the same, and final profits are slightly lower.

FIGURE 5.4 A comparison between the fixed ratio method and a version taking things slow to keep everything under control.

Figure 5.4 shows the comparison between the two lines. It's easy to see that these complications in terms of calculations didn't produce the benefits we'd hoped for.

■ 5.5 Timid Bold Equity

The above test was run in an attempt to try and 'calm' the roller-coaster ride of an equity line in relation to the increase in the number of contracts.

Obviously, there are also those whose reasoning is exactly the opposite, who are happy to safeguard the initial capital and risk all the profits they've made. In a certain sense, the fixed ratio method behaves intrinsically in this way, increasing the number of contracts only as profits increase. In fact, the formula considers the difference between the level of the equity and the initial capital, therefore excluding the latter when calculating the number of contracts.

The fixed ratio method, on the other hand, has proven to be a rather 'conservative' method as your available capital increases, and might not be the ideal solution for someone who wanted to use a more aggressive approach on the market, while still treating your initial capital with kid gloves.

On this subject, K. Van Tharp proposes the idea of splitting your capital into two parts, the first to be traded at a low risk and the second at a high risk (which he calls timid and bold). His idea is to calculate the number of contracts to use with the fixed fractional method, but applying two different percentages to the two parts of the capital, in particular a low-risk percentage to the part to keep and a high-risk/returns percentage to the remaining part.

In particular, he considers it expedient to apply the optimal f percentage to the high-risk part.

Finally, as far as the division is concerned, he suggests considering the initial capital low risk and the profits made on the market high risk. This can be done using any thresholds you want. In particular, once the capital has doubled, it would be advisable to start again from scratch, keeping double the initial capital that was kept previously and applying the risk percentage to what's left over.

Starting with €50,000, for example, you'd trade with a percentage of 5% applied to €50,000, the result of which is 2,000. To this you'd add the value you get from applying the optimal percentage to the profits. Remember, optimal f for this system was 23.4%. Therefore, if you reached a capital of €60,000 you'd calculate the number of contracts as follows:

$$\text{contracts} = \text{ENT}\left(\frac{((50,000 * 5\%) + (60,000 - 50,000) * 23.4\%)}{1,250}\right)$$
$$= \text{ENT}(3.872) = 3.$$

On the other hand, by applying 5%, as we would traditionally, to the entire €60,000, we would have obtained:

$$\text{contracts} = \text{ENT}\left(\frac{(60,000 * 5\%)}{1,250}\right) = \text{ENT}(2.4) = 2.$$

After €100,000, you'd apply 5% to 100,000 and 23.4% to anything over that, up to 150,000 where the capital up to 150,000 would be calculated at 5%, and so on.

Figure 5.5 compares the trend of this line with a fixed fractional method, always using 5%.

Note that the result is almost double, but the drops during the drawdown periods are worse, too. Note also that, in fact, although a higher percentage is used on anything over the initial capital (or multiples of the same), the

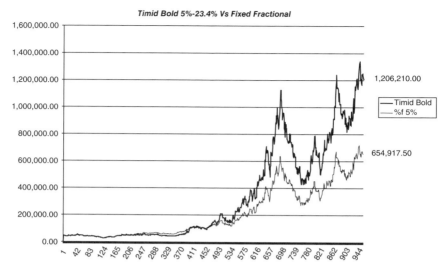

FIGURE 5.5 A comparison between a standard line and one that risks more on accumulated gains.

final result represents a higher percentage for all the capital. Starting with three contracts instead of two is simply more risky. It doesn't matter if the third contract is used applying an imaginative formula; you're simply risking more. To prove this, we could apply the same concept to a base percentage of 4% and 23.4% to anything over the initial capital. The results are shown in Figure 5.6.

Note how the fixed 4% line proceeds as usual without a hitch (remember 3.75 was the minimum that could be used for the series of trades using this system), while the timid/bold line is blocked.

This is because more was risked at the beginning and the initial negative period brought the line to €30,997.5, which wasn't enough for even one contract:

$$\text{contracts} = \text{ENT}\left(\frac{(30,997.5 * 4\%)}{1,250}\right) = \text{ENT}\,(0.99192) = 0.$$

Risking always and only 4% the equity never dropped this low so the system could continue to trade.

This is an example of how a more aggressive strategy can produce both damage and benefits. What's important is to know this, and therefore be prepared for the negative consequences such a choice might entail.

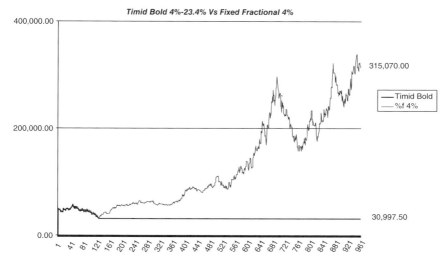

FIGURE 5.6 Reducing the base percentage from 5% to 4% blocks the mixed curve.

5.6 Equity Curve Trading

One concept that's very popular with traders is adapting your trading to the principal equity, the original equity with just one contract. This means trying to stay in the saddle as far as possible, making the most of good times and leaving it be during the bad.

One method is to calculate a moving average of the equity and check when the two lines (the equity line and the average equity line) cross in order to find, more or less, favourable or unfavourable trend periods. The number of periods to use to calculate the moving average depends to a great extent on the type of system, although often traders use 30 periods of good results.

Figure 5.7 shows the trend of the principal equity of the system and the average of the same over 30 periods.

What this method does is prevent trading when the equity curve is below its moving average.

Figure 5.8 shows a comparison between the lines produced by a 5% risk using the fixed fractional method. The thick line shows that obtained blocking the system when the principal equity was below its average over 30 periods.

Note that the final result of this method, ceasing trading in negative times, is worse than the complete method but, without a doubt, the trend of the

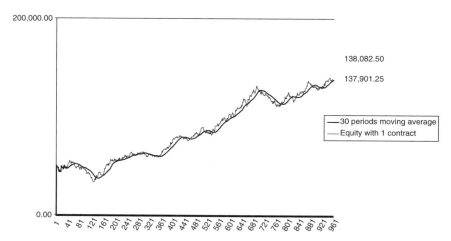

FIGURE 5.7 Trend of the principal equity and the crossover with the moving average of the same over 30 periods.

FIGURE 5.8 Trend of the equity with %f = 5%, blocking some trades.

equity is more 'benevolent.' The drawdowns are much more acceptable, and the worst period of the system is kept 'frozen' to start trading again only during the subsequent positive recovery.

Let's take a look at what would have happened if we used the system in a more aggressive way, respectively, with risk percentages of 7.5%, 10%, and finally, 15%, which, as you may recall, was a disaster.

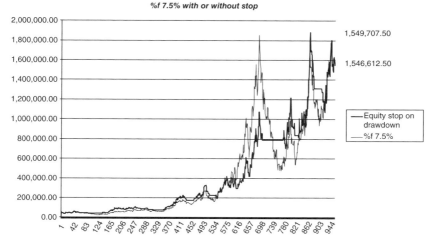

FIGURE 5.9 A %*f* of 7.5% produces results that are practically the same for the two methods.

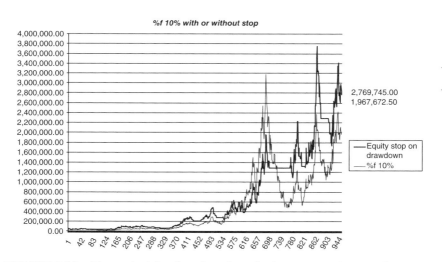

FIGURE 5.10 The method that doesn't trade in the downturns ends up producing much better results with an aggressive %*f*.

It's worth taking the time to reflect on what we can see in this line. It isn't an invitation to increase risk percentages with no limits, ceasing trading when the system goes into a stall; but it does show how a system one might call 'irregular' with nasty drawdown periods, as every moving average crossover system tends to be, can be improved by adapting your trading

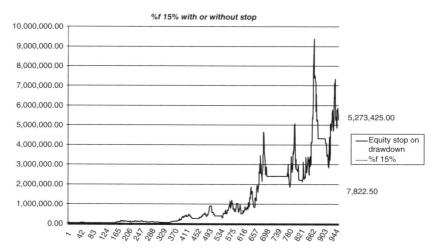

FIGURE 5.11   Ceasing trading at the worst times can produce impressive results.

to the trend of the system. Note that, for a moving average crossover system more than others, the trend reflects the market period and, adjusting to the results of the system means adjusting to the market's behaviour in that particular period.

This is what happens using the fixed fractional method, ceasing trading below the average.

FIGURE 5.12   With stops below average the fixed ratio equity improves.

Now let's take a look at the fixed ratio methods using the same technique, in other words making no trades in the periods in which the equity with 1 contract is below the average of that equity over 30 periods. We'll consider cases with a delta of €5,000, €2,500 and €1,250 respectively; in other words starting with a 'normal' delta and getting more aggressive.

FIGURE 5.13 Fewer drawdowns with an aggressive delta and stops below the moving average.

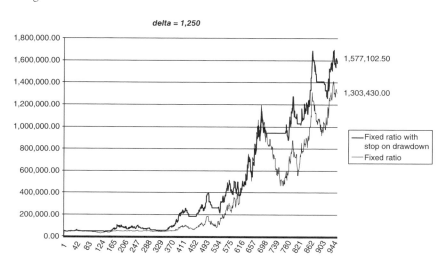

FIGURE 5.14 A very aggressive delta, which produces good results with acceptable fluctuations.

FIGURE 5.15   %vol of 3%; the results are the same but the line is more regular with stops below the average.

To conclude this analysis, let's take two cases applying the percent volatility method with an allowed volatility of 3% and 15%, the first quite a delicate approach, the second very aggressive.

Note that, for lower values of the allowed percent volatility, the result doesn't change a great deal. The only difference is that there are some more easygoing periods at the times when the market was unfavourable for the strategy. You'll recall that at low *%vol* values the system itself prevents trading at various entry points, automatically filtering potentially hazardous ones.

The scenario with a very aggressive percentage, such as an allowed volatility of 15%, is very different. The final result, ceasing trading at times when the principal equity is below the 30-day average, produces almost 10 times what we would have obtained if we continued trading. A look at Figure 5.16 shows this is mainly due to keeping equity high after the seven-hundredth trade.

Obviously, while on the one hand the final result is certainly remarkable, the drawdown suffered from the highest equity levels is also quite painful. In fact, I believe this example should only be taken as mathematical proof of the method, and I wouldn't want to encourage anyone to use such levels of risk.

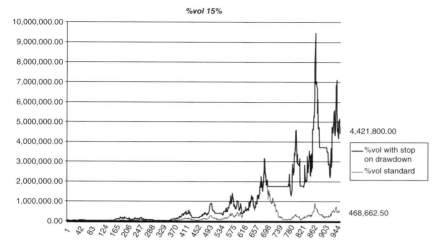

FIGURE 5.16 An extreme %vol, not trading at unfavourable times, changes the results considerably.

It must be said that blocking the system below the moving average improves the final situation for systems that suffer marked drawdown periods. Ceasing trading, in fact, more often than not, prevents following the signals during prolonged depreciations in the equity. Often, the very configuration of a system alternates good and bad periods, and this method aims to cease trading in the bad ones. Remember, we're working with a banal moving average crossover system, and it's well known that these systems work well in trend periods, while suffering heavy drawdowns when the market becomes congested. It's also well understood that the market alternates trend periods with congested periods, and by ceasing trading below the equity's moving average we can often stay away from long periods of congestion.

That's not all. This type of stop also protects you from the risk of finding yourself with a system that, for whatever reason, no longer works. If the system is doing badly, this acts as a sort of emergency brake applied before you lose the profits you managed to accumulate up to that point.

There are other systems, though, that – thanks to special filters – produce a much more regular equity line with much less marked drawdowns. If we tried to apply a system stop of this kind to one of these systems, we'd always and inevitably obtain worse historical results. We should consider, however, that these systems already have a filter upstream that cleans up the equity trend. (It would be very difficult for a system without special filters, intended as additional conditions, to produce a regular equity line.) Applying this filter is a good idea for the purpose of protecting yourself from the possible 'demise' of the system.

■ 5.7 z-Score

Another trading technique based on past system data analyzes consecutive trade sequences, attempting to establish whether the result of a trade (in terms of a positive or negative result) is dependent (or not) on previous trades.

If there was such a thing as a system that *always* alternated between gain/loss anyone, after a gain, would halt trading at the following signal and wait for the next one. This is obviously an ideal situation that's all but impossible to encounter, but we can study the correlations to provide trading guidelines. There's room in this subject for digression if we get into statistics. In the same way as in a coin toss, there's a 50% probability of each toss coming up 'heads,' also in trading if a system has a winning percentage of 54% (to choose any old percentage) every trade should have a 54% chance of winning. The above would make the whole subject of dependence of trades, invalid; but we can consider that, as trades derive from market behaviour, said behaviour may crop up again continuously in trades of the same characteristics. In other words, the event isn't merely a question of statistics related to one particular case, but is driven by external factors.

These are lines of reasoning everyone is free to consider, and decide whether to get your teeth into the subject (or not). Personally, I'm not a firm believer in the effectiveness of the same, but I do think they're worthy of consideration.

The z-score is used to measure how much dependence there is between trades, with the following equation:

$$z\text{-score} = \frac{N * (R - 0.5) - X}{\sqrt{\dfrac{X * (X - N)}{N - 1}}}$$

In which N is the number of trades, R the number of series (a sequence of positive trades is one series, a sequence of negative trades is another) and

$X = 2 * W * L$ in which W is the number of winning trades and L is the number of losing or null trades.

Positive z-scores show a tendency for alternating trades, so after a win you could expect a loss, and vice versa. Negative scores, on the other hand, show a tendency of strings of consecutive trades producing the same result. In fact, the higher R is, the more alternation there is in the positive/negative result of the trades and the higher the equation numerator will be (if there was perfect win/loss/win/loss alternation R would be equal to the number of trades N). If R decreases on the other hand (if all the trades were somehow positive, R would be equal to one as there is just one sequence of trades), the numerator would become negative and decrease more and more.

But it's not enough for the calculated score to be positive or negative to take decisions. There must be considerable presumed dependence to give us a real advantage and, the higher the z-score is in terms of an absolute value, the greater the probability the dependence found will occur again in the future.

In particular, 1.96 (or -1.96 if negative) is a value that's often used as a limit value. This value gives weight to the significance of the information. In particular, 1.96 means the information is 95% valid, which is obviously a good value.

The z-score is similar to standard deviations in a Gaussian distribution. In said distribution, 95% of the data comes within a wide range from -2 to $+2$ standard deviations ($-1.96 +1.96$ to be precise, and again we've found our limit number).

If the z-score is 3 or -3, the level of confidence would be 99.73%.

If we obtained a z-score of over 1.96 for a system we might risk considering that after a winning trade it would be highly probable there'd be a losing trade, and after two winning trades it would be even more probable there'd be a losing trade. We could analyze the system report to check how many series of single trades there are, and how many trades in sequences of two, and trade as a consequence, ceasing after one or two winning trades, until there's a losing trade (obviously only a signal; as we'd be faithfully following the z-score).

Vice versa with a negative z-score of less than -1.96, we could cease trading after the first losing trade, confident that it would be followed by other, numerous, losing trades; and only start trading again after the first winning trade. With a negative z-score in fact, the trades should tend to maintain the same sign for quite long sequences.

Unfortunately, the system we've been using for all these examples, isn't well-suited to this theory. Let's calculate the z-score.

An analysis of the sequence of the 964 trades produces the following data:

$$N = 964$$

$$R = 486 \text{ (243 winning sequences and 243 losing sequences)}$$

$$W = 473$$

$$L = 491$$

$$X = 2 * W * L = 2 * 473 * 491 = 464{,}486$$

$$\text{z-score} = \frac{964 * (486 - 0.5) - 464{,}486}{\sqrt{\dfrac{464{,}486 * (464{,}486 - 964)}{964 - 1}}} = 0.2364$$

As can be seen, the result is extremely low, too low to base any sort of specific strategy on.

Apart from the fact that this method can't really be effectively applied to the example we've been using, it must be said that, usually the more trades that are used to calculate the z-score, the more this method can be considered valid. In our case, 964 is a significant number; but doing the same thing on fewer than 300 trades wouldn't produce very reliable results. We could, for example, calculate the z-score trade by trade, and see how it can change considerably, and therefore be quite untrustworthy.

■ 5.8 Conclusions

Once you know the basic methods that can be used to apply money management strategies to your trading, it's also important to know these can be tweaked in various ways. A trader should have a clear idea of his goal, maximum risk or maximum results, limited drawdown, low exposure always, and in any case, etc. Once you know your goals, you can adapt the money management method to your own risk profile.

We've looked at various ways to make an approach more aggressive in the initial stages of the system, and make it more docile at later stages. Other methods go in the opposite direction, attempting to risk more as profits are added to the system.

Some methods try to follow market trends or 'standby' when they are unfavourable for the system.

Finally, we considered an instrument that can be used to try and define the predictability of the next trade and decide whether to follow it or wait for the next one.

The possibilities of studying new techniques and combining those mentioned above offer a multitude of scenarios, so even the most demanding of traders can calculate the optimal number of contracts to use.

■ References

Jones, Ryan. *The Trading Game: Playing by the Numbers to Make Millions*. New York: John Wiley & Sons, 1999.

Tharp, Van K. *Trade Your Way to Financial Freedom*. New York: McGraw-Hill, 2007.

CHAPTER 6

The Monte Carlo Simulation

At this point, you could already choose the money management method you want to use. In fact, you already have enough information to roll your sleeves up and get to work, after deciding how you want to use your strategy.

But I must once again dampen the enthusiasm of those who, having seen the firepower a money management strategy can bring to bear, can't wait to put the pedal to the metal and start trading with high-risk percentages using the fixed fractional method, or a very low delta using the fixed ratio method. In the previous chapter, I always emphasized that there's another side of the coin, which, apart from drawdowns that can be difficult for anyone to withstand, can also put an end to your strategy if your capital is now insufficient.

■ 6.1 Using the Monte Carlo Simulation

Let's take a look at an example. Supposing a trader has €20,000 and uses a strategy with a stop-loss of €1,500. On the basis of an analysis of his strategy's historical data, he decides on an extremely aggressive approach (the only one possible with a low initial capital) using the fixed fractional method with a 10% risk.

Let's suppose his sequence of trades is as shown in Table 6.1.

TABLE 6.1

Capital	No. of contracts	Trade
20000	1	500
20500	1	600
21100	1	450
21550	1	800
22350	1	−3000
19350	1	−2100
17250	1	10000
27250	1	2750
30000	2	1000
32000	2	. . .

There are two losing trades, and both lose more than the theoretical stop-loss (one even twice as much). We've seen, and I've said several times, that this isn't something that can be excluded and, on the contrary, it's something that happens more often than one might imagine.

The final result, though, is quite respectable and paves the way for the trader to proceed with his work.

If this series was the series of trades obtained in the back testing, the trader would have been able to rely on it and choose a risk percentage of 10%, considering the 50% gain (from €20,000 to €30,000) at the end of the series.

But let's see what would have happened if the order of the trades was simply different to that in Table 6.1, and was as shown in Table 6.2, for example.

As you can see, the final result is very different to the previous one. While still making a discrete profit, the trader is certainly in a worse condition than he thought he'd be in.

But that's not all; Table 6.3 shows another case with a different distribution of trades.

What happened? It's simple. With just €14,900 remaining after the first two losing trades, the trader no longer has sufficient capital to continue using a studied strategy; in fact, 10% of €14,900 is 1,490, which isn't enough to cover the system stop-loss of €1,500.

Obviously, the trader could increase his risk percentage and continue, but this stratagem should be avoided, as it's better to stop using a strategy

TABLE 6.2

Capital	No. of contracts	Trade
20000	1	10000
30000	2	−3000
24000	1	2750
26750	1	800
27550	1	500
28050	1	600
28650	1	450
29100	1	1000
30100	2	−2100
25900	2	...

TABLE 6.3

capital	No. of contracts	Trade
20000	1	−300
17000	1	−2100
14900	0	450
14900	0	800
14900	0	500
14900	0	600
14900	0	10000
14900	0	1000
14900	0	2750
14900	0	...

that's already put you in a condition from which you can't continue. In this case, there would have been an excellent recovery, but the future is always an unknown factor and the market might not return what you've just put into it.

This is an example of how the fortuitous nature of events can change the final scenario considerably. If the trader used just one contract, those trades would always have produced the same final result anyway, but that wouldn't be the case if he used a money management strategy. If those trades are a reflection of the market on which they were made, there's nothing to say they won't occur in exactly that way, but in a totally different order to what was predicted.

If, instead of 10%, the same trader risked 11% of his capital, with the same sequence in Table 6.3, he would have obtained the result in Table 6.4.

TABLE 6.4

Capital	No. of contracts	Trade
20000	1	−3000
17000	1	−2100
14900	1	450
15350	1	800
16150	1	500
16650	1	600
17250	1	10000
27250	1	1000
28250	2	2750
33750	0	...

This is a case in which a greater risk than what is already considered aggressive, produces completely different results. This doesn't mean you should risk more, but it does mean that apparently insignificant details like the order in which the trades occur can produce substantial differences. Also note that the above example is totally fictitious for the sole purpose of illustrating these differences on the basis of the order of events. What increases the risk from 10% to 11% could also be considered finding a minimum risk percentage to continue without worrying about the order of the trades. In the real example in the previous chapter, the minimum percentage for the fixed fractional method was 3.75%, below which the system ceased trading.

So, is there a way to protect yourself from such hazards?

There is certainly not a definitive way, above all, because the market can change radically, but we can at least evaluate the effect of various sequences of trades using simulations, and try to choose the best approach.

This is why a version of the Monte Carlo simulation is used in trading.

The Monte Carlo simulation is a method that, on the basis of some of the data at your disposal, you attempt to extrapolate other data to produce a more varied series of cases. In practice, you analyze the known sample, and by studying the statistical characteristics you 'prepare' other data with the same characteristics.

One quite well known application of the Monte Carlo simulation was during World War II, when it was used to try and optimize bombing raids. Another classic application of this method is calculating how long a person will wait at a bus stop on the basis of how often the buses pass, the number of people travelling, etc.

The Monte Carlo simulation fell on fertile ground in the trading world, and it's used in various ways.

One of the most popular methods consists of taking a series of trades you have at your disposal and using them to create a high number of permutations of the same; in other words, creating new series of the same trades, but in different positions.

Let's take a look at an example of the permutation of three elements: A, B, and C. We could end up with the following cases:

TABLE 6.5					
A	A	B	B	C	C
B	C	A	C	B	A
C	B	C	A	A	B

The number of permutations of n numbers is $n!$ (factorial n), which is equal to $n*(n - 1)*(n - 2)* \ldots *1$, in our case $3*2*1 = 6$, exactly the number of cases found.

In general, the approach simulates 1,000 or more new series of trades and applies the chosen money management strategy to each of these. This creates a statistical sample of results, and we can see how they change. The greater the distribution of the final profits, or the maximum percentage drawdowns, the less reliable the choice made is, which clearly depends a lot on how the events occur, and a change in the expected order can make a notable difference (for better or naturally for worse).

This approach gives you an idea of how things can change compared to what you experienced while following pretty much the same pattern as the one you've just seen.

A more complex method lets you reutilize the trades you've already used in the new series. In practice, it doesn't create permutation of the principal series, but creates new series picking trades randomly from a list. A trade might appear several times in the new series, and therefore its effect would be multiplied. If this repeatedly used trade is by chance the worst-ever loss of the system it would have a pessimistic effect, in favour of safety.

We'll use this simulation system in our examples, creating a certain number of new lists of trades picked randomly from the original list of our trading system.

There are also even more complex methods that, for example, let you forcibly add the maximum historical loss of the original system a certain number of times, or randomly add a value that's double the same. This would simulate a day on which a particular event produces a notable crash (never a good thing for traders, who almost always find themselves flat on their faces when something unexpected happens).

A much more complex method goes even further and studies the history of every trade. In particular, it examines how the market has moved since the trade opened until when it closed, for the entire duration of the trade, recording the percentage fluctuations of each bar, and remixing these fluctuations at random, it creates a new history for the trade, changing the final result in fact. In practical terms, let's say this system creates new series of trades in which the individual results are different to the original ones. The only thing they have in common is a certain harmony with the market you are trading on. This is certainly a very sophisticated method, but in my opinion it goes beyond the spirit of a simulation and almost leaves the world of trading behind to become an exercise in statistics. Furthermore, in order to apply a method of this kind, you'd need to use tools more sophisticated than I can imagine, and the amount of information necessary would be considerable too. A good software tool for this and other methods is Monte Carlo-Lab, to be used with Wealth-Lab, but I must warn you that it can be quite complicated to program strategies in Wealth-Lab, and use Monte Carlo-Lab.

If you want to create new series of trades you can start also on the basis of the statistical distribution of the original trades, using the average and the standard deviation, to create new values using these parameters.

I've included a program in Excel with the book you can use to run money management strategy simulations with the fixed fractional and fixed ratio methods.

Enter the list of trades and principal data in the spreadsheet to run the simulation, in particular the number of available trades, the type of money management method you want to use in the simulation, the risk profile (the risk percentage if you choose the fixed fractional method, or delta if you choose the fixed ratio method) and, just as important, the number of simulations you want to run.

As a number of reference, it's a good idea to run at least 1,000 simulations, 5,000 will give you a more reliable result, and even 10,000 will make the results more trustworthy, although there's not that much improvement to make the longer computing times worth it.

The other data to enter includes the margin per contract (to limit the number of contracts when the available capital isn't sufficient to cover the margins), and the maximum number of contracts you want to work with. This number is a limit put on trading to avoid disrupting the market. If you're lucky and find your capital has increased considerably, you might find yourself in a situation in which, when calculating the number of contracts to use, the result is a very high number. If, for example, the calculation suggests trading with 100 SPMIB futures, it's obvious that this number of contracts will be difficult to manage, not because you'll cause problems for other traders on the market (100 new contracts wouldn't upset the market) but it will be problematic to enter trades with 100 contracts at the desired price in a reasonable amount of time. 100 is in any case just an example, and you could even find yourself faced with higher numbers, which would be impossible to implement, so the maximum number of contracts is a limit you set in order to be able to effectively trade on the market.

The program extrapolates the maximum historical loss on the basis of the list of trades; you can choose to use this figure as the maximum loss, or continue using the theoretical stop-loss.

It's definitely better to use the maximum historical loss if you want to protect yourself from similar events in the future. In any case, the examples in the previous chapters were all concluded using a theoretical stop-loss. Later, we'll see what difference choosing one parameter rather than another can make.

Apart from entering the initial capital as a start point, there's another important figure to enter, the number of trades to simulate. For the basic purpose of our work, this number could be the same as the historical trades. Later on, we'll go into how this could be used in a different way.

The first simulation we'll study applies the fixed fractional method with a 5% risk percentage and a maximum loss equal to the €1,250 stop-loss. An initial capital of €50,000 is used, in line with the examples in the previous chapters.

The first chart to analyze is the distribution of the percentage returns. A histogram was created in which each column shows the number of cases with a percentage return of that level.

Figure 6.1 shows the histogram.

The histogram provides a great deal of information. The first thing that's evident is there's a 50% probability of making more than 1,000% over a period of roughly six years (the 964 available trades represent six years using our system). Note, in fact, that 476 of the 1,000 simulations closed above 1,000% (for practical purposes, results over 1,000% are always grouped together).

This information might already be sufficient for a trader to go to work with the much-celebrated 5%.

Figure 6.1, however, tells another story. For example, we can see that the distribution of the cases is very 'flat.' The peak over 1,000% is the result of grouping together all the cases with percentages higher than this figure and, if we created other percentage classes above this figure, we'd probably end up with an even flatter histogram. Some might say there's a significant column also before the last with 175 cases. The truth is that this column shows the cases with returns from 500% to 1,000%, which is quite an extensive range. All the other ranges are 50 percentage points from 200% up (200%, 250%, 300%, etc.) and the range is 10 points for lower values.

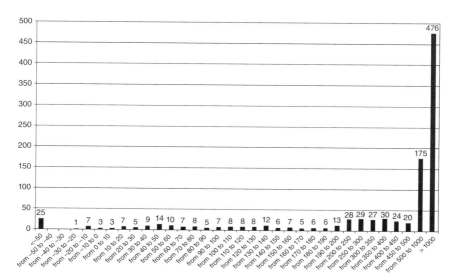

FIGURE 6.1 Distribution of percentage returns with a 5% risk.

A distribution of this kind substantially indicates that a 5% risk creates an outcome that isn't easy to predict. We know that in 50% of the cases, returns will be over 1,000%, but above this percentage or in the other half of the histogram it's impossible to predict the final result in a reliable way (in other words, you can't confidently aim for 400%, for example).

We've considered the positive aspects of the histogram, boldly going over 1,000%, but it's important to consider the left part too, where various simulations produced negative results.

In particular, 25 cases left less than half the capital intact, and in another 11 cases the final capital was less than the initial capital (three with losses of up to 10%, seven from −10% to −20%, and one from −30% to −20%).

If we add all the negative cases, in total there are 36 cases in which the system is a losing one: 36 out of 1,000 is 3.6%, which means that using a 5% risk, there's a 3.6% probability of the result being a loss after six years.

We've considered the returns and their range of percentage values, but the software provides other information that's just as important when assessing the approach: the maximum percentage drawdown.

Figure 6.2 shows the chart with the distribution of this parameter.

The distribution is much more regular than that of the percentage returns. At a glance, we can see the most populated zone around 49%, but we can also say without a doubt that most of the results are between a 34% and a 70% percentage drawdown.

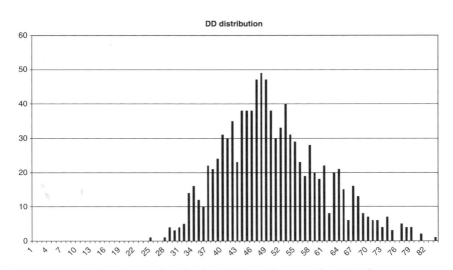

FIGURE 6.2 Drawdown values for the 1,000 simulations with a 5% risk.

So, trading with a 5% risk and a maximum loss equal to the system stop-loss, there'd be a 50% probability of making over 1,000% but with a drawdown that would most probably be between 35% and 70%. Considering the other aspects of these results it's now up to the trader to decide whether this is acceptable or not. For example, is the trader willing to have an almost 4% probability of losing money after trading for six years? Let's not forget in any case that, apart from the cases in which there's a loss, there are various cases in which the percentage gain in six years might not be considered sufficient for some traders.

Now let's take a step back and consider the number of simulations again. I said 1,000 was a good number, but you could run up to 5,000, for more precise and reliable results. Out of curiosity, let's see what the histogram would look like with 5,000 simulations.

Figure 6.3 shows more or less the same situation as Figure 6.1, with 2,394 cases out of 5,000 that make over 1,000% and 210 out of 5,000 that produce a loss. The cases that produce high returns are still just less than 50% while 210 out of 5,000 is 4.2%, which is quite close to the 3.6% calculated previously.

Figure 6.4 shows the drawdown.

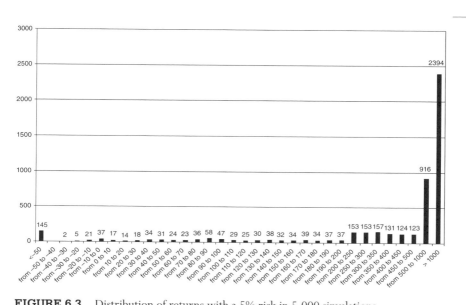

FIGURE 6.3   Distribution of returns with a 5% risk in 5,000 simulations.

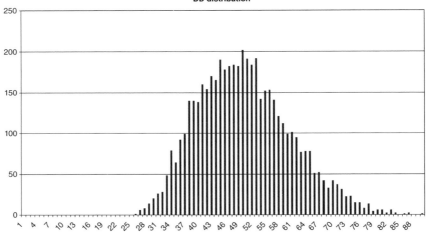

FIGURE 6.4   Trend of the percentage drawdown with a 5% risk in 5,000 simulations.

Also in this case, there is an evident similarity with Figure 6.2. The curve shows the maximum population density in the zone around 50%. Compared to the previous histogram, though, it looks like there are slightly more cases with a drawdown of around 50%, but below this value there are more bars from 35% to 50% than in the previous case.

So you can obtain useful information from 1,000 simulations, and if you wish, when close to taking your final decision, you could run 5,000 simulations to create a more detailed histogram.

Let's proceed with some additional analysis to see what sorts of possibilities might be presented and how to face them. We'll look at this step by step, just as if we were making a trading decision.

Let's suppose you're a particularly conservative and prudent trader, who absolutely doesn't want to go too far with the risk percentages. On the basis of the analyses in the previous chapters we saw that, below 3.75%, the system would inevitably cease trading. But this belongs to the past, and what we want to do now is look at what might happen if we risk very little.

The stop-loss is 1,250, which is 2.5% of the initial capital. Obviously, if we try to use a 2.5% risk percentage, all it would take would be one first losing trade to block the system. In fact, we'd end up with a capital of less than €50,000, and 2.5% of the new capital would in any case be less than the estimated loss of 1,250, making it impossible to continue.

Being an overly prudent trader you might in any case test a 2.5% risk, perhaps with the option of using a higher percentage if the system was blocked immediately.

Figure 6.5 shows the equity trend.

Well, the histogram leaves little room for doubt, in 89.5% of the cases you'd end your adventure with a loss of up to 10%. In actual fact, these losses would be closer to 0 than −10%; but, in any case, they're sufficient to cease trading. There's nothing to say these are all losses on the first trade, all it takes is one trade that reduces the equity to less than €50,000 and your run is over.

Note that there are very few cases in which the system really took off, and of these, 18 (1.8%) produce returns over 500%.

No matter how prudent you are, you probably wouldn't want to start trading in these conditions, and it's no use looking at the drawdown chart as we already know that, with a risk of just 2.5% there's very little chance of continuing to the end.

The real system needed at least 3.75% to function, but if we want to try something more conservative, let's try 3%.

Figure 6.6 shows what might happen.

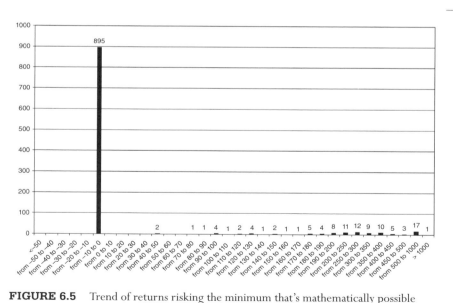

FIGURE 6.5 Trend of returns risking the minimum that's mathematically possible equal to 2.5%.

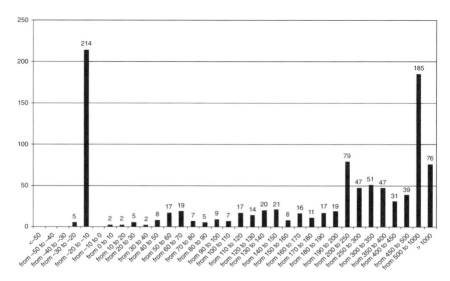

FIGURE 6.6 Trend of returns for 1,000 simulations with a 3% risk.

The scenario has changed considerably compared to the previous test and now there are 219 cases out of 1,000 that close at a loss (probably blocked before the end due to insufficient capital) but the rest make a profit and most of the cases are in the high percentage zone.

Would you be willing to risk being blocked in 21.9% of the cases (219 out of 1,000) with a probability of 26.1% (185 + 76 cases out of 1,000) of making over 500%?

It's worth thinking about that question before answering yes or no, and to do so let's take a look at the percentage drawdowns.

As can be seen, most of the drawdowns are between 15% and 40%, with the highest probability around 25%. Frankly, this trend leaves room for doubt; the idea was not to risk much as you know you can't withstand high drawdown percentages. It can't be said that the values in Figure 6.7 are high, but perhaps there's something better suited to a very prudent trader.

If you remember, I mentioned the fixed ratio method appears to be better suited to limiting drawdowns.

First, let's run a simulation with the 'usual' delta of 5,000 just to see what the scenario looks like (Figures 6.8–6.9).

Though the trend of the percentage returns is certainly interesting, the drawdown trend isn't. Note that just 21 cases out of 1,000 close with a loss, while 500 close making over 1,000%. The results are similar to those

THE MONTE CARLO SIMULATION

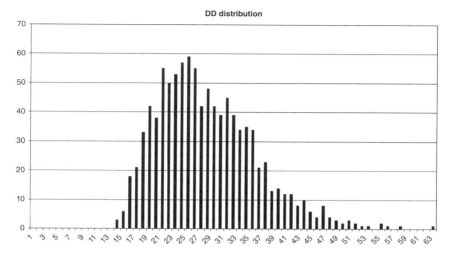

FIGURE 6.7 Trend of the percentage drawdowns for 1,000 simulations with a 3% risk.

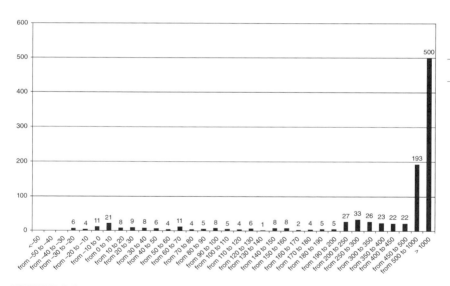

FIGURE 6.8 Percentage returns for 1,000 simulations using the fixed ratio method with a delta = 5,000.

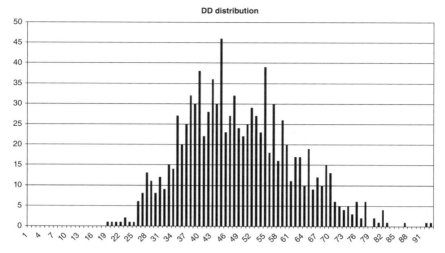

FIGURE 6.9 Drawdown trend for 1,000 simulations using the fixed ratio method with a delta = 5,000.

in Figure 6.1, but in terms of returns, we can consider them to be better, as there are more high-return cases and slightly fewer cases that close with a loss.

In terms of drawdowns, the situation doesn't change much as far as the average is concerned, which we could consider to be around 50%; but, note that the distribution is a little wider than in Figure 6.2, although there are a few cases of around 20% that weren't seen with the fixed fractional method. This could be one of those cases in which it's worth running more simulations to see a more precise drawdown distribution. Figure 6.10 shows the trend with 5,000 simulations.

This histogram confirms that the drawdown risk is very similar to that with the fixed fractional method using a 5% risk, but the bulge of bars has moved slightly to the left, and now there is a certain (limited) number of less-dramatic cases.

Remember, you're a very prudent trader, who feels decidedly uneasy with these drawdown values. Knowing you can produce less aggressive lines by increasing delta with the fixed ratio method, you can run a test with a delta that's very close to the maximum historical drawdown of the original system with one contract. Remember, this drawdown was about €22,000, so we'll run the test with a delta of 20,000.

Figure 6.11 shows the result.

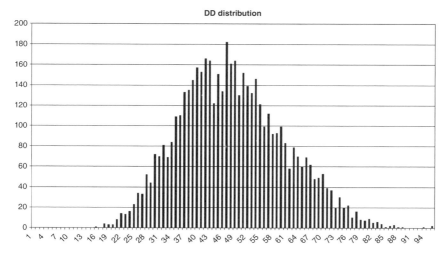

FIGURE 6.10 5,000 simulations to verify the percentage drawdown distribution using the fixed ratio method with delta = 5,000.

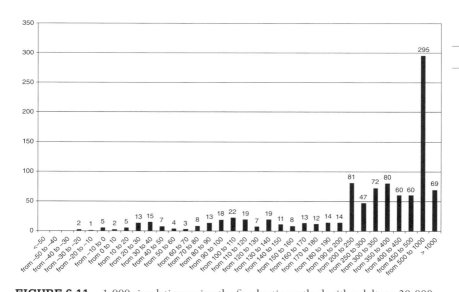

FIGURE 6.11 1,000 simulations using the fixed ratio method with a delta = 20,000.

What's not to like? The percentage returns are respectable, although certainly it's not easy to do better than 1,000% with just 69 cases out of 1,000 that did so, but there are as many as 295 cases between 500% and 1,000%. What's more, most of the results are 200% or more.

In terms of losses, there are 8 cases out of 1,000 that close with less than the initial capital, which is certainly an interesting result.

Satisfied with this scenario, let's take a look at the drawdowns.

This histogram boosts your confidence further. Note that the average is around 30%, with most of the cases below that value and very few above 50%.

Being a conservative and prudent trader, you decide without further ado to take this route!

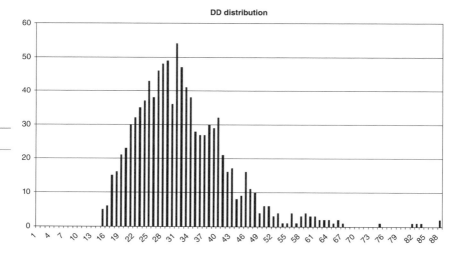

FIGURE 6.12 Percentage drawdowns using the fixed ratio method with a delta = 20,000.

Now let's put ourselves in the shoes of a very aggressive but not totally crazy/reckless trader, a trader who wants to maximize profits while attempting to survive the market's adversities as best he can.

Well aware of the fact that to reach ambitious goals you have to take bigger risks, let's immediately test the scenario with the fixed fractional method and a 10% risk, again using the system stop-loss as the maximum loss.

This is the trend of the percentage returns in this case.

There's no denying the good news, almost 70% of the cases close with returns above 1,000%. It's definitely an interesting result. The negative cases

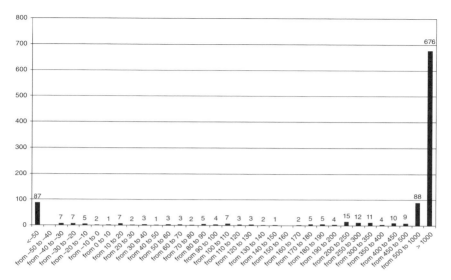

FIGURE 6.13 Distribution of percentage returns with a 10% risk.

might make you turn up your nose though, as 87 left less than half the initial capital intact. A total of 108 were losing, and this means, at the end of the day, you'd have just over a 10% chance of losing money. There aren't many cases between 0 and 500%. Which means, broadly speaking, you could consider that, with a 10% risk, you'd either make a big profit or go bankrupt, but the probability of making a healthy profit is seven times that of losing your money. It is without a doubt an interesting scenario, as is also that shown in Figure 6.1 with a 5% risk. In the previous case, though, the distribution was less biased towards the right than in this case, meaning a lower probability of very high returns, with most of the cases in a zone, where the returns are 'simply' high.

No matter how valiant and stubborn your resolve- and, above all, no matter how tempted you might be by potential profits- it's always a good idea to go a little further and analyze possible percentage drawdowns you might encounter using this risk profile, as shown in Figure 6.14.

This histogram might dampen your initial enthusiasm quite brusquely. Note that the drawdown percentages are very high, with a 10% risk. An 80% drawdown looks like a real possibility and worth thinking seriously about to see whether you think you'll have sufficient fortitude and faith in the system to serenely face such events.

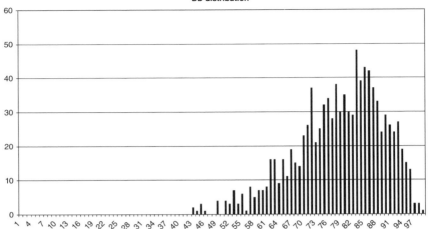

FIGURE 6.14 Distribution of percentage drawdowns with a 10% risk.

Considering the type of system in question (a moving-average crossover), it's understandable that there are high drawdowns. It's quite normal, but considering the type of market we've applied it to (a market split in half after eliminating all the afternoon bars, which are those with the greatest fluctuations), you might be worried about possible losses that are higher than the stop-loss (bad news in the afternoon could produce a loss on the market that's much higher than expected). So, take a moment to study new scenarios before making a decision.

Before testing a possible reduction of the risk, let's try to see if we can obtain some benefits by applying the fixed ratio method instead of the fixed fractional method.

As we're trading aggressively, we'll use a delta of 2,500 and run 1,000 simulations.

Let's take a look at the results (Figure 6.15).

It's immediately obvious that potential profits are more limited, a little under 60% of the cases are over 1,000%, and frankly there's not a notable difference between these results and those with a delta of 5,000 (Figure 6.8). There are cases with higher profits, but not enough for there to be a real competitive advantage in using this approach. Note that, in terms of losses the situation is certainly more lenient than with the fixed fractional method, but slightly worse (as could be expected) than the data in Figure 6.8 with a delta of 5,000.

THE MONTE CARLO SIMULATION

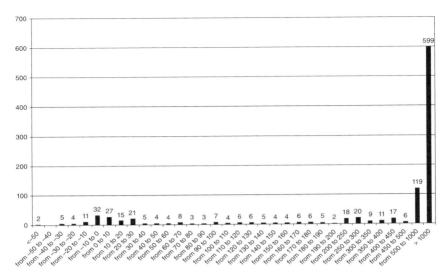

FIGURE 6.15 Distribution of percentage returns using the fixed ratio method with a delta of 2,500.

The distribution of the drawdowns is strange, with two peaks. It would appear probable you'd suffer a drawdown of 48% to 50% or 60%, values that are notably better than those in the fixed fractional simulation but worse than those in Figure 6.9, so it's fair to say that the advantage in terms of the probability of high profits isn't offset in terms of drawdown percentages, which are worse than expected. This approach doesn't appear to be what we're looking for, either.

As the drawdowns with the fixed ratio method seem far worse than the improvement in percentage gains as delta decreases (and therefore the trader trades in a more aggressive way), we won't test lower delta values and we'll go back to using the fixed fractional method to try something else.

We know that a 5% risk won't fully satisfy our ambition for profit; but we also know that the percentage drawdowns with a 10% risk would be harsh. Let's look at a compromise and run 1,000 simulations at 7.5% (Figure 6.17).

This looks good in terms of returns. Compared to Figure 6.13, returns over 1,000% have dropped slightly, and there's an increase in those from 500% to 1,000%. The losing cases have been all but halved (Figure 6.18).

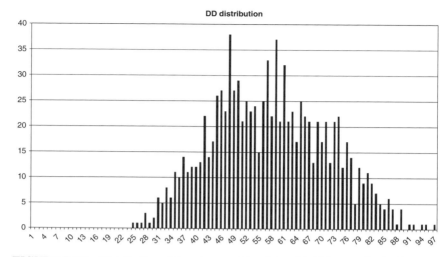

FIGURE 6.16 Distribution of drawdowns with a delta of 2,500 using the fixed ratio method.

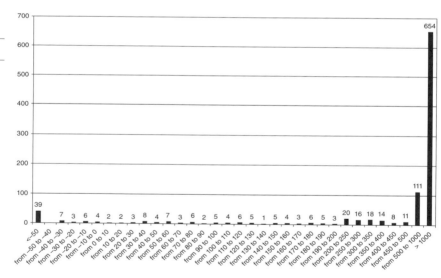

FIGURE 6.17 Returns with a 7.5% risk percentage.

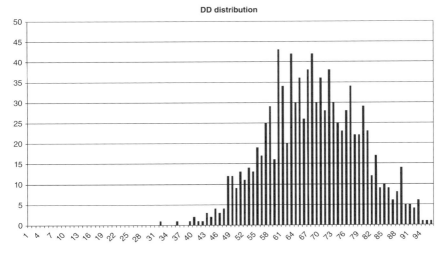

FIGURE 6.18 Trend of the drawdowns with a 7.5% risk using the fixed fractional method.

As for the drawdowns, there is an improvement, but the values are still quite high. Note, in fact, that there is a high probability of 60% to 80% drawdowns.

Again, the scenario is perplexing, and the wisest decision seems to be to use our resources elsewhere. This trading system isn't what we're looking for.

As seen above, the Monte Carlo simulation can also make you take quite drastic decisions you might not have taken, based on data from the principal trading system alone. It's very important to try and take a step back to analyze the results of the simulation objectively, to try and consider the possible scenarios in terms of what your feelings might be at the time. It's no use kidding ourselves and 'ignoring' a 10% possibility that a certain negative event might occur. 10% isn't exactly a remote chance, and if you find yourself in that situation it can be hard to continue.

■ 6.2 Maximum Loss

In the previous simulations, we deliberately used the same value as the system stop-loss to calculate the maximum loss. We all know, both as is evident from the figures and after due and considerable reflection, that the stop-loss isn't actually the maximum loss that occurred or might occur in a system.

Too many events change the rules of the game, and often the results in the field are worse than what was expected.

In our example, we're using a stop-loss of –€1,250; but, if we take a look at the system performance report (Figure 3.2), you'll see that the actual maximum loss in the 6 years in question was €2,757.5, more than double that!

This goes to show that, in actual fact, we're using percentages that are too aggressive, something that could get you into serious trouble. Risking 10%, for example, when that loss occurred you would have lost 20% of your capital, which is certainly not something to look forward to.

Despite the fact that this maximum loss is a past event, and no one can guarantee that a worse event might not occur in the future, it can be taken as a point of reference for a more in-depth study, related to actual system events. From a certain point of view, using the maximum loss instead of the stop-loss is the same as halving the risk percentage (in this specific case, in which the loss is roughly twice the stop-loss):

$$ff \text{ contracts} = INT \left(\frac{C * f}{Maxloss} \right).$$

Doubling the value of the denominator is the same as halving the value of the numerator, but using the maximum loss protects you from possible adverse effects when rounding off.

In actual fact, studying the trend of the system, based on the real maximum loss, gives you a much more precise idea and follows events much more closely.

Note also that optimal f is calculated by definition using the maximum loss of the system.

So, let's now take a look at what would happen to the Monte Carlo simulation if we use the maximum loss instead of the stop-loss.

A first attempt using a risk percentage of 5% is a failure and the program doesn't provide us with any data. Why is that? Simply because 5% of our initial capital of €50,000 is €2,500, which doesn't cover the maximum loss of €2,757.5, so in this case the system can't start trading.

Now let's try with 10% and take a look at the results (Figure 6.19).

We can immediately see there's been a significant change in the results. In the previous case, in Figure 6.13, there were almost 70% of the cases with returns of over 1,000%; this time, in Figure 6.19, they're just over 40%. Note the scenario in terms of negative cases is particularly lenient, and there are very few results below 0 (Figure 6.20).

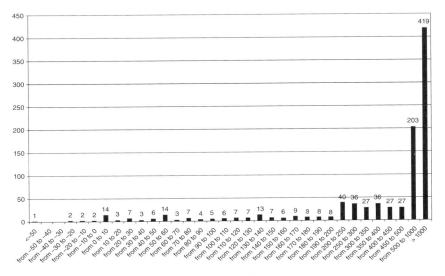

FIGURE 6.19 10% risk, this time considering the real maximum loss.

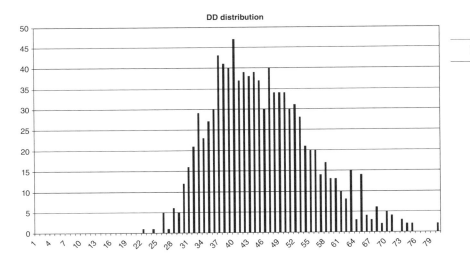

FIGURE 6.20 Trend of the drawdowns risking 10% with reference to the real maximum loss.

In terms of the drawdowns, there's more good news. The grouping is in zones with percentages significantly lower than those in Figure 6.14.

We did, however, say that doubling the maximum loss produced roughly the same effect as halving the risk percentage. We have double the loss, and by testing the system using the same risk percentages we will, in a certain sense, be comparing apples and oranges.

As the above-mentioned aggressive trader turned up his nose at results with a 7.5% risk, testing the same percentage now wouldn't really provide a concrete comparison at the same level.

It makes more sense to run the same simulation with a 15% risk, which is twice the 7.5% that definitively blocked the aggressive trader (we'll use double the value as the maximum loss is approximately double the stop-loss).

This is what the trader would obtain with a 15% risk and the real maximum loss (Figures 6.22 and 6.21).

Note that the profit percentages are slightly lower, but the histogram showing the drawdowns is slightly 'easier to digest' as can be seen if we compare Figure 6.21 to Figure 6.18 (the differences aren't great).

So, which is the best parameter to use? The choice, once again, is up to the person using the method.

Bear in mind that, if the maximum loss diverges greatly from the stop-loss (as in this case), you should check to see if it's an isolated case, or whether there have been other trades that suffered losses much higher than those estimated. If it's just one isolated case, the best idea is to use the stop-loss, considering that particular loss as an unfortunate one-off; which does, however, in the simulations illustrate the idea of the vicissitudes one has to deal with on the market quite well.

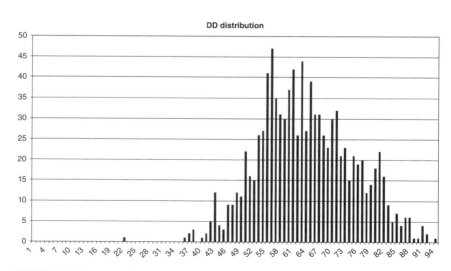

FIGURE 6.21 Drawdowns with a 15% risk, using the real maximum loss.

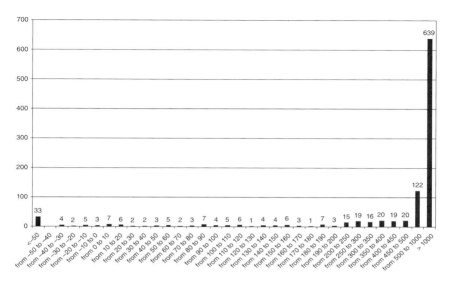

FIGURE 6.22 Returns with a 15% risk, using the real maximum loss.

If, on the other hand, there are many cases in which the loss was greater than the stop-loss, it's definitely better to use the maximum loss, especially to calculate the number of contracts when using the system.

In fact, it all depends on what you intend to do when you start using the system. If you intend to use the stop-loss in all the calculations, then you should also use it for the simulations; the choice of the risk percentage in fact depends on the result of the simulations, and it wouldn't make sense to run these with different parameters to those you intend to use.

Vice versa, if you choose to use the maximum loss to calculate the number of contracts, the best thing is to run the simulations using the same value. In this case, it wouldn't be that much of a problem if you ran the simulations using the stop-loss as the simulations were done in a more unfavourable environment than the real one (the simulations would produce various cases with losses greater than those expected), and using a higher maximum loss would put us in more cautious conditions.

■ 6.3 Conclusions

Being able to simulate cases that might occur, but aren't included in the historical data, lets you analyze more cases you might find yourself in on the basis of your money management decisions.

Rounding off to whole numbers of contracts, and increasing the number of the same as the capital increases, are important to make the strategy you intend to use bear fruit. It's just as important to consider the order in which events occurred. The Monte Carlo simulation lets you create a certain number of scenarios, based on the original, simply by mixing up the order in which events happened; so the same might be repeated or some events might not occur at all.

The data obtained from the simulations can be used to evaluate the probability of the results you might obtain when making a certain choice, to help you make the right one.

CHAPTER 7

The Work Plan

■ 7.1 Using a Work Plan

It's a good idea to use a strategy with a clear idea of the field you're going to use it in. If you simply start using a strategy without a clear idea of how you're going to use it, this can often put you in situations where you don't know what to do. As long as you're making a healthy profit everything is fine, but as soon as you suffer a period of drawdowns you'll begin to worry. At other times, if you know the rules of the strategy (perhaps one you created yourself), you can try to change it to improve things in the unfavourable period you're in. A good trader stands out from the crowd also in these cases due to his abilities, and one of the essential qualities of a good trader is knowing how to react to losses.

141

If the trader did a preliminary study of the strategy (and therefore planned potential goals but also, and above all, planned for potential hazards) he'd be able to assess difficult periods more calmly, knowing whether they were part of the game or whether he should be worried if something is effectively going wrong.

Planning is often a job that's given very little consideration or is done superficially, perhaps because people just want to get started as soon as possible, or because they think it's boring and won't be a great help anyway. But, when you find yourself in difficulty (and inevitably sooner or later everyone does), if you know how to react, all the work you've done, and the time you've put into planning up to that point, will pay off.

In this chapter, we'll lay the foundations to give you an idea of a planning method you can use with the Monte Carlo simulation software described in the previous chapter. The purpose is to give you a few ideas you can base your own work on, in the way that suits you best.

Let's suppose we have the usual €50,000 and want to start using the by now well-known moving average crossover strategy we discussed earlier in the book.

In the previous chapter we looked at various ways to size a position when entering the market, and how the equity trend changed over the six years in question.

Planning an activity that will last for six years will certainly mean developing some interesting medium-term goals; but it doesn't leave much room for intermediate checks, as it's a reflection of the situation when everything is said and done.

There's a parameter in the software we haven't discussed yet, the number of trades to simulate; in the previous chapter this number was set to be equal to the number of available trades.

This number simply represents the length of each series of trades you'll create.

Let me explain: in the previous chapter we were working with 964 available trades, and we were picking randomly from the list 964 times (copying the chosen value but keeping it, so there were always 964 trades right up to the end); and then we created a second series of 964 trades, then a third, a fourth and so on up to 1,000, or 5,000, or any other number. We were creating 1,000 series as long as the original one. This was the most obvious procedure to follow to see what would have happened to that series in the case of a different sequence of events.

In any case, the 964 trades were those from six years of using the system, and if we take another look at Figure 3.3 you'll see that around 160 trades were placed every year, a figure that can also be obtained by dividing the 964 trades by 6.

As each of the 1,000 simulations was created from the first to the 964th trade, it's as if each simulation was traded for those same six years. At this point, it's easy to see that, if instead of tabulating 964 values, we used just the first 160, it would be as if we just studied the first year of the simulation. If we continued to 320, it's as if we're simulating two years of the system's history, etc.

I'm sure you'll see what I'm getting at. What I want to do is verify the probable history after one, two, or three years (or other chosen periods of time) to create a sort of roadmap to be able to check how close (or not) we are to predicted performance.

Note that, by applying money management strategies, the profits (which hopefully there are) grow exponentially, compared to the linear growth of single contract strategies. Therefore, the scenario after one or two years will be a lot different to that after 6. As soon as the strategy starts making a profit, and more contracts are used, the growth of the equity soars. The flip side of the coin is that this increase in the number of contracts also increases drawdown percentages, which are therefore not the same when trading with just a few contracts as when you're trading at full steam.

The 70% drawdowns in the previous chapter shouldn't therefore be taken as a reference for the first year of the strategy, when one would presume they would be lower; at the start you should run specific analyses.

If you don't take a close look at things year by year, there's the risk of accepting a negative scenario that shouldn't actually exist at that particular time. If, for example, we started working on a strategy accepting the possibility of a 70% drawdown and after six months suffered a 70% loss, we might erroneously believe it to be within acceptable limits, while actually, in the first year the drawdowns should probably be a lot less harsh. A case such as this should have started an alarm bell ringing previously.

To plan your activities, you should therefore simulate the trend of profits and drawdowns after one year, after two years and so on, for as far as you intend to go. The simulations will provide information on the potential results of the strategy, so the effective performance can be monitored during the period in question.

The thing that's most worrying is the drawdown that might be suffered and it's important to have parameters that can be used to halt trading if necessary before it's too late. So you have to set limits on using the strategy, abandoning it if the real results are within these limits (obviously the limits for lowest acceptable profits and, above all, the limits for maximum drawdowns).

If one of the limits set is exceeded, this should ring an alarm bell, as the results of the strategy are very different to those expected, so it may no longer be valid. Anyone who knows a bit about trading systems or methods based on repetitive phenomena knows that sooner or later, things may change and no longer continue, as they have even for a long time in the past. At this point, it's important to pause and take a good look at the whole setup on which your approach is based. So how do you do this?

By simply looking at the drawdown histograms in the previous chapter, you'll notice the distribution in all of them is like that of classic statistical curves. In particular, the distribution of the percentage drawdowns is log-normal. For lovers of statistics let's say the distribution of the natural logarithm of the percentage drawdowns is normal, so the percentage drawdowns are distributed log-normally.

This means that in order to calculate an average drawdown, first we have to calculate the natural logarithms of the various drawdown values, then find the arithmetic mean, and finally calculate the result of e raised to that mean.

On the basis of the percentage drawdown values DD%1, DD%2, DD%3, ... DD%n we'll calculate:

$$DDIn_m = \frac{\text{In}(DD\%1) + \text{In}(DD\%2) + \text{In}(DD\%3) + ... + \text{In}(DD\%n)}{n}$$

$$DD\%_m = e^{DDIn_m}$$

where e is equal to 2.7182818, a number maths lovers will be sure to recognize. These are, in any case, all functions you can find in Microsoft Excel, and the software that comes with the book will run the calculations, to save the trader who wants to use it the bother.

Returning to statistical concepts, let's consider the standard deviation. This measures the dispersion around a series of mean values of the same. The greater the standard deviation, the greater the dispersion of the values around the mean.

A normal distribution has approximately 68% of its values within one standard deviation from the mean, 95% within approximately two standard deviations and 99.7% within approximately three standard deviations. (The concept of the z-score is also based on the standard deviation and the value 1.96 isn't used by chance. In fact, it guarantees a 95% probability of dependence for the trades.)

In practice, we could calculate the average drawdown and the standard deviation (also on the basis of the logarithmic series of the drawdowns, to be carried over for usable values) and estimate zones that are acceptable.

In consideration of the fact that two standard deviations constitute a boundary within which 95% of the cases considered lie, we could use these two values as expected limits within which our percentage drawdown should be after the period in question.

Obviously, every trader is free to calculate the values they want, using more restrictive limits on the basis of their own particular disposition to risk.

If, for example, the results of the strategy indicated that the average drawdown in one year of work, should be around 20% with a standard deviation of 5, this would mean that 95% of the values calculated would be in the range 20 ± 2*5 or between 10 and 30. If the maximum percentage drawdown after one year is 34% you might think the strategy is no good and should be abandoned. To tell the truth, one could say the probability of this case occurring was less than 5%, and decide whether this is dangerous.

If we considered three standard deviations as an acceptable limit we would, however, have continued as the upper limit would be 35% (20 + 3*5).

Once you've chosen the risk profile and the money management method you intend to use, it's a good idea to run simulations for at least one to two years, taking note of the probable results, especially in terms of drawdowns. If you decide to abandon a strategy when a drawdown suffered in the field is more than two standard deviations over the calculated mean, at regular intervals you would check you're still within the set limits.

As a concrete example, let's suppose we're using a moving average crossover strategy, and we're at the end of the third year, so only have the first 480 trades to work with. We'll plan our trading for the next three years on the basis of that data.

So, we'll run simulations with the 480 trades to choose the most suitable approach to risk.

Let's run simulations on 480 trades to see the result after another 480 trades if we used the strategy for three years.

Starting with a hypothesis of using a fixed fractional method based on a stop-loss with a 5% risk, Figure 7.1 shows the results in terms of profits.

The distribution of the percentage profits is also basically log-normal. The peaks in the figure between 200% and 250% and between 500% and 1,000% are due to the fact that, in these zones, the ranges are a lot more extensive, so naturally they include more data. We could show everything with a 10% range, but the histogram would be huge and quite difficult to read.

Let's take a look at what we could expect from the drawdowns.

Note that the value of the drawdowns is basically in the zone around 35%. In particular, the program tells us that the average drawdown is 38.65%, the values of the first standard deviation are shown as between 30.24% and 49.39%, which means that, for approximately 68% of the

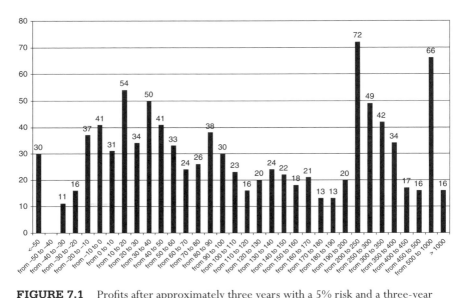

FIGURE 7.1 Profits after approximately three years with a 5% risk and a three-year database.

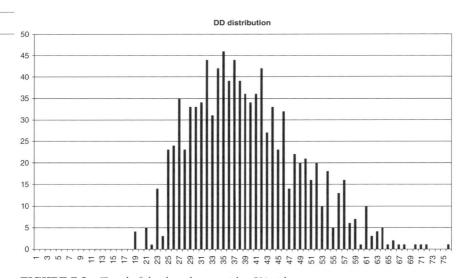

FIGURE 7.2 Trend of the drawdowns with a 5% risk.

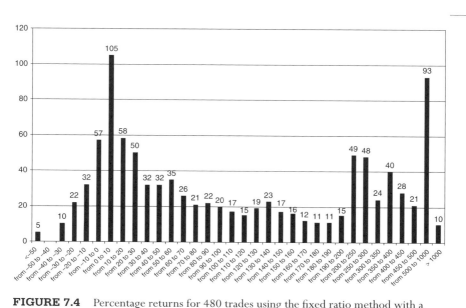

drawndown results		
average drawdown	**38,65**	
drawdown +/-1 std dev	**30,24**	**49,39**
drawdown +/-2 std dev	**23,66**	**63,11**
drawdown +/-3 std dev	**18,52**	**80,66**
hide		

FIGURE 7.3 Summary of the drawdown data.

cases, the percentage drawdown values are in this range. With the values of two standard deviations, we obtain the range of approximately 95% of the values. This range is from 23.66% to 63.11%.

Figure 7.3 shows a summary.

These values might be acceptable, but let's see what could happen in these three years using the fixed ratio method with a delta of 5,000.

FIGURE 7.4 Percentage returns for 480 trades using the fixed ratio method with a delta = 5,000.

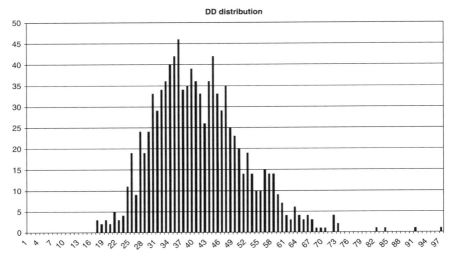

FIGURE 7.5 Percentage drawdown trend for 480 trades using the fixed ratio method with a delta = 5,000.

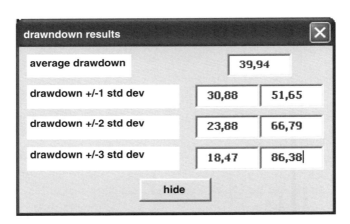

FIGURE 7.6 Data on the distribution of the drawdowns in Figure 7.5.

Here are the same three figures for this case.

Note that in this case, the summary data on the drawdowns is very similar for both the fixed fractional and the fixed ratio method, with the latter slightly more extreme in terms of the limit of the second standard deviation. The results of the equity, however, make the fixed ratio method the obvious choice as there is less dispersion in the negative zone and greater solidity in the zone of limited percentages.

A drawdown of over 60% is still worrying though, so let's try to run a simulation with the fixed fractional method and a risk limited to 4%.

Here are the results.

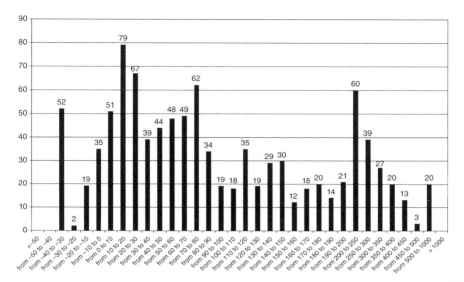

FIGURE 7.7 Trend of profits with a 4% risk after 480 trades.

It's immediately obvious that the situation in terms of negative performance has improved considerably compared to that in Figure 7.1. In fact, there are no longer any cases with losses of over 50%. Finally, the number of cases with modest returns have increased, but there are still a considerable number of cases with profits up to 100%. Obviously, there are fewer cases with very high profits, as is to be expected with a lower risk.

Figure 7.8 looks similar to Figure 7.2 but the curve has moved left, which is what we expected and wanted.

Figure 7.9 is reassuring. If we decide to keep trading only if we remain within 95% of the expected cases, we'd suffer a maximum percentage drawdown of 51.69%, which, although notable, is less harsh than the values of over 60% in the previous simulations.

So we decide to proceed with the fixed fractional method using a 4% risk.

We've taken the first step by choosing the risk profile we want to trade on the market with. The second thing to do is build the plan for growth, step by step.

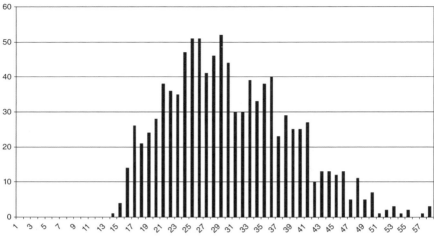

FIGURE 7.8 Trend of the drawdowns with a 4% risk.

drawndown results		
average drawdown	29,69	
drawdown +/-1 std dev	22,50	39,18
drawdown +/-2 std dev	17,05	51,69
drawdown +/-3 std dev	12,93	68,21
hide		

FIGURE 7.9 Summary of the data on drawdown distribution with a 4% risk.

Now, let's see what we might expect after one year (160 trades) and after two years (320 trades).

We'll run the simulation again, first with 160 and then 320 trades, then take a look at the data on equity and drawdowns (Figures 7.10–7.13).

Note that after one year, it's quite probable that profits will be at least 20% but, above all, we can expect a drawdown of around 18%; we will be willing to stick it out as long as the maximum drawdown isn't over 37.16%.

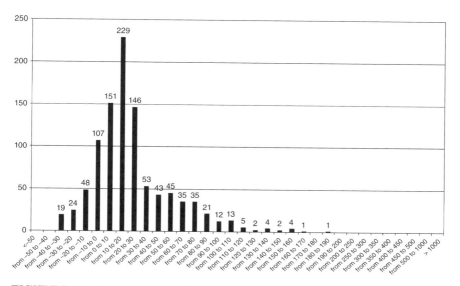

FIGURE 7.10 Expected returns after the first 160 trades (after about 1 year) with a 4% risk.

drawndown results		
average drawdown		18,29
drawdown +/-1 std dev	12,83	26,07
drawdown +/-2 std dev	9,00	37,16
drawdown +/-3 std dev	6,31	52,96
	hide	

FIGURE 7.11 Expected drawdowns after the first year with a 4% risk.

After two years, the returns will be a lot more spread out, luckily with positive results. Obviously, there will also be harsher drawdowns, and in the second year we should expect to have to suffer a drawdown of up to 46.1%.

We chose this method because we thought we'd be able to withstand drawdowns of up to about 51%. In the first two years, though, the limit

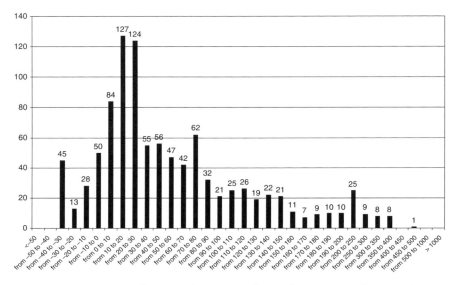

FIGURE 7.12 Expected returns after 2 years of using the strategy with a 4% risk.

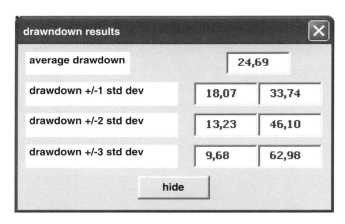

FIGURE 7.13 Expected drawdown values after 2 years of using the strategy with a 4% risk.

is lower and we might only have to withstand this level of drawdowns during the third year of using the strategy. If it occurred during the first two years it would be better to cease trading.

Now let's see what happened after the first 480 trades when the plan had been prepared, in a period of actual trading.

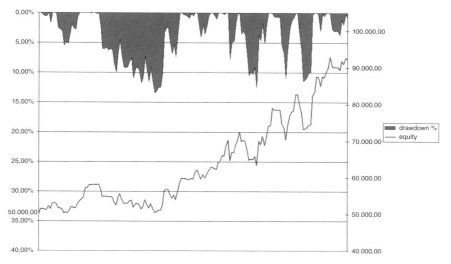

FIGURE 7.14 Trend of profits and drawdowns during the first year.

We'll proceed year by year and first we'll take a look at the situation after placing the first 160 trades.

Figure 7.14 shows the trends of the drawdowns and profits superposed. Note that the year closes just over €90,000 at €92,300. The maximum percentage drawdown of 13,46% was in the sixtieth trade. Note that this isn't the maximum drawdown in terms of absolute value. Also, at a glance, in fact you can see that harshest drawdown from the maximum levels reached is in the second part of the year – but we chose (for the reasons explained in detail in previous chapters) to use the percentage drawdown as a measure of the level of sufferance.

According to the values in Figure 7.11, we could 'suffer' a drawdown of up to 37.16% so we are well within the limits. Actually, these values look particularly benevolent, below the average and near the first standard deviation.

The particularly favourable period is also confirmed by the results of the percentage profits, with profits just over 80% and as can be seen in Figure 7.10 very few cases above these values (a total of 65 starting with 21 in the 80% to 90% range).

Let's continue to incorporate also the second year of results.

Figure 7.15 shows one of those bad periods that every trader finds himself in sooner or later. After having reached a peak of around €150,000 at the

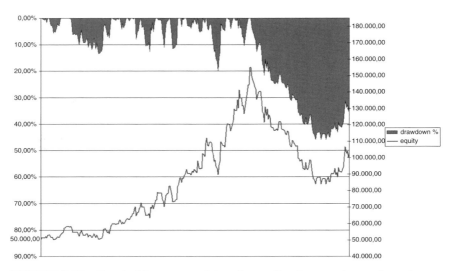

FIGURE 7.15   Trend of the equity and drawdowns after the second year of actual trading.

beginning of the second year, we suffered a period of losses that reduced the equity to less than €85,000, which is less than what we started the year with. A period like this would put the nerves of any trader to the test and many would probably throw in the towel before they reached the lowest point.

So why did we continue? It's simple. In Figure 7.13, we had an 'acceptable' drawdown limit of 46.10%. Well, the maximum drawdown in the worst period for the system reached 45.9%! (This result came really close to the limit merely by chance, and there was no intention of using these values to astonish the reader.) We were going to call it a day. Another losing trade and we probably would have passed the barrier we'd set, and at these levels we certainly wouldn't have made any excuses and extended the limits of tolerance to three standard deviations, so we would have closed up shop; but at 45.9%, we decided it was still acceptable to continue, and the plan that had been prepared proved to be right with a subsequent recovery that closed the year at €102,875 with profits of just over €10,000. Of course, €10,000 isn't much compared to the €42,500 of the previous year (we started with €50,000), but it did make the close of the year a positive one, and kept hopes up for the future.

Now let's see the outcome after the three forecasted years (Figure 7.16).

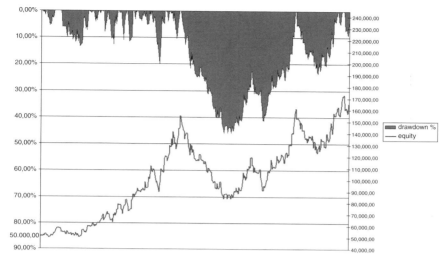

FIGURE 7.16 Final equity and drawdowns after three years of real trading.

At the end of our adventure (we decided to use the strategy for three years) we have an equity of €165,015.5, with profits of around 230% on the initial capital of €50,000. The maximum drawdown is the above-mentioned 45.9%. Note that at the beginning of the third year the equity drops again, but this time it stops at €95,000 to then recover and finally let us breathe easy.

The 230% profits are at the limit of the first standard deviation of the values in Figure 7.7 (this figure is calculated by the software, which gives an extremely wide range of 54,107 – 155,604 for the first standard deviation) and is therefore in line with the best estimates. As for the drawdown suffered, 45.9% was particularly harsh in the first two years, but now this can be considered in perspective, as it's lower than the 51.69% estimated as being the maximum allowed drawdown (Figure 7.9).

A well-constructed work plan helped bring our work to a successful conclusion and, above all, get through a very ugly period without getting into a panic (there were of course a few frayed nerves, but having a plan helped in the decision-making process).

■ 7.2 Conclusions

The correct use of the tools at our disposal to simulate how a strategy might behave can help in the decision-making process when considering whether to continue or cease trading with the same strategy. Meticulously preparing a plan that clearly sets limits of acceptance and those that need monitoring, before starting, helps the trader at difficult times when you might fall prey to your emotions.

At this point, you must, of course, be unmoving in your resolve and stick to the set guidelines, because sometimes you can be walking the razor's edge, and only sticking faithfully to the rules will let you continue and conclude the work you started with the best possible outcome.

With the Monte Carlo simulation, you can prepare possible scenarios after various periods of time using the strategy, and can prepare a list of potential profits (in general, these are much more difficult to predict when using more aggressive strategies), and potential drawdowns (to be considered on the basis of how difficult it will be for the trader to withstand the same).

CHAPTER 8

Combining Forces

At this point you could stop reading and start working, but first let's take a detailed look at some of the other things you might encounter as a trader.

One theme that's definitely worth looking into is diversification, how combining various strategies improves the overall situation.

We've seen that the aim of applying money management techniques is to find the best amounts to adopt to maximize profits while limiting drawdowns to acceptable values.

■ 8.1 Using a Combination of Systems

Up to now we've worked with a strategy that, while it certainly can't be considered excellent, is quite suitable for analyzing most of the techniques we're interested in. Now let's take a look at what would happen to the equity lines if we combined various systems.

To do so we'll use a new system, which this time is based on hourly bars, and simply buys on the breakout of the 50-bar high and sells on the breakout of the low in the same period.

This concept, known as *Donchian Channel Breakout*, is one of the most classic trend-following models found in literature, and it's based on the conviction that when a market is strong enough to exceed the highest highs of a certain period, then it is highly probable that it will continue in that direction (and therefore give us the chance to follow a long trend) and vice versa, on a breakout of the lowest lows in the same period (50 bars, in our case) it shows signs of weakness that suggests further down movements will follow (and it's therefore a good opportunity for trading short).

We'll apply the model to three futures' markets that usually have good trending characteristics, the Crude Oil, Gold, and Soybean markets.

The strategy will be applied with a 1,500 USD stop-loss per contract to protect the position.

First, let's look at results on the crude oil market only, in the period from the 1 January 2010 to the end of 2017 (Figures 8.1–8.3).

The trend of the strategy isn't exactly exceptional despite for the fact that there are profits in time. If we look at the results year by year, we'll see that some years close with a loss.

Now let's take a look at the results using the same approach with Gold futures (Figures 8.4–8.6).

As can be seen, the results in numerical terms for Gold and Crude Oil are very similar, although the trend of gold is much more regular over the years.

COMBINING FORCES

Strategy Performance Summary			
	All Trades	Long Trades	Short Trades
Net Profit	$81,110.00	$18,880.00	$62,230.00
Gross Profit	$496,900.00	$225,080.00	$271,820.00
Gross Loss	($415,790.00)	($206,200.00)	($209,590.00)
Adjusted Net Profit	$25,482.78	($18,286.82)	$20,746.91
Adjusted Gross Profit	$462,772.77	$203,114.44	$245,542.17
Adjusted Gross Loss	($437,289.99)	($221,401.27)	($224,795.26)
Select Net Profit	($320.00)	($6,190.00)	$5,870.00
Select Gross Profit	$415,470.00	$200,010.00	$215,460.00
Select Gross Loss	($415,790.00)	($206,200.00)	($209,590.00)
Account Size Required	$40,800.00	$31,790.00	$27,310.00
Return on Account	198.8%	59.39%	227.87%
Return on Initial Capital	81.11%	18.88%	62.23%
Max Strategy Drawdown	($47,580.00)	($36,910.00)	($33,460.00)
Max Strategy Drawdown (%)	(31.78%)	(28.21%)	(25.61%)
Max Close To Close Drawdown	($40,800.00)	($31,790.00)	($27,310.00)
Max Close To Close Drawdown (%)	(28.55%)	(25.14%)	(21.94%)
Return on Max Strategy Drawdown	1.7	0.51	1.86
Profit Factor	1.2	1.09	1.3
Adjusted Profit Factor	1.06	(0.92)	1.09
Select Profit Factor	(1)	(0.97)	1.03
Max # Contracts Held	1	1	1
Slippage Paid	$0.00	$0.00	$0.00
Commission Paid	$17,595.00	$8,685.00	$8,910.00
Open Position P/L	$2,575.00	$2,575.00	n/a
Annual Rate of Return	10.16%	2.37%	7.8%
Monthly Rate of Return	0.85%	0.2%	0.65%
Buy Hold Return	($52,253.54)	($52,253.54)	($52,177.38)
Avg Monthly Return	$871.72		
Monthly Return StdDev	$5,648.16		

FIGURE 8.1   Crude Oil strategy performance report.

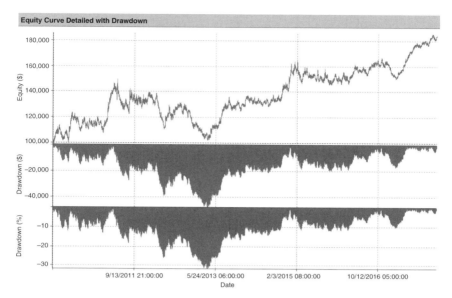

FIGURE 8.2   Crude Oil equity line.

Annual Period Analysis

Period	Profit $	%	Gross Profit	Gross Loss	# Trades	% Profitable
2017	$22,870.00	14.22%	$46,375.00	($23,505.00)	60	45%
2016	$12,180.00	8.19%	$50,800.00	($38,620.00)	71	36.62%
2015	($7,210.00)	(4.63%)	$53,610.00	($60,820.00)	81	35.8%
2014	$26,740.00	20.71%	$67,070.00	($40,330.00)	65	43.08%
2013	$16,190.00	14.34%	$55,230.00	($39,040.00)	70	42.86%
2012	($24,210.00)	(17.66%)	$56,245.00	($80,455.00)	88	25%
2011	$22,450.00	19.58%	$94,395.00	($71,945.00)	85	35.29%
2010	$14,675.00	14.68%	$76,790.00	($62,115.00)	74	32.43%

FIGURE 8.3   Annual result for Crude Oil

As mentioned above we'll also consider Soybean futures and verify the system metrics on that market (Figures 8.7–8.9).

In this case, there's a flattening in the returns in the later years after a start that produced higher profits (but also a harsher drawdown in the initial period).

Strategy Performance Summary			
	All Trades	Long Trades	Short Trades
Net Profit	$84,220.00	$52,720.00	$31,500.00
Gross Profit	$522,470.00	$257,890.00	$264,580.00
Gross Loss	($438,250.00)	($205,170.00)	($233,080.00)
Adjusted Net Profit	$26,972.19	$14,075.75	($10,949.17)
Adjusted Gross Profit	$487,245.08	$234,249.26	$238,253.31
Adjusted Gross Loss	($460,272.89)	($220,173.52)	($249,202.48)
Select Net Profit	($10,680.00)	$26,350.00	($37,030.00)
Select Gross Profit	$427,570.00	$231,520.00	$196,050.00
Select Gross Loss	($438,250.00)	($205,170.00)	($233,080.00)
Account Size Required	$15,640.00	$19,160.00	$33,200.00
Return on Account	538.49%	275.16%	94.88%
Return on Initial Capital	84.22%	52.72%	31.5%
Max Strategy Drawdown	($21,320.00)	($22,480.00)	($36,060.00)
Max Strategy Drawdown (%)	(16.69%)	(14.72%)	(33.96%)
Max Close To Close Drawdown	($15,640.00)	($19,160.00)	($33,200.00)
Max Close To Close Drawdown (%)	(14.03%)	(12.74%)	(31.95%)
Return on Max Strategy Drawdown	3.95	2.35	0.87
Profit Factor	1.19	1.26	1.14
Adjusted Profit Factor	1.06	1.06	(0.96)
Select Profit Factor	(0.98)	1.13	(0.84)
Max # Contracts Held	1	1	1
Slippage Paid	$0.00	$0.00	$0.00
Commission Paid	$18,495.00	$9,195.00	$9,300.00
Open Position P/L	$5,395.00	$5,395.00	n/a
Annual Rate of Return	10.55%	6.61%	3.95%
Monthly Rate of Return	0.88%	0.55%	0.33%
Buy Hold Return	$7,846.20	$7,846.20	$8,696.37
Avg Monthly Return	$933.49		
Monthly Return StdDev	$4,899.95		

FIGURE 8.4 Gold future strategy performance report.

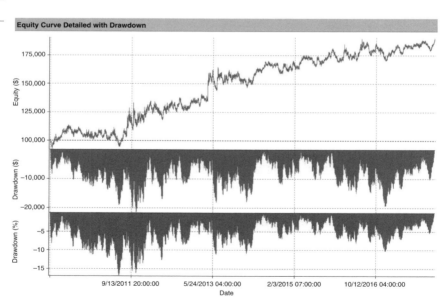

FIGURE 8.5 Gold equity line.

Annual Period Analysis

Period	Profit $	Profit %	Gross Profit	Gross Loss	# Trades	% Profitable
2017	$17,580.00	10.22%	$53,460.00	($35,880.00)	67	35.82%
2016	$1,600.00	0.94%	$61,595.00	($59,995.00)	83	36.14%
2015	$5,930.00	3.6%	$52,505.00	($46,575.00)	73	36.99%
2014	$12,640.00	8.32%	$53,860.00	($41,220.00)	72	41.67%
2013	$16,600.00	12.27%	$86,660.00	($70,060.00)	83	28.92%
2012	$9,960.00	7.95%	$71,505.00	($61,545.00)	80	36.25%
2011	$19,590.00	18.53%	$98,225.00	($78,635.00)	88	31.82%
2010	$5,715.00	5.71%	$54,775.00	($49,060.00)	78	41.03%

FIGURE 8.6   Annual result for Gold.

Strategy Performance Summary

	All Trades	Long Trades	Short Trades
Net Profit	$64,350.00	$45,947.50	$18,402.50
Gross Profit	$274,207.50	$145,087.50	$129,120.00
Gross Loss	($209,857.50)	($99,140.00)	($110,717.50)
Adjusted Net Profit	$30,885.59	$22,057.41	($5,014.81)
Adjusted Gross Profit	$253,538.33	$129,793.93	$115,196.63
Adjusted Gross Loss	($222,652.74)	($107,736.53)	($120,211.45)
Select Net Profit	($7,162.50)	$20,167.50	($27,330.00)
Select Gross Profit	$202,695.00	$119,307.50	$83,387.50
Select Gross Loss	($209,857.50)	($99,140.00)	($110,717.50)
Account Size Required	$18,130.00	$13,345.00	$13,407.50
Return on Account	354.94%	344.3%	137.26%
Return on Initial Capital	64.35%	45.95%	18.4%
Max Strategy Drawdown	($21,835.00)	($15,312.50)	($15,607.50)
Max Strategy Drawdown (%)	(18.28%)	(10.78%)	(14.56%)
Max Close To Close Drawdown	($18,130.00)	($13,345.00)	($13,407.50)
Max Close To Close Drawdown (%)	(15.66%)	(8.8%)	(12.66%)
Return on Max Strategy Drawdown	2.95	3	1.18
Profit Factor	1.31	1.46	1.17
Adjusted Profit Factor	1.14	1.2	(0.96)
Select Profit Factor	(0.97)	1.2	(0.75)
Max # Contracts Held	1	1	1
Slippage Paid	$0.00	$0.00	$0.00
Commission Paid	$13,365.00	$6,690.00	$6,675.00
Open Position P/L	$2,535.00	n/a	$2,535.00
Annual Rate of Return	8.88%	6.34%	2.54%
Monthly Rate of Return	0.74%	0.53%	0.21%
Buy Hold Return	$103,777.66	$173,623.19	$103,777.66
Avg Monthly Return	$760.06		
Monthly Return StdDev	$3,708.25		

FIGURE 8.7   Soybean strategy performance report.

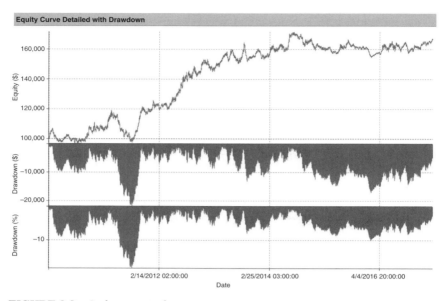

FIGURE 8.8 Soybean equity line.

Annual Period Analysis

Period	Profit $	Profit %	Gross Profit	Gross Loss	# Trades	% Profitable
2017	$6,050.00	3.76%	$8,942.50	($2,892.50)	11	63.64%
2016	$192.50	0.12%	$28,650.00	($28,457.50)	70	32.86%
2015	($887.50)	(0.55%)	$21,390.00	($22,277.50)	66	33.33%
2014	$6,402.50	4.13%	$34,142.50	($27,740.00)	63	47.62%
2013	$5,175.00	3.45%	$43,067.50	($37,892.50)	66	40.91%
2012	$27,100.00	22.06%	$56,482.50	($29,382.50)	61	52.46%
2011	$13,642.50	12.49%	$49,752.50	($36,110.00)	55	36.36%
2010	$9,210.00	9.21%	$36,960.00	($27,750.00)	61	34.43%

FIGURE 8.9 Annual result for Soybean.

For the first analysis on the concept of collaboration between systems, we'll combine the three systems in a portfolio in the hypothesis of investing with an initial capital of 100,000 USD to check the resulting behaviour (Figures 8.10–8.12).

	All Trades	Long Trades	Short Trades
Net Profit	$229,680.00	$117,547.50	$112,132.50
Gross Profit	$1,293,577.50	$628,057.50	$665,520.00
Gross Loss	($1,063,897.50)	($510,510.00)	($553,387.50)
Account Size Required	$74,570.00	$64,295.00	$73,917.50
Return on Account	308.01%	182.83%	151.7%
Return on Initial Capital	229.68%	117.55%	112.13%
Profit Factor	1.22	1.23	1.2
Slippage Paid	$0.00	$0.00	$0.00
Commission Paid	$49,455.00	$24,570.00	$24,885.00
Open Position P/L	$10,505.00	$7,970.00	$2,535.00
Select Net Profit	$213,720.00		
Adjusted Net Profit	$144,212.57		
Max Portfolio Drawdown	($47,400.00)		
Max Portfolio Drawdown (%)	(27.79%)		
Max Portfolio Close To Close Drawdown	($38,322.50)		
Max Portfolio Close To Close Drawdown (%)	(23.64%)		
Return on Max Portfolio Drawdown	4.85		

FIGURE 8.10   Portfolio of systems without money management.

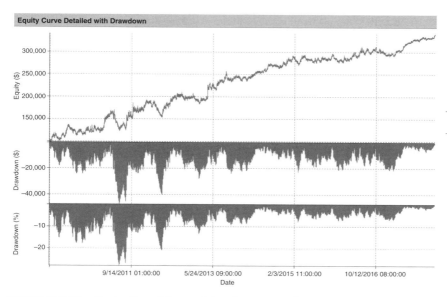

FIGURE 8.11   Equity line of the portfolio of systems without money management.

The turbulence in the initial years has an effect also on the performance of the portfolio, but in the last periods there's a certain improvement in the trend of the equity line with evident greater stability in terms of drawdowns. The percentage drawdown figure doesn't make much sense, as it's calculated each time on the basis of the level the equity line has reached at that particular time, so it depends on accumulated profits and when the analysis starts.

Annual Period Analysis

Period	Net Profit	% Gain	Profit Factor	# Trades	Percent Profitable
2017	$46,500.00	15.83%	1.75	138	42.03%
2016	$13,972.50	5%	1.11	224	35.27%
2015	($2,167.50)	(0.77%)	(0.98)	220	35.45%
2014	$45,782.50	19.39%	1.42	200	44%
2013	$37,965.00	19.16%	1.26	219	36.99%
2012	$12,850.00	6.94%	1.07	229	36.24%
2011	$55,682.50	42.96%	1.3	228	34.21%
2010	$29,600.00	29.6%	1.21	213	36.15%

FIGURE 8.12   Annual trend of the portfolio of systems without money management.

The absolute drawdown does, however, provide a valid point of reference and is a measure of the stability already mentioned. We can make other considerations on the lines we'll draw when we analyze the application of the money management models.

Now, to evaluate the effect of both the application of position sizing on the systems, and whether a portfolio approach is effective or not, first we'll consider the individual systems applying different money management algorithms, starting with the Crude Oil system and evaluating the performance with a percent f of 2% calibrated to the stop-loss, a fixed ratio with a delta of 10,000 USD and a percent volatility of 2% (Figures 8.13–8.15).

No matter how you look at it, you'll see that the Crude Oil performance shows no substantial improvement after applying money management. On the contrary, with some models the performance is even worse than the single contract model.

The cause of this is the irregularity of the equity line and the volatility of the instrument, evidently too aggressive for a capital of 100,000 USD (partial confirmation of this comes from the fact that the percent volatility model is the only one for which performance has improved with one single contract and, as we know, this model prevents trading in market conditions that are too turbulent for the available capital).

Performance Summary

	All Trades	Long Trades	Short Trades
Net Profit	$79,190.00	$20,060.00	$59,130.00
Gross Profit	$536,090.00	$246,130.00	$289,960.00
Gross Loss	($456,900.00)	($226,070.00)	($230,830.00)
Account Size Required	$40,800.00	$39,040.00	$27,310.00
Return on Account	194.09%	51.38%	216.51%
Return on Initial Capital	79.19%	20.06%	59.13%
Profit Factor	1.17	1.09	1.26
Slippage Paid	$0.00	$0.00	$0.00
Commission Paid	$19,590.00	$9,660.00	$9,930.00
Open Position P/L	$5,150.00	$5,150.00	$0.00
Select Net Profit	($57,070.00)		
Adjusted Net Profit	$18,745.45		
Max Portfolio Drawdown	($47,580.00)		
Max Portfolio Drawdown (%)	(31.78%)		
Max Portfolio Close To Close Drawdown	($40,800.00)		
Max Portfolio Close To Close Drawdown (%)	(28.55%)		
Return on Max Portfolio Drawdown	1.66		

FIGURE 8.13   Performance report for the system with Crude Oil and a percent f of 2%.

Performance Summary

	All Trades	Long Trades	Short Trades
Net Profit	$69,300.00	$31,510.00	$37,790.00
Gross Profit	$657,340.00	$321,110.00	$336,230.00
Gross Loss	($588,040.00)	($289,600.00)	($298,440.00)
Account Size Required	$81,110.00	$64,900.00	$40,110.00
Return on Account	85.44%	48.55%	94.22%
Return on Initial Capital	69.3%	31.51%	37.79%
Profit Factor	1.12	1.11	1.13
Slippage Paid	$0.00	$0.00	$0.00
Commission Paid	$25,290.00	$12,510.00	$12,780.00
Open Position P/L	$10,300.00	$10,300.00	$0.00
Select Net Profit	$45,690.00		
Adjusted Net Profit	($6,253.12)		
Max Portfolio Drawdown	($94,145.00)		
Max Portfolio Drawdown (%)	(56.6%)		
Max Portfolio Close To Close Drawdown	($81,110.00)		
Max Portfolio Close To Close Drawdown (%)	(52.91%)		
Return on Max Portfolio Drawdown	0.74		

FIGURE 8.14   Performance report for the system with Crude Oil using the fixed ratio method with a delta $= 10,000$ USD.

Performance Summary

	All Trades	Long Trades	Short Trades
Net Profit	$102,280.00	$8,300.00	$93,980.00
Gross Profit	$551,030.00	$236,600.00	$314,430.00
Gross Loss	($448,750.00)	($228,300.00)	($220,450.00)
Account Size Required	$44,730.00	$52,740.00	$22,060.00
Return on Account	228.66%	15.74%	426.02%
Return on Initial Capital	102.28%	8.3%	93.98%
Profit Factor	1.23	1.04	1.43
Slippage Paid	$0.00	$0.00	$0.00
Commission Paid	$20,505.00	$10,095.00	$10,410.00
Open Position P/L	$7,725.00	$7,725.00	$0.00
Select Net Profit	($24,360.00)		
Adjusted Net Profit	$38,387.89		
Max Portfolio Drawdown	($52,190.00)		
Max Portfolio Drawdown (%)	(36.71%)		
Max Portfolio Close To Close Drawdown	($44,730.00)		
Max Portfolio Close To Close Drawdown (%)	(33.2%)		
Return on Max Portfolio Drawdown	1.96		

FIGURE 8.15   Performance Report for the system with Crude Oil and a percent volatility of 2%.

In any case, let's take a look at the results, applying the same position sizing models to the Gold futures market (Figures 8.16–8.18).

The situation isn't exactly idyllic for the Gold futures, either. Using the fixed ratio method there are no results (Figure 8.17), and only the percent volatility method shows some improvement, although in this case probably due to the halt imposed when the market is too turbulent.

Now let's take a look at Soybean futures, applying the same position sizing algorithms (Figures 8.19–8.21).

Performance Summary

	All Trades	Long Trades	Short Trades
Net Profit	$99,240.00	$60,480.00	$38,760.00
Gross Profit	$732,430.00	$362,420.00	$370,010.00
Gross Loss	($633,190.00)	($301,940.00)	($331,250.00)
Account Size Required	$29,580.00	$28,840.00	$33,200.00
Return on Account	335.5%	209.71%	116.75%
Return on Initial Capital	99.24%	60.48%	38.76%
Profit Factor	1.16	1.2	1.12
Slippage Paid	$0.00	$0.00	$0.00
Commission Paid	$27,330.00	$13,620.00	$13,710.00
Open Position P/L	$10,790.00	$10,790.00	$0.00
Select Net Profit	$5,080.00		
Adjusted Net Profit	$18,040.58		
Max Portfolio Drawdown	($38,400.00)		
Max Portfolio Drawdown (%)	(20.88%)		
Max Portfolio Close To Close Drawdown	($29,580.00)		
Max Portfolio Close To Close Drawdown (%)	(15.23%)		
Return on Max Portfolio Drawdown	2.58		

FIGURE 8.16 Performance report for the system with Gold futures and a percent f of 2%.

Performance Summary

	All Trades	Long Trades	Short Trades
Net Profit	$6,080.00	$28,820.00	($22,740.00)
Gross Profit	$651,560.00	$335,990.00	$315,570.00
Gross Loss	($645,480.00)	($307,170.00)	($338,310.00)
Account Size Required	$36,040.00	$42,050.00	$41,330.00
Return on Account	16.87%	68.54%	(55.02%)
Return on Initial Capital	6.08%	28.82%	(22.74%)
Profit Factor	1.01	1.09	(0.93)
Slippage Paid	$0.00	$0.00	$0.00
Commission Paid	$26,175.00	$13,095.00	$13,080.00
Open Position P/L	$5,395.00	$5,395.00	$0.00
Select Net Profit	$11,150.00		
Adjusted Net Profit	($70,284.75)		
Max Portfolio Drawdown	($44,325.00)		
Max Portfolio Drawdown (%)	(31.55%)		
Max Portfolio Close To Close Drawdown	($36,040.00)		
Max Portfolio Close To Close Drawdown (%)	(27.04%)		
Return on Max Portfolio Drawdown	0.14		

FIGURE 8.17 Performance report for the system with Gold futures using the fixed ratio method with a delta = 10,000 USD.

Performance Summary			
	All Trades	Long Trades	Short Trades
Net Profit	$150,540.00	$96,040.00	$54,500.00
Gross Profit	$766,230.00	$387,210.00	$379,020.00
Gross Loss	($615,690.00)	($291,170.00)	($324,520.00)
Account Size Required	$38,080.00	$34,670.00	$46,620.00
Return on Account	395.33%	277.01%	116.9%
Return on Initial Capital	150.54%	96.04%	54.5%
Profit Factor	1.24	1.33	1.17
Slippage Paid	$0.00	$0.00	$0.00
Commission Paid	$28,770.00	$14,490.00	$14,280.00
Open Position P/L	$21,580.00	$21,580.00	$0.00
Select Net Profit	$86,700.00		
Adjusted Net Profit	$63,034.43		
Max Portfolio Drawdown	($46,770.00)		
Max Portfolio Drawdown (%)	(18%)		
Max Portfolio Close To Close Drawdown	($38,080.00)		
Max Portfolio Close To Close Drawdown (%)	(15.14%)		
Return on Max Portfolio Drawdown	3.22		

FIGURE 8.18 Performance report for the system with Gold futures and a percent volatility of 2%.

Performance Summary			
	All Trades	Long Trades	Short Trades
Net Profit	$73,922.50	$55,207.50	$18,715.00
Gross Profit	$399,162.50	$210,292.50	$188,870.00
Gross Loss	($325,240.00)	($155,085.00)	($170,155.00)
Account Size Required	$30,355.00	$26,690.00	$19,700.00
Return on Account	243.53%	206.85%	95%
Return on Initial Capital	73.92%	55.21%	18.72%
Profit Factor	1.23	1.36	1.11
Slippage Paid	$0.00	$0.00	$0.00
Commission Paid	$21,270.00	$10,680.00	$10,590.00
Open Position P/L	$5,070.00	$0.00	$5,070.00
Select Net Profit	$14,627.50		
Adjusted Net Profit	$24,004.26		
Max Portfolio Drawdown	($34,165.00)		
Max Portfolio Drawdown (%)	(18.28%)		
Max Portfolio Close To Close Drawdown	($30,355.00)		
Max Portfolio Close To Close Drawdown (%)	(16.39%)		
Return on Max Portfolio Drawdown	2.16		

FIGURE 8.19 Performance report for the system with Soybean futures and a percent f of 2%.

Performance Summary			
	All Trades	Long Trades	Short Trades
Net Profit	$159,510.00	$102,960.00	$56,550.00
Gross Profit	$982,065.00	$498,677.50	$483,387.50
Gross Loss	($822,555.00)	($395,717.50)	($426,837.50)
Account Size Required	$93,610.00	$81,747.50	$57,870.00
Return on Account	170.4%	125.95%	97.72%
Return on Initial Capital	159.51%	102.96%	56.55%
Profit Factor	1.19	1.26	1.13
Slippage Paid	$0.00	$0.00	$0.00
Commission Paid	$54,330.00	$27,240.00	$27,090.00
Open Position P/L	$15,210.00	$0.00	$15,210.00
Select Net Profit	$135,620.00		
Adjusted Net Profit	$35,332.00		
Max Portfolio Drawdown	($106,090.00)		
Max Portfolio Drawdown (%)	(33.13%)		
Max Portfolio Close To Close Drawdown	($93,610.00)		
Max Portfolio Close To Close Drawdown (%)	(30.21%)		
Return on Max Portfolio Drawdown	1.5		

FIGURE 8.20 Performance report for the system with Soybean futures using the fixed ratio method with a delta = 10,000 USD.

	All Trades	Long Trades	Short Trades
Net Profit	$107,225.00	$85,932.50	$21,292.50
Gross Profit	$638,327.50	$344,012.50	$294,315.00
Gross Loss	($531,102.50)	($258,080.00)	($273,022.50)
Account Size Required	$77,745.00	$58,617.50	$46,247.50
Return on Account	137.92%	146.6%	46.04%
Return on Initial Capital	107.23%	85.93%	21.29%
Profit Factor	1.2	1.33	1.08
Slippage Paid	$0.00	$0.00	$0.00
Commission Paid	$37,905.00	$19,380.00	$18,525.00
Open Position P/L	$17,745.00	$0.00	$17,745.00
Select Net Profit	$73,880.00		
Adjusted Net Profit	$26,727.36		
Max Portfolio Drawdown	($86,870.00)		
Max Portfolio Drawdown (%)	(36.08%)		
Max Portfolio Close To Close Drawdown	($77,745.00)		
Max Portfolio Close To Close Drawdown (%)	(33.25%)		
Return on Max Portfolio Drawdown	1.23		

FIGURE 8.21 Performance report for the system with Soybean futures and a percent volatility of 2%.

'Finally,' one of the systems shows signs of improvement on all fronts, although still nothing to write home about; but in comparison to the disappointing Crude Oil and Gold results the Soybean results prove the effectiveness of money management.

■ 8.2 Portfolio Money Management

We've reached the point where it's time to put everything we've learnt into practice and consider using a portfolio.

So what's the best way to proceed now we have three instruments? How does the approach change?

Substantially, there's little change to the logic illustrated in the previous chapters. We're still thinking in terms of risk percentages for the fixed fractional method and in terms of delta for the fixed ratio method, while for percent volatility we'll consider the usual allowable percentage fluctuation.

Also in this case we'll use the system stop-loss or the largest losing trade actually recorded in the period being studied as the maximum loss. In both the first and the second case, it's important to use the values that refer to each system/instrument on the basis of the input signal received. In our case, using the stop-loss eliminates any problems as the value is the same for all instruments.

Someone might object that we're using the profits from one instrument to increase the number of contracts on another, or that the performance of a strong system is hampered by the losses of another system in crisis with the number of its contracts increased thanks to the first.

In money management, you don't think in terms of single systems. Always remember that the number of contracts depends on the available capital. If you're using the fixed fractional method and have 100,000 USD and use one contract, you'll use two (or even three, depending on how much that one for the first contract was rounded down) if you have 200,000 USD. So if you start with 100,000 USD, and the system performs well from the start and brings your equity to 200,000, it's only natural for the second system to take that 200,000 as a reference, just as if you're starting from that point with that capital.

The fixed ratio method is slightly different. In this case, when you start using the system you'll start with just one contract, so the profits accumulated using other instruments shouldn't be taken into consideration when calculating the number of contracts to use in the first trade. In actual fact, starting with just one contract is something you can of course decide to change. The basic concept is that, without prejudice to the initial capital, you increase the number of contracts in a way that's more or less linked to what you make on the market. In fact, you'd go back to using one contract if your equity dropped back to below the level of your initial capital. Following this line of reasoning, starting with 100,000 USD, once we've reached 200,000 USD perhaps thanks to the Soybean system, we'd simply calculate the number of contracts to use with the Gold system as if it produced those profits. In fact, also the Gold system in practice starts with 100,000 USD, and we'd adjust the number of contracts from this value on, so at 200,000 we'd run the necessary calculations and wouldn't consider this as the initial capital any longer.

■ 8.3 Which Capital?

This matter is more complex than one might think. Which capital should be considered when calculating the number of contracts?

When we were working with just one single instrument and a single system, the situation was simple enough. You calculate the capital at the close of the trade and use it as the point of reference for calculating the number of contracts for the next trade. Cases with reverse orders might seem complex, but using the correct setup for the calculations lets you bypass this obstacle.

Now we're using several instruments at the same time, and one of these might be in position when there's a signal to enter a trade using another instrument.

Various methods can be used as ways to consider your capital of reference, and everyone is free to choose the one they find most suitable.

The first method, invented by Van Tharp called the core equity model, considers the available capital to be that remaining after deducting the potential losses allowed by the money management strategy.

In practice, if, for example, you have an available capital of 500,000 USD and adopt the above strategy with Gold using a percent f of 2%, you'd be able to enter the trade with six contracts:

$$\text{capital risked} = 500,000 * 2/100 = 10,000$$

$$\text{contracts} = \text{ENT}(10,000/1,500) = 6.$$

This means you'd be willing to withstand a loss of 9,000 USD. Now, if you received a signal to enter a Crude Oil trade, you'd consider your capital to be the initial 500,000 USD less the 9,000 risked and would therefore use the value 491,000 to calculate the number of Crude Oil contracts.

A second Van Tharp method is called the total equity model. In this case, the capital of reference is the total available liquid capital added to the current value of the portfolio. Taking the same previous example, let's suppose you have a gain of 2,000 USD for each Gold contract in position when you decide to enter the Crude Oil trade. In this case the capital to be considered would be

$$500,000 + 6 * 2,000 = 512,000.$$

It's immediately evident that the situation is quite different, and a different choice could produce very different results.

Van Tharp also came up with a third method called the reduced core equity model, although he later changed the name to reduced total equity model. This method is based on the reasoning behind the core equity model and subtracts the risk values from the initial capital. If some values change while the position is open, however, as a result of a dynamic trailing stop or take profit, the method returns the staked parts to the value of the capital to be considered.

If, for example, in the above case you reached a point in which the Gold contract provided for a move to a closer exit level (this isn't provided for by the system we're taking as an example but is often used in many other systems), and instead of a loss of 1,500 USD now provided for a loss of 500 USD, the 1,000 USD 'gained' from the dynamics of the trade for each contract would be added to the value of the capital to be considered.

So before we had:

$$500,000 - 6 * 1,500 = 491,000.$$

Now we have:

$$491,000 + 6 * 1,000 = 497,000.$$

We're simply subtracting what remains as the risk of a loss from the total capital, in other words 500 USD for each contract trading, in fact:

$$500,000 - 6 * 500 = 497,000.$$

The substantial difference with this approach, though, is when another increase in profits from the Gold contracts once again results in changing the exit level, to this time guarantee: for example, 500 USD of profits from each contract.

At this point, we'll have changed the level of risk by another 1,000 USD per contract (from a 500 loss to 500 in profit) and based on the previous 497,000 of reference, we'd calculate:

$$497,000 + 6 * 1,000 = 503,000,$$

which also corresponds to the sum of the capital and the profits guaranteed by the open trade, which, we've assumed, is equal to 500 USD per contract.

$$500,000 + 6 * 500 = 503,000.$$

The last method (the last we'll look at in this book, but certainly not the last in terms of possibilities, which are limited only by the trader's imagination) is, for every trade, to consider the equity when the last trade closed. In practice the evolution of the open trades and their potential repercussions on the capital, aren't considered. As far as I know, this method doesn't have a name, and I do sometimes use it as the calculations are intrinsically very simple.

Apart from the implications in terms of results, there are also practical aspects to consider when deciding whether to use one method rather than another.

The core equity model is quite well-suited to evaluating series of trades in Excel. If you have the date and time when each trade was opened and closed, it's easy to build the above-mentioned model. You can't go further without the detailed history of the evolution of the trade, so you can't apply the total equity model or the reduced total equity model.

The total equity model, however, is easy to use for those who can monitor their portfolio in real time, and therefore have a constantly updated value of the amount of cash and the projection of the positions. Not all trading platforms make this information available for it to be used immediately, so each individual should see whether they can use the model described, and above all, what sort of 'feeling' they have for it.

The reduced total equity model is definitely more complex but lets you follow the trend of your system in the best possible way. While the core equity model considers the limits of the trade (stop-loss or maximum loss) only at the beginning of the trade, for the reduced total equity model you have to record the evolution of said parameters during the entire life of the trade. If a stop is increased in the base system, the model must also take this into account.

The last method described comes in handy if you keep accounts of closed trades, which are only updated when each trade does in fact close. This, therefore, refers to the total equity, which is updated each time a new amount is added or subtracted.

It can be said that the core equity model is certainly the most conservative. In fact, every time you open a position it considers the worst event. In other words, it considers your capital to be that which remains after docking the estimated loss for that position. As we've seen, a more conservative approach can often offer some protection from adverse events, but it's also important to consider that this approach can limit the potential of the system in the case of long-term trades.

In fact, let's suppose you open a position for a month. Obviously, during that month the position could be very profitable, and using the core equity model for the whole month it's as if you have the initial capital after docking the estimated loss (let's suppose 1,500 USD per contract) available for the open position. If you opened a second position after 20 days, the number of contracts of this position would therefore refer to the portion of your capital earmarked for the loss of the first position. Let's imagine, though, that the first position is doing extremely well and produces open profits of 10,000 USD per contract. You use the core equity model to calculate the number of contracts for the second position:

$$500,000 - 6 * 1,500 = 491,000.$$

With the total equity model, on the other hand, this would give you:

$$500,000 + 6 * 10,000 = 560,000.$$

As is easy to imagine, it's highly probable you'd end up with quite a different number of contracts.

Personally, I also use another method to assess the impact of money management on portfolios of strategies, which consists of calculating the total equity at the close of the day before any new trades are entered. This approach is an approximation (from the previous close to the moment when a new trade is placed the available capital will certainly change), but it makes it easy to manage placing contracts as they are fixed at the start of each day, and there's no risk of having to calculate them at the same time as entering the trade with the same.

■ 8.4 The Effects of Portfolio Money Management

So, now let's take a look at what effect applying known money management strategies can have with our system of three instruments.

We'll apply the same models to each single instrument and calculate the total equity as described at the end of the previous paragraph.

We'll start using percent *f* with a 2% risk and the loss based on a stop-loss of 1,500 USD for all instruments (Figure 8.22).

It's immediately obviously that the net profit is much higher than the sum of the three single results. It's over 530,000 USD, while the sum of the three single systems, adopting the position sizing model we've used here on each, is approximately 250,000 USD; we've more than doubled the final result!

Performance Summary			
	All Trades	Long Trades	Short Trades
Net Profit	$531,652.50	$224,992.50	$306,660.00
Gross Profit	$3,755,712.50	$1,794,140.00	$1,961,572.50
Gross Loss	($3,224,060.00)	($1,569,147.50)	($1,654,912.50)
Account Size Required	$250,690.00	$294,415.00	$193,290.00
Return on Account	212.08%	76.42%	158.65%
Return on Initial Capital	531.65%	224.99%	306.66%
Profit Factor	1.16	1.14	1.19
Slippage Paid	$0.00	$0.00	$0.00
Commission Paid	$161,250.00	$79,980.00	$81,270.00
Open Position P/L	$78,970.00	$63,760.00	$15,210.00
Select Net Profit	$191,995.00		
Adjusted Net Profit	$279,316.29		
Max Portfolio Drawdown	($137,540.00)		
Max Portfolio Drawdown (%)	(40.78%)		
Max Portfolio Close To Close Drawdown	($114,912.50)		
Max Portfolio Close To Close Drawdown (%)	(35.69%)		
Return on Max Portfolio Drawdown	3.87		

FIGURE 8.22 Performance report of the portfolio with a percent *f* of 2%.

The DD has also been affected, and from just over 30%; in this case, it's increased to over 40%.

Let's take a look at the trend of the equity line (Figure 8.23).

It's an interesting trend. The maximum percentage drawdown (remember that, in the evaluation, with position sizing the DD% is more representative than the absolute drawdown, unlike when considering a single contract) is in the initial phases, where there were difficulties, especially with the Crude Oil system – while it stabilizes at around 20% in the subsequent phases.

A look at the results year by year shows good progression, with again the false note of 2015 that closes at a loss.

Now, let's take a look at the results when applying the fixed ratio method, again with a delta of 10,000 USD. (This was chosen as it represents a value that's on average near the required margins of these instruments and therefore in line with the consequent trading.)

These results are to a certain extent surprising, as the fixed ratio method wasn't exactly the highest performer when applied to individual systems; but, when applied to a portfolio, it produces a notably higher final profit compared to the same portfolio with percent f. The drawdown is worse,

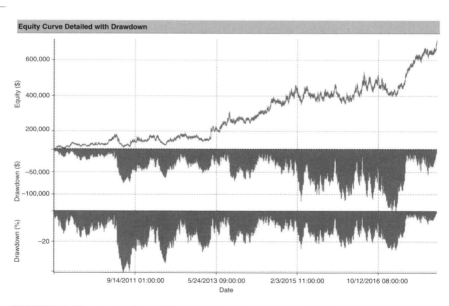

FIGURE 8.23   Equity line of the portfolio with a percent f of 2%.

Period	Net Profit	% Gain	Profit Factor	# Trades	Percent Profitable
2017	$300,257.50	73.17%	1.72	138	42.03%
2016	$32,665.00	8.65%	1.05	224	35.27%
2015	($32,397.50)	(7.9%)	(0.95)	220	35.45%
2014	$160,735.00	64.46%	1.37	200	44%
2013	$81,277.50	48.35%	1.22	219	36.99%
2012	$2,615.00	1.58%	1.01	229	36.24%
2011	$35,870.00	27.68%	1.15	228	34.21%
2010	$29,600.00	29.6%	1.21	213	36.15%

FIGURE 8.24   Annual performance of the portfolio with a percent f of 2%.

Performance Summary

	All Trades	Long Trades	Short Trades
Net Profit	$739,887.50	$285,190.00	$454,697.50
Gross Profit	$5,772,422.50	$2,746,720.00	$3,025,702.50
Gross Loss	($5,032,535.00)	($2,461,530.00)	($2,571,005.00)
Account Size Required	$397,135.00	$476,457.50	$307,525.00
Return on Account	186.31%	59.86%	147.86%
Return on Initial Capital	739.89%	285.19%	454.7%
Profit Factor	1.15	1.12	1.18
Slippage Paid	$0.00	$0.00	$0.00
Commission Paid	$252,480.00	$125,460.00	$127,020.00
Open Position P/L	$120,990.00	$95,640.00	$25,350.00
Select Net Profit	$372,342.50		
Adjusted Net Profit	$349,657.49		
Max Portfolio Drawdown	($224,047.50)		
Max Portfolio Drawdown (%)	(56.55%)		
Max Portfolio Close To Close Drawdown	($195,220.00)		
Max Portfolio Close To Close Drawdown (%)	(51.68%)		
Return on Max Portfolio Drawdown	3.3		

FIGURE 8.25   Performance report of the portfolio using the fixed ratio method with a delta of 10,000 USD.

however, and over 50%, which would certainly be difficult for even the most tenacious of traders to withstand.

Figure 8.26 shows the trend of the equity line and Figure 8.27 shows the profits year by year.

As can be seen in Figure 8.26, there were prolonged periods of significant drawdowns and, in the last period, with levels over 25% while percent f showed levels around 20% only.

Figure 8.27 shows that 2012 would have also closed with a loss.

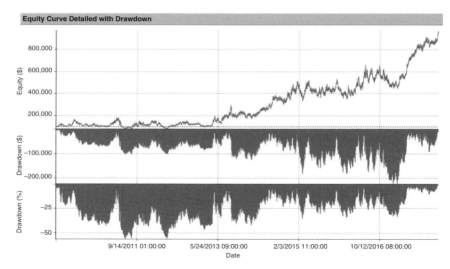

FIGURE 8.26 Equity line of the portfolio using the fixed ratio method with a delta of 10,000 USD.

Annual Period Analysis

Period	Net Profit	% Gain	Profit Factor	# Trades	Percent Profitable
2017	$491,825.00	104.86%	1.73	138	42.03%
2016	$81,570.00	21.05%	1.07	224	35.27%
2015	($41,580.00)	(9.69%)	(0.96)	220	35.45%
2014	$244,752.50	132.79%	1.35	200	44%
2013	$62,017.50	50.71%	1.12	219	36.99%
2012	($13,337.50)	(9.83%)	(0.96)	229	36.24%
2011	$29,207.50	27.44%	1.08	228	34.21%
2010	$6,422.50	6.42%	1.03	213	36.15%

FIGURE 8.27 Annual performance of the portfolio using the fixed ratio method with a delta of 10,000 USD.

	All Trades	Long Trades	Short Trades
Net Profit	$1,539,895.00	$628,415.00	$911,480.00
Gross Profit	$7,836,192.50	$3,709,860.00	$4,126,332.50
Gross Loss	($6,296,297.50)	($3,081,445.00)	($3,214,852.50)
Account Size Required	$753,155.00	$619,905.00	$544,002.50
Return on Account	204.46%	101.37%	167.55%
Return on Initial Capital	1539.89%	628.41%	911.48%
Profit Factor	1.24	1.2	1.28
Slippage Paid	$0.00	$0.00	$0.00
Commission Paid	$364,020.00	$181,455.00	$182,565.00
Open Position P/L	$327,500.00	$233,705.00	$93,795.00
Select Net Profit	$1,146,727.50		
Adjusted Net Profit	$1,017,404.26		
Max Portfolio Drawdown	($340,650.00)		
Max Portfolio Drawdown (%)	(32.18%)		
Max Portfolio Close To Close Drawdown	($330,715.00)		
Max Portfolio Close To Close Drawdown (%)	(30.99%)		
Return on Max Portfolio Drawdown	4.52		

FIGURE 8.28 Performance report of the portfolio with a percent volatility of 2%.

These evaluations weaken the case for using the fixed ratio method, despite the better performance in terms of final returns.

But let's continue and take a look at the results using a 2% percent volatility model (Figure 8.28).

Well, the model that attempts to weigh entering trades to avoid suffering overly from movements in more turbulent times produces results that are astonishing, to say the least, when compared to the other approaches.

Now, let's take a look at the trend of the equity line and the annual distribution of profits (Figures 8.29, 8.30).

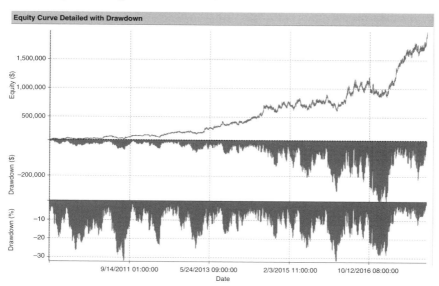

FIGURE 8.29 Equity line of the portfolio with a percent volatility of 2%.

Annual Period Analysis

Period	Net Profit	% Gain	Profit Factor	# Trades	Percent Profitable
2017	$1,087,837.50	123.68%	1.76	138	42.03%
2016	$167,205.00	23.47%	1.1	224	35.27%
2015	$7,720.00	1.1%	1.01	220	35.45%
2014	$331,537.50	88.86%	1.38	200	44%
2013	$135,452.50	57%	1.3	219	36.99%
2012	$58,192.50	32.43%	1.22	229	36.24%
2011	$58,720.00	48.64%	1.35	179	34.64%
2010	$20,730.00	20.73%	1.13	199	37.19%

FIGURE 8.30 Annual performance of the portfolio with a percent volatility of 2%.

It's immediately obvious that the drawdown in the initial years is more contained, and finally there are no years that close with a loss (although 2015 can practically be considered to have broken even). It's interesting to see that, in Figure 8.28, the maximum drawdown is just over 30%.

Having judged the fixed ratio method too 'unpredictable' in terms of drawdowns, we could compare the percent f of 2% with the percent volatility method that produces similar results in terms of net profit to compare the risks for the same results.

In order to produce similar results, we can trade by limiting the fluctuations to less than 1.55%. This choice (instead of 2%) produces the results shown in Figures 8.31–8.33.

Performance Summary

	All Trades	Long Trades	Short Trades
Net Profit	$571,852.50	$226,290.00	$345,562.50
Gross Profit	$2,901,977.50	$1,368,902.50	$1,533,075.00
Gross Loss	($2,330,125.00)	($1,142,612.50)	($1,187,512.50)
Account Size Required	$259,452.50	$223,490.00	$183,235.00
Return on Account	220.41%	101.25%	188.59%
Return on Initial Capital	571.85%	226.29%	345.56%
Profit Factor	1.25	1.2	1.29
Slippage Paid	$0.00	$0.00	$0.00
Commission Paid	$133,965.00	$66,900.00	$67,065.00
Open Position P/L	$104,685.00	$71,730.00	$32,955.00
Select Net Profit	$311,475.00		
Adjusted Net Profit	$368,487.81		
Max Portfolio Drawdown	($107,150.00)		
Max Portfolio Drawdown (%)	(24.79%)		
Max Portfolio Close To Close Drawdown	($106,032.50)		
Max Portfolio Close To Close Drawdown (%)	(21.91%)		
Return on Max Portfolio Drawdown	5.34		

FIGURE 8.31 Performance report of the portfolio with a percent volatility of 1.55%.

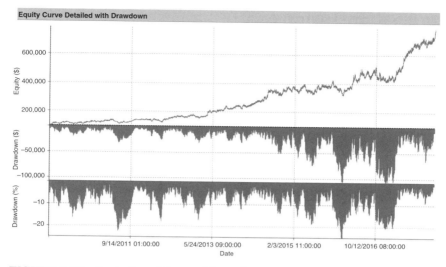

FIGURE 8.32   Equity line of the portfolio with a percent volatility of 1.55%.

Annual Period Analysis

Period	Net Profit	% Gain	Profit Factor	# Trades	Percent Profitable
2017	$354,185.00	83.86%	1.77	138	42.03%
2016	$62,547.50	17.38%	1.11	224	35.27%
2015	$2,722.50	0.76%	1.01	220	35.45%
2014	$132,065.00	58.69%	1.4	200	44%
2013	$53,502.50	31.19%	1.27	215	37.67%
2012	$29,850.00	21.07%	1.2	196	37.76%
2011	$15,890.00	12.63%	1.21	107	34.58%
2010	$25,775.00	25.77%	1.27	151	36.42%

FIGURE 8.33   Annual performance of the portfolio with a percent volatility of 1.55%.

The most interesting piece of information is provided by Figure 8.31, where we can see that, with results for profits close to those using a percent *f* of 2%, the drawdown is less than 25%!

A result of this kind tips the scales in favour of the percent volatility model.

■ 8.5 Conclusions

The aim of this chapter was, first and foremost, to show you how combining several strategies that refer to the same capital increases the potential of money management methods exponentially. In fact, the number of contracts are gradually increased in a more marked way the more trades there are. (Paradoxically, imagine a strategy that makes just one good trade: there would be no point in applying a money management method to this strategy, as there are no other trades for which you could use different numbers of contracts.) Combining several strategies increases the total number of trades and, therefore, intensifies the effect described.

We looked at how various methods might behave on moving average crossover strategies and drew our conclusions. These conclusions should not be taken as gospel for all types of strategies, though. What matters is the process used to reach this point, and it's this process that must be learnt in order to be able to replicate it with other systems.

■ Reference

Tharp, Van K. *Trade Your Way to Financial Freedom*. New York: McGraw-Hill, 2007.

CHAPTER 9

Money Management When Trading Stocks

Until now, we've focused on trading futures. These instruments are often erroneously considered risky, but the real risk is not knowing them, and therefore not being able to assess the risks. If you know the risks, and take steps to keep them under control, derivatives are nothing more nor less than simple trading instruments.

In any case, what we've discussed up to this point also applies to other trading instruments, and in particular to the stock market, which remains as always the most popular and populated trading market in the world.

■ 9.1 Trading in the Stock Market

When choosing a market to trade on a trader should consider all the pros and cons, and know what sort of limits they might encounter. In the case of the futures' market, often there are limits in terms of the margins required to trade with a certain instrument, and if the available capital isn't enough to cover these margins trading will be blocked. On the stock market we could say this limit is all but nonexistent: you can buy as many shares as you want and therefore size the trade you're entering in a way that doesn't create obstacles (unless, of course, the price of the share chosen is already higher than the capital in your trading account).

In many cases, you can also trade using leverage; in other words, buy (or sell) more stocks than you could with the capital in your account. There are, of course, a series of limits to be observed, but this option can certainly offer new levels of freedom that could be useful.

Trading on the stock market in fact involves an approach that's instinctively different to trading derivatives. In fact, when buying stocks it's natural to think in terms of exposure, so the question you need to answer is, 'How' much money should I 'invest?' With derivatives, one's reasoning is almost always along other lines, and if you're buying a DAX contract it would be unlikely for you to think how much it's really worth in monetary terms. In other words, you won't calculate the result of multiplying the current price for the BigPointValue (value of each point), not because it's wrong but because it simply doesn't come spontaneously; but, it's exactly this lack of spontaneity that makes it almost always easier to think in terms of how much you could lose on each trade you're going to open. With derivatives in general, we think of where to enter and exit trades and how much the difference between the two levels costs for each contract purchased. So, we start on the basis of a concept of potential loss and arrive, as a consequence, at the point in which we can size the position. (In reality, I say this in the hope that this is what the reader who has reached this point is now doing, because I know many beginners use much more hazardous approaches. But in this case, let's assume one is trading on the basis of the notions acquired in the previous chapters of the book.)

On the stock market, you'd usually think of how much of your available capital you're going to invest and, while this may be considered the correct approach (if you answer the question allowing for the risk), it is still quite hazardous.

On the basis of this premise, let's make a hypothesis that we have just one system and want to trade any stock on the US market – Amazon, for example. Well aware of the mean-reverting nature of the principal stocks on the US market, we decide to trade after a significant fall in the market, counting on a rebound.

To develop the trade we use intraday data and refer to the daily time frame to construct our setup.

If, at the close of the previous day, the price has dropped to a new low over the last three days, we decide, today, to buy at yesterday's low price, but we don't send the entry order right away, we keep it active only from 10:00 to 14:30 (remember the US stock exchange trades from 9:30 to 16:00) to avoid entering the trade at the time of maximum market volatility.

The position will be closed, either by a 2% stop-loss or a take profit that's double the stop.

Figure 9.1 shows an example of the trade.

FIGURE 9.1   Entry at lowest low of the previous three days and take-profit exit.

The following EasyLanguage code corresponds to the above concepts.

```
if low of data2 <= lowest(l of data2, 3) and time > 1000 and time
    < 1430 then buy next bar at (low of data2) limit;

if marketposition > 0 then sell("LXSL") next bar at entryprice
    *(1-Mypercloss/100) stop;

if marketposition > 0 then sell("LXTP") next bar at entryprice
    *(1+(Mypercloss*2)/100) limit;
```

We start trading in the hypothesis of having an initial capital of 10,000 USD paying 10 USD per contract in commission. The first assessment will be done imagining we use all the available capital; this choice, which might seem absurd, isn't exactly ill-advised because we've decided to use a 2% stop-loss; so, trading with all the available capital is the equivalent of an own risk of 2% per trade which, as we've seen in the previous chapters, is absolutely acceptable.

Figure 9.2 shows the performance report, the subsequent trend of the equity line and returns year by year. Results are appreciable.

Some may feel a drawdown that's often over 20% is too much, and therefore prefer a more conservative trading strategy.

Above, I said that always using all the available capital is the equivalent of a 2% risk per trade. If we want to use a much less aggressive strategy, we could risk just 1%; in other words, use only half the capital available to open positions. What would happen if we halved our exposure? Let's take a look at the performance report in Figure 9.5.

Perhaps many will be astonished to see no results when, with a bigger risk, we obtained such a satisfactory performance. In the previous chapters, we

Strategy Performance Summary			
	All Trades	Long Trades	Short Trades
Net Profit	$14,665.96	$14,665.96	n/a
Gross Profit	$106,430.09	$106,430.09	n/a
Gross Loss	($91,764.13)	($91,764.13)	n/a
Adjusted Net Profit	$1,969.53	$1,969.53	n/a
Adjusted Gross Profit	$98,996.69	$98,996.69	n/a
Adjusted Gross Loss	($97,027.16)	($97,027.16)	n/a
Select Net Profit	$15,878.72	$15,878.72	n/a
Select Gross Profit	$101,102.75	$101,102.75	n/a
Select Gross Loss	($85,224.03)	($85,224.03)	n/a
Account Size Required	$4,739.44	$4,739.44	n/a
Return on Account	309.44%	309.44%	n/a
Return on Initial Capital	146.66%	146.66%	n/a
Max Strategy Drawdown	($5,652.31)	($5,652.31)	n/a
Max Strategy Drawdown (%)	(28.27%)	(28.27%)	n/a
Max Close To Close Drawdown	($4,739.44)	($4,739.44)	n/a
Max Close To Close Drawdown (%)	(27.24%)	(27.24%)	n/a
Return on Max Strategy Drawdown	2.59	2.59	n/a
Profit Factor	1.16	1.16	n/a
Adjusted Profit Factor	1.02	1.02	n/a
Select Profit Factor	1.19	1.19	n/a
Max # Contracts Held	358	358	0
Slippage Paid	$0.00	$0.00	$0.00
Commission Paid	$10,190.00	$10,190.00	n/a
Open Position P/L	$396.05	$396.05	n/a
Annual Rate of Return	10.17%	10.17%	n/a
Monthly Rate of Return	0.85%	0.85%	n/a
Buy Hold Return	$284,409.08	$284,409.08	n/a
Avg Monthly Return	$86.56		
Monthly Return StdDev	$714.12		

FIGURE 9.2 Performance report starting with 10,000 USD always investing all the capital.

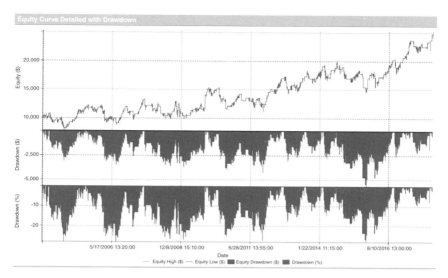

FIGURE 9.3 Equity line starting with 10,000 USD always investing all the capital.

Annual Period Analysis

Period	Profit $	%	Gross Profit	Gross Loss	# Trades	% Profitable
2018	$2,607.73	11.61%	$4,017.36	($1,409.63)	8	62.5%
2017	$3,522.02	18.6%	$6,438.33	($2,916.31)	14	50%
2016	$1,013.68	5.66%	$7,339.90	($6,326.22)	26	42.31%
2015	$202.90	1.15%	$5,457.39	($5,254.49)	19	36.84%
2014	($156.67)	(0.88%)	$8,308.82	($8,465.49)	34	35.29%
2013	$2,386.55	15.41%	$7,210.20	($4,823.65)	27	48.15%
2012	$2,955.01	23.58%	$8,995.48	($6,040.47)	34	47.06%
2011	($848.37)	(6.34%)	$7,234.51	($8,082.88)	44	34.09%
2010	($1,604.66)	(10.71%)	$4,981.20	($6,585.86)	29	34.48%
2009	$4,556.21	43.69%	$8,243.66	($3,687.45)	29	48.28%
2008	($877.12)	(7.76%)	$12,407.04	($13,284.16)	80	36.25%
2007	$352.86	3.22%	$5,706.53	($5,353.67)	34	38.24%
2006	($594.90)	(5.15%)	$6,365.62	($6,960.52)	42	40.48%
2005	$1,764.99	18.04%	$6,269.68	($4,504.69)	33	45.45%
2004	($372.26)	(3.67%)	$6,936.75	($7,309.01)	53	37.74%
2003	$154.04	1.54%	$1,504.18	($1,350.14)	10	40%

FIGURE 9.4 Annual profits starting with 10,000 USD always investing all the capital.

saw that, by pressing harder on the accelerator, we could earn more but also suffer more marked drawdowns; but we never came across a case in which a greater risk with a losing system could suddenly start making profits. So how can we explain this phenomenon?

Comparing Figures 9.5 and 9.2 you'll see they have one thing in common, and that is the total commission paid.

When we were trading futures we paid a certain amount per contract, and increasing or decreasing the exposure as a consequence increased or decreased the commission paid; on the stock market on the other hand, apart from some exceptions that can in any case be even more costly, a per-trade commission is paid. It doesn't matter whether said trade is for a lot of 10,000 USD or 5,000 USD, and this is what makes a difference using our approach: the impact of the 10 USD commission, set to simulate realistic calculations, becomes too burdensome when opening smaller positions. In short, a single trade can often be invalidated, or even make a loss, due to the impact of the commissions, and this can destroy what would otherwise be a good system.

I don't want to imply that trading derivatives is cheaper and trading stocks is too costly, but I do want to emphasise you should always consider the

Strategy Performance Summary

	All Trades	Long Trades	Short Trades
Net Profit	($3,194.27)	($3,194.27)	n/a
Gross Profit	$29,203.38	$29,203.38	n/a
Gross Loss	($32,397.65)	($32,397.65)	n/a
Adjusted Net Profit	($7,092.06)	($7,092.06)	n/a
Adjusted Gross Profit	$27,163.73	$27,163.73	n/a
Adjusted Gross Loss	($34,255.78)	($34,255.78)	n/a
Select Net Profit	($2,420.56)	($2,420.56)	n/a
Select Gross Profit	$28,139.68	$28,139.68	n/a
Select Gross Loss	($30,560.24)	($30,560.24)	n/a
Account Size Required	$4,087.36	$4,087.36	n/a
Return on Account	(78.15%)	(78.15%)	n/a
Return on Initial Capital	(31.94%)	(31.94%)	n/a
Max Strategy Drawdown	($4,236.06)	($4,236.06)	n/a
Max Strategy Drawdown (%)	(41.08%)	(41.08%)	n/a
Max Close To Close Drawdown	($4,087.36)	($4,087.36)	n/a
Max Close To Close Drawdown (%)	(39.98%)	(39.98%)	n/a
Return on Max Strategy Drawdown	(0.75)	(0.75)	n/a
Profit Factor	(0.9)	(0.9)	n/a
Adjusted Profit Factor	(0.79)	(0.79)	n/a
Select Profit Factor	(0.92)	(0.92)	n/a
Max # Contracts Held	160	160	0
Slippage Paid	$0.00	$0.00	$0.00
Commission Paid	$10,190.00	$10,190.00	n/a
Open Position P/L	$44.14	$44.14	n/a
Annual Rate of Return	(2.21%)	(2.21%)	n/a
Monthly Rate of Return	(0.18%)	(0.18%)	n/a
Buy Hold Return	$284,409.08	$284,409.08	n/a
Avg Monthly Return	($18.10)		
Monthly Return StdDev	$219.25		

FIGURE 9.5 Performance report with a 1% risk per trade (exposure 50% of available capital).

various scenarios and never underestimate anything that could in any way throw a spanner in the works.

I mentioned other commissions, and some brokers offer proportional transaction costs (in other words, the commission is calculated in proportion to the sum traded) but apart from some very rare exceptions (the only broker that comes to mind is the Italian broker Directa, who may have changed their conditions in the meantime) these commissions do have a minimum fee: which, again, has a negative effect when trading smaller amounts.

At this point, we could obviously consider doing the opposite and increase the risk to minimize the impact of commission. While, in mathematical terms, this idea holds water, it does, however, go against risk containment logic, and there might also be problems with the limits imposed on trading by the broker you've chosen.

In fact, if the broker doesn't allow any kind of leverage, it will be impossible to open positions that could result in exposure to risks of over 2%, as this is how much we'd lose using all the available capital (as it coincides with the percentage stop of the strategy). If we wanted to risk 3% per trade we'd have to open positions that, if stopped at 2% from the entry point, would lose 3%, so positions 1.5 times the whole account, and this could only be done with leverage.

Let's imagine, just to see what might happen, that we could use 200% leverage and therefore could adopt a 3% risk per trade. Figure 9.6 and the following shows the results we would have obtained.

These are very interesting results, although the drawdown is definitely starting to be too much. It would be interesting to see what sort of impact a percent volatility model might have, and whether it was more or less effective. To obtain a performance near that with a percent f of 3% in Figure 9.6, we'd have to use a volatility percentage of 4%, which produces the results shown in Figure 9.9 and the following.

Note that the max. drawdown with percent volatility is higher than that with percent f for the same results. Comparing Figures 9.7 and 9.10, you'll see that, with percent f the drawdown is more regular, while with percent volatility there are two spikes and then lower values on average (around 20%). It's down to the individual trader to decide whether they prefer one approach or the other. Leverage for both was 200%.

Strategy Performance Summary

	All Trades	Long Trades	Short Trades
Net Profit	$47,957.08	$47,957.08	n/a
Gross Profit	$247,572.61	$247,572.61	n/a
Gross Loss	($199,615.53)	($199,615.53)	n/a
Adjusted Net Profit	$19,217.12	$19,217.12	n/a
Adjusted Gross Profit	$230,281.39	$230,281.39	n/a
Adjusted Gross Loss	($211,064.27)	($211,064.27)	n/a
Select Net Profit	$40,067.51	$40,067.51	n/a
Select Gross Profit	$213,032.43	$213,032.43	n/a
Select Gross Loss	($172,964.92)	($172,964.92)	n/a
Account Size Required	$12,643.75	$12,643.75	n/a
Return on Account	379.29%	379.29%	n/a
Return on Initial Capital	479.57%	479.57%	n/a
Max Strategy Drawdown	($15,309.48)	($15,309.48)	n/a
Max Strategy Drawdown (%)	(37.78%)	(37.78%)	n/a
Max Close To Close Drawdown	($12,643.75)	($12,643.75)	n/a
Max Close To Close Drawdown (%)	(35.96%)	(35.96%)	n/a
Return on Max Strategy Drawdown	3.13	3.13	n/a
Profit Factor	1.24	1.24	n/a
Adjusted Profit Factor	1.09	1.09	n/a
Select Profit Factor	1.23	1.23	n/a
Max # Contracts Held	607	607	0
Slippage Paid	$0.00	$0.00	$0.00
Commission Paid	$10,190.00	$10,190.00	n/a
Open Position P/L	$1,478.85	$1,478.85	n/a
Annual Rate of Return	33.24%	33.24%	n/a
Monthly Rate of Return	2.77%	2.77%	n/a
Buy Hold Return	$284,409.08	$284,409.08	n/a
Avg Monthly Return	$284.11		
Monthly Return StdDev	$1,760.97		

FIGURE 9.6   Performance report with a 3% risk per trade (exposure 150% of available capital).

MONEY MANAGEMENT WHEN TRADING STOCKS

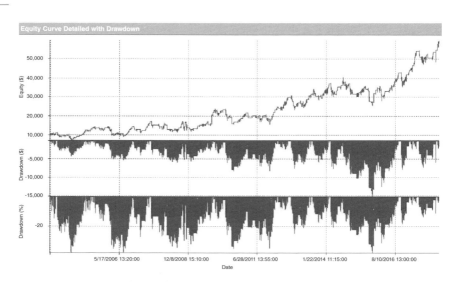

FIGURE 9.7   Equity line with a 3% risk per trade (exposure 150% of available capital).

Period	Profit $	%	Gross Profit	Gross Loss	# Trades	% Profitable
2018	$9,215.02	18.35%	$13,933.10	($4,718.08)	8	62.5%
2017	$11,608.52	30.06%	$21,292.89	($9,684.37)	14	50%
2016	$3,871.99	11.15%	$22,247.09	($18,375.10)	26	42.31%
2015	$1,136.54	3.38%	$15,510.24	($14,373.70)	19	36.84%
2014	$382.45	1.15%	$23,927.51	($23,545.06)	34	35.29%
2013	$7,021.67	26.8%	$19,358.09	($12,336.42)	27	48.15%
2012	$7,634.94	41.13%	$22,497.20	($14,862.26)	34	47.06%
2011	($1,043.59)	(5.32%)	$16,128.02	($17,171.61)	44	34.09%
2010	($3,142.46)	(13.81%)	$11,003.91	($14,146.37)	29	34.48%
2009	$9,758.48	75.11%	$16,978.09	($7,219.61)	29	48.28%
2008	($625.83)	(4.6%)	$23,573.82	($24,199.65)	80	36.25%
2007	$989.37	7.83%	$10,385.66	($9,396.29)	34	38.24%
2006	($678.00)	(5.1%)	$10,543.82	($11,221.82)	42	40.48%
2005	$3,188.07	31.51%	$10,620.76	($7,432.69)	33	45.45%
2004	($189.36)	(1.84%)	$10,435.85	($10,625.21)	53	37.74%
2003	$308.12	3.08%	$2,305.25	($1,997.13)	10	40%

FIGURE 9.8 Annual profits with a 3% risk per trade (exposure 150% of available capital).

Strategy Performance Summary

	All Trades	Long Trades	Short Tr:
Net Profit	$46,019.33	$46,019.33	n/a
Gross Profit	$209,085.22	$209,085.22	n/a
Gross Loss	($163,065.89)	($163,065.89)	n/a
Adjusted Net Profit	$22,063.71	$22,063.71	n/a
Adjusted Gross Profit	$194,482.07	$194,482.07	n/a
Adjusted Gross Loss	($172,418.36)	($172,418.36)	n/a
Select Net Profit	$33,465.74	$33,465.74	n/a
Select Gross Profit	$174,022.41	$174,022.41	n/a
Select Gross Loss	($140,556.67)	($140,556.67)	n/a
Account Size Required	$14,146.38	$14,146.38	n/a
Return on Account	325.31%	325.31%	n/a
Return on Initial Capital	460.19%	460.19%	n/a
Max Strategy Drawdown	($17,002.97)	($17,002.97)	n/a
Max Strategy Drawdown (%)	(45.61%)	(45.61%)	n/a
Max Close To Close Drawdown	($14,146.38)	($14,146.38)	n/a
Max Close To Close Drawdown (%)	(41.98%)	(41.98%)	n/a
Return on Max Strategy Drawdown	2.71	2.71	n/a
Profit Factor	1.28	1.28	n/a
Adjusted Profit Factor	1.13	1.13	n/a
Select Profit Factor	1.24	1.24	n/a
Max # Contracts Held	814	814	0
Slippage Paid	$0.00	$0.00	$0.00
Commission Paid	$10,190.00	$10,190.00	n/a
Open Position P/L	$1,939.04	$1,939.04	n/a
Annual Rate of Return	31.9%	31.9%	n/a
Monthly Rate of Return	2.66%	2.66%	n/a
Buy Hold Return	$284,409.08	$284,409.08	n/a
Avg Monthly Return	$275.62		
Monthly Return StdDev	$1,737.15		

FIGURE 9.9 Performance report with a percent volatility of 4%.

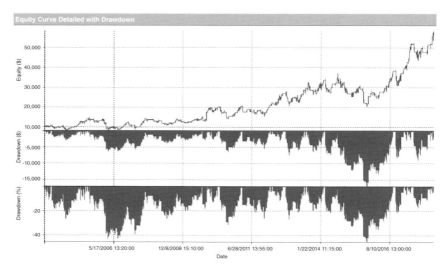

FIGURE 9.10 Equity line with a percent volatility of 4%.

Annual Period Analysis

Period	Profit $	%	Gross Profit	Gross Loss	# Trades	% Profitable
2018	$10,566.94	22.3%	$12,321.13	($1,754.19)	8	62.5%
2017	$13,856.00	41.32%	$25,635.72	($11,779.72)	14	50%
2016	$5,948.42	21.56%	$21,113.17	($15,164.75)	26	42.31%
2015	($1,595.74)	(5.47%)	$12,854.43	($14,450.17)	19	36.84%
2014	($1,988.90)	(6.38%)	$19,752.92	($21,741.82)	34	35.29%
2013	$7,154.16	29.79%	$20,077.56	($12,923.40)	27	48.15%
2012	$6,663.85	38.4%	$21,658.75	($14,994.90)	34	47.06%
2011	($787.29)	(4.34%)	$12,292.53	($13,079.82)	44	34.09%
2010	($1,395.00)	(7.14%)	$9,576.49	($10,971.49)	29	34.48%
2009	$7,258.76	59.12%	$12,366.14	($5,107.38)	29	48.28%
2008	($132.96)	(1.07%)	$9,222.49	($9,355.45)	80	36.25%
2007	$1,697.14	15.84%	$7,711.17	($6,014.03)	34	38.24%
2006	($1,909.99)	(15.13%)	$7,999.67	($9,909.66)	42	40.48%
2005	$2,170.24	20.76%	$10,573.45	($8,403.21)	33	45.45%
2004	$450.76	4.51%	$8,438.99	($7,988.23)	53	37.74%
2003	$1.98	0.02%	$1,465.11	($1,463.13)	10	40%

FIGURE 9.11 Annual profits with a percent volatility of 4%.

Here's the complete code, with all the variables and inputs you can use for various evaluations.

```
var: myshares(1000), MyATR(1);

var: MP(0), MyEquity(10000);

MP = marketposition;

input:MyInitialBalance(10000),Mypercloss(2), Myrisk(1), MM(1),
    percvol(2), marg(100);

MyATR= AvgTrueRange(5) of data2;

MyEquity= MyInitialBalance+ netprofit + openpositionprofit-commission;

if MM = 2 then myshares= minlist(Intportion((MyEquity*percvol/100)/
    MyATR),(marg/100)*Intportion(MyEquity/close));

if MM = 1 then myshares= minlist(Intportion((MyEquity*Myrisk/
    Mypercloss)/close),(marg/100)*Intportion(MyEquity/close));

if MM = 0 then myshares= Intportion(MyEquity/close);

if low of data2 <= lowest(l of data2,3) and time > 1000 and time
    < 1430 then buy myshares shares next bar at (low of data2) limit;

//setexitonclose;

if marketposition > 0 then sell("LXSL") next bar at entryprice
    *(1-Mypercloss/100) stop;

if marketposition > 0 then sell("LXTP") next bar at entryprice
    *(1+(Mypercloss*2)/100) limit;
```

I didn't mention or use a fixed ratio model in the calculations. This model could certainly be used, but the calculations would be complicated due to the construction of this particular algorithm. In fact, you'd have to use a lot of shares to be considered as if it was a futures' contract and multiply this lot to calculate the total number of shares to buy each time. You could, of course, just buy one share, as we did with the futures' contracts; but, in this case, the delta would have to be so small it would be an exercise in futility. Due to these complications, and the potential doubts concerning any advantages, we won't use this technique to trade shares.

■ 9.2 Conclusions

The stock market, like any other, is well suited to the application of position-sizing algorithms. The impact of commissions does, however, play a significant role, especially in terms of more modest investments. It's important to evaluate each model, including the impact of the commissions in the tests as, on the stock market, they are almost always per trade rather than proportional to the amount invested.

When permitted, you can also trade with a margin, although this should be properly coded and taken into account when sizing positions.

CHAPTER 10

Portfolio Management

We're nearing the end of the book, and it's important to explore a field that's definitely one of the most interesting in a trader's work. If you're using a good strategy and applying correct money management principles to the same produces indubitable benefits, the management of significant assets for the range of stocks in your basket is certainly something that gives you a great deal of satisfaction if done correctly.

Portfolio management will assume completely different aspects, depending on the final client it's done for.

If you have your own capital and set up a strategy to manage the same, the development plan can be calibrated to suit your own personality, and the events that characterize the progress of the equity will be monitored with a critical, but above all knowledgeable, eye. Managing your capital and planning your activities to "control" the movements of your assets in a way that's sustainable makes it possible to react in an appropriate way when problems occur. In other words, you'll have a good idea whether the drawdown you're suffering is part of the plan or whether something isn't going according to plan and has broken the mold (probably in a definitive way), and it's better to cut your losses and call it a day.

Managing your own funds makes you personally responsible for the development of the same and, apart from the implications that profits can have on the family (or more probably not making a profit might have) the only person you have to answer to is yourself.

If you're running a professional fund management company, on the other hand, part of a business setup to manage capital for others, your clients will be the subscribers of the fund you're working with. In this case, it will be a lot harder to 'justify' the trends of the capital you're managing to people who might not know that much about financial investments, and they certainly won't have had a hand in drawing up the investment plan. The classic example is the different way you'll see a 40% drawdown. If you're managing your own capital, a drawdown of that kind might have been part of the plan, and your risk profile will make such a retracement from the highs reached easier to withstand. If, on the other hand, a fund managed by a fund management company suffers such a drawdown, the company will probably lose a few clients, who might leave with a sour taste in their mouths; or in any case. at the very least, it would be hard to find new subscribers. A 40% drawdown, in fact, would be interpreted as the fund management company's inability to limit losses, rather than the natural consequence of an approach that's not overly conservative and that, in happier times on the market, would probably produce very interesting results.

As mentioned above, if you work for a company that manages other people's capital, you'll have to plan a strategy that makes the equity line trend as regular as possible.

In fact, while a heavy drawdown can discourage your clients, there's also another factor to consider, when trying to keep your subscribers as happy as possible. If you're using what's basically an aggressive system, and it's a favourable period, the results will certainly be good, to say the least; and, if there are no particular difficulties in the following period; but also no major market fluctuations, there shouldn't be any particular problems in terms of drawdown. But, obviously, you won't see the excellent results obtained in the previous period either. Once again, your clients might be dissatisfied, expecting a repeat performance in terms of profits made (or that they read about in the brochure) during the previous period. You have to consider that someone who puts their savings in a fund expects to see a trend similar to the one they read had already occurred in previous periods, and disclaimers on future trends will be ignored. The client choses a fund and expects it will continue to perform as it has until then, and as they'll obviously choose a fund that performed well up to that point they'll also obviously expect good performance in the future.

This is another reason to consolidate the idea that the more regular and 'gentle' the trend of the capital is, the better it will look for a professional fund management company.

The methods used to manage exposure in a stock portfolio, in conceptual terms, are no different from those we've discussed and applied for a single strategy (or three strategies in Chapter 8).

If you have to monitor several shares, you'll have signals to enter trades for some of these stocks at different times or, in rare cases, also at exactly the same time. The problem for the person managing the capital is, once again, how much to invest for each single position.

■ 10.1 A Portfolio Approach

In the previous chapters, we discussed futures, and looked at the effect that different approaches might have on the same. We considered approaches that quantified the entry points on the basis of the risk the same represented, therefore establishing parameters for the number of contracts on the basis of the worst possible event that could occur: the stop-loss.

Other approaches attempted to limit variations in the available capital by measuring the movement of the instrument before entering the trade and, on the assumption the fluctuations would continue along the same lines during the trade, the number of contracts on the basis of said variations.

Still other methods started with the minimum possible (one contract for futures) and increased them in a constant way on the basis of profits made on the market.

There are pros and cons with each of these approaches, one better suited than another for the purpose the trader wants to use it for, and also in relation to the type of market it would be applied to.

When trading on the stock market, we considered the role leverage plays when choosing the best strategy, and how it can change the limits within which we can trade.

All these concepts can be adapted to a more consistent basket, and similar ones can be used, too, based on different logic in line with the same basic method.

The first step is to refer to Chapter 8, and stress the importance of the concept of capital to which you refer in each single trade.

The method you use to calculate the equity changes the final result, especially with systems the positions of which remain open for some time.

So, here once again are the three principal methods:

1. *Core equity model.* This considers the available capital to be that available in the portfolio, before opening the position, minus the amounts that would be lost if the stop-losses of the open positions were triggered. So, this is quite conservative.

2. *Total equity model.* This method considers the capital to be the liquidity in the portfolio, plus the market exchange value of the open positions. In practice, it allows for the fact that, if an open position is making a lot of profit, it's as if the capital has increased even if you haven't liquidated the position yet.

3. *Reduced total equity model.* Like the core equity model, this model considers the amount of funds before opening positions minus the losses related to those positions. If stop values are changed, or profits are committed, these values are added to the capital; it's as if you consider the position to be closed at preset values at any time.

After deciding which method to use to calculate the equity, now comes the hard part: choosing the money-management technique.

In the case of a stock portfolio, there are several different methods you could use, and many are based on very simple assumptions.

Let's take a look at the most well known and most commonly used methods.

The simplest method to use by far is *equally weighting positions,* which sounds more complicated than the extremely simple principle behind it. In practice, once you know the number of stocks you intend to monitor, you divide the available capital into the same number of parts and each part constitutes the capital used for each stock.

So, if you have 10 stocks to monitor and €1,000,000 available, you allocate €100,000 to each stock and, when a signal is triggered, you buy €100,000 of the indicated stock at the exchange value.

The method can develop in two different ways as capital increases. The first, most obvious way, is to recalculate each time the amount to use for each single stock. So if the initial €1 million is now €1,050,000, for each new signal you'd use €105,000, instead of the initial €100,000. In practice, in the same way as each stock constitutes a fraction of the total number of stocks you're monitoring, the capital used for the same constitutes the same fraction of the total capital of reference.

The second method you could adopt is to continue to use €100,000 for each signal; once you've reached €1,100,000, you'd add another stock to the basket to make a total of 11.

The first method is certainly the one that lets you manage your portfolio most effectively, so it grows in a way that's more in line with the ups and downs of the market. Using the first method increases exposure on the market as your capital increases in proportion to available funds. The second method, in practice, represents an obstacle to a constant percentage growth of the capital. In fact, if we consider that it would be quite improbable to be trading on the market with all 10 stocks monitored at the same time, and therefore even more improbable that you'd increase your exposure with an eleventh, there's no real increase in exposure. This choice, however, allows greater diversification of the investments. This may mean a higher probability of staying on the market, with more stocks for which buy signals could be triggered, but the level of exposure for each single stock would always be the same. We would always be using €100,000, and at a certain point in the growth of the capital, the method might appear to be too conservative.

One method that's very similar to the previous one is the *percent of equity* method: in practice, you decide to use a fixed percentage of your capital for each position.

It's different from the previous method in that the chosen percentage isn't necessarily linked to the number of stocks you're monitoring. In the example in which we equally weighted positions, we had 10 stocks and €1,000,000, using 1/10 or 10% for each stock.

With the percent of equity method we can arbitrarily choose a percentage that's different from 10%, and this could be higher (a more aggressive method) or lower (a more conservative method). It's obvious that in this case, if we used a higher percentage than that represented by the stock in relation to the total number of stocks monitored, we could find ourselves in a situation in which we couldn't make a trade because we didn't have sufficient available capital. If, for example, with €1,000,000 we decided to use a percent of equity method with a percentage of 20%, and we found ourselves contemporarily with open positions for 5 of the 10 stocks monitored, we couldn't open a trade for a signal that would have triggered a sixth stock, as all our capital is tied up on the market (5 stocks using 20% of the capital each makes a total of 100% of the capital).

In any case, it must be said that the percent of equity method is one of the most used methods: it's extremely simple as you always know how much capital you have available. (Remember, though, that this does in any case depend on the initial choice you made on how you'll consider the capital; in other words, in terms of core equity, total equity or reduced total equity.) All you have to do is calculate the percentage chosen and buy the appropriate number of stocks for the resulting amount.

The two methods described give you an idea of how to 'distribute' available funds and that it's not a good idea to stay too long with a single stock. Thinking initially though in terms of capital held, and adjusting the number of shares bought only on the basis of this parameter, there's the risk of creating an imbalance in your portfolio.

It's certainly important to consider the consequences of an investment and not just consider things in terms of before (the capital held), but also in terms of after (the trend of the trade).

One way to follow the evolution of an entry into the market is, as we saw in previous chapters, to consider how much this investment could lose and decide beforehand to limit the global effect of said negative event.

You simply decide beforehand what part of the capital you are willing to risk if you close the trade with a loss; and, in consideration of the open position risks, you adjust the relevant number of shares as a consequence. This method is better known as *percent risk* as it's a percentage risk on which the your choice is based.

So, if you have €1,000,000 and don't want to risk more than 2% of the entire capital, you'd analyze the worst event for the position you intend to open. If, for example, the position has a 4% stop-loss, you'll see we can buy using as much as €500,000, which is half the available capital; in fact, if a stop-loss is triggered half of the capital would lose 4%, which would obviously be 2% of the total capital.

Even with this straightforward example, it's easy to see that, when using this type of approach, you might easily not be in a position to make some trades as you won't have enough capital (in the above example, in fact, we used half the capital to enter one trade, and all it would take would be another similar trade to have committed all our available capital on the market).

It's true that this example is only used to illustrate the method. In fact, when using this method the risk percentages are very low, in order to create the least possible disturbance to the trend of the equity line and allow for greater diversification, always on the condition you have capital available.

The first methods described, as mentioned above, don't consider the consequences of the trade but just the capital. Percent risk attempts to calibrate entering a trade in terms of the worst event that could occur. It's true that, if we adopt the same strategy for all the stocks in the basket in question, and this strategy had a 5% stop-loss, for example, once again all the stocks would be considered in the same way. This would certainly give you a good deal of control over the equity trend in terms of loss containment, but the exposure would be practically the same for each single stock. If we risked 0.5% of the capital and the strategy had a 5% stop-loss, this would mean we would risk €5,000 of the €1,000,000. So this €5,000 would be 5% of the capital allocated to each single trade, as this is how much we would lose if the stop-loss was triggered. The stock would therefore be bought for €100,000. In fact, if the 5% stop-loss is triggered with €100,000, we would lose €5,000, which is 0.5% of the entire capital.

So it's clear that you don't start with the available capital but with the losses, and this is positive, but you continue to treat each stock in the same way, the strategy is the same and the capital allocated to each trade is the same regardless of which stock is chosen. This is obviously true in the case in which the strategy provided for a percentage stop-loss, as in the above example.

Once again, there's the risk that the portfolio in question wouldn't be balanced in the best possible way.

If we take a banal example, it's easy to see that holding €10,000 in ENEL isn't the same thing as holding €10,000 in Tiscali. Volatile stocks cause more disruption in the equity line than 'quiet' stocks.

So, in order to effectively deal with this, let's once again consider the volatility of stocks, just as we did with the percent volatility model in Chapter 4.

As we saw in that chapter, the volatility of stock can be measured by calculating an average of the fluctuations of said stock during the day. As is well known, the difference between the day's high and low is called the *range,* and the bigger it is, the more volatile the stock is.

True range was introduced to replace range in order to provide a more accurate figure for the multiday trend, allowing for the possibility that the previous day's close lies outside the daily range and, if applicable, it shows the distance of the same from the bar high or low to the range value (see Figures 4.18 and 4.19).

In Chapter 4, we considered an average of five days for the true range. It must be said that for medium- to long-term strategies it's preferable to consider longer periods. We said that 20 days serve as a good compromise (on daily charts, this is approximately the equivalent of a one trading month). Therefore, calculating an average at 20 days (or another period, depending on the type of system chosen) of the true range gives you an idea of the average stock fluctuation. This fluctuation is measured in terms of absolute value, and may, for example, be 1.5, which means that the stock in question on average moves 1.5 points during the day (for example, from 30 to 31.5). In this case, of the stocks in our list and standard trading, this value also corresponds to the value in euros. If, in fact, a stock moves from 30 to 31.5, we would say it moved €1.5. What we want to do is measure the volatility value in euros in order to evaluate the effect on the capital. With futures it's different, as the volatility in euros is usually not the same as the movement in points. With Italian futures, for example, each point is worth €5, and a true range average of 500 points is the equivalent of a volatility of €2,500.

Returning to stocks in order to simplify things, we've seen that one stock has an average volatility of €1.5 (in the above, example). If we buy 1,000, we'll have an average of €1,500; buying 2,000 will be €3,000, and so on.

Now let's consider our available capital to be €1,000,000. We deem the possibility of suffering variations of over 0.5% to be too onerous; in other words, if there were fluctuations of over €5,000 in the open positions, at this point, with our stock that has an average volatility of 1.5 points we can buy 3,333 shares. So:

$$5,000/1.5 = 3,333.333.$$

If we buy more, we run the risk of suffering greater fluctuations than the chosen €5,000.

The volatility of the stock can be used in two ways that translate into the same number of different money management methods. The first of the two is the *percent risk with ATR* method, which practically uses the same steps as the percent risk method but, instead of using the stop-loss to limit negative events, it uses a multiple of the average true range (ATR) as the limit value for the fluctuation.

If, for example, we take the 10-day ATR as a significant volatility value, we might consider a fluctuation that's twice said value to be a significant level at which to limit the trade. At this point, you establish the percentage of the capital you're willing to let fluctuate to this limit and calculate the number of stocks to buy on the basis of this figure.

Let's take, for example, the *Canistracci Oil* stock, which has a 10-day ATR of two points (the choice of this number is also arbitrary and in general is linked in different ways to different strategies). Supposing we have an available capital of €100,000 and we don't want to expose more than 1% of said capital to the risk of excessive portfolio fluctuation. This means we want to prevent the portfolio losing more than €1,000 during the trade we're going to open, considering that we want to avoid this event in cases of exceptional volatility, so we multiply the 10-day ATR by 2 and take this value as a reference. The result is volatility in exceptional cases of 4 points (2 measured multiplied by 2). We don't want this to produce losses of over €1,000, so it's easy to calculate $1,000/4 = 250$, which is the maximum number of Canistracci Oil shares we can buy.

Often, this method is combined directly with the basic strategy in which, instead of a percentage stop-loss, you use a stop level or a trailing stop equal to a multiple of the ATR. In this case, the value of the stop in the strategy corresponds to a multiple of the measured volatility of the instrument (which is also logical if we consider it's better to close a position if the instrument starts moving in the opposite direction).

The second method that uses volatility is the actual *percent volatility model*. In this case, you don't consider the system stop-loss but simply its ATR – let's say, over 20 days. This value is used as the volatility of reference for the instrument. Now, if we establish how much we're willing to let our total capital fluctuate, we can calculate the number of shares to buy on the basis of the ratio of the two values.

If the 20-day ATR of the above Canistracci Oil stock was 1.8 points and we decided that for our capital of €100,000 we didn't want to suffer fluctuations of over 1%, this means we mustn't buy more than:

$$\frac{100,000 * \dfrac{1}{100}}{1.8} = 555.55,$$

so we should buy no more than 555 shares.

The above lays the foundations for correct portfolio management, but as always, it's important to take a look at some results to fully appreciate the different ways the equity line can behave depending on the method chosen.

In Chapter 8, we saw how combining different strategies can produce astonishing results. In that chapter, we limited the trading to three futures, adopting the same strategy for all.

In this case, however, we'll study a stock portfolio, and to simplify things we'll limit ourselves to only 10 stocks as an example, in consideration of the fact that the principles described can easily be applied also to more consistent baskets.

Once again, we're interested in the trends produced by different money management techniques, so we'll take the case of just one single strategy applied in the same way to all the stocks.

We'll compare the results using the same percentage of capital for each stock with that to using percent volatility and see which approach limits drawdown most effectively in relation to profit made.

First, let's take a look at the rules of the strategy we'll be using to trade both long and short on daily bars.

We'll use a faster moving average with 20 periods and a slower moving average with 45 periods, as well as a trend reference average of 200 periods.

The long positions will only be opened if the last close is above the 200 periods moving average and the short positions will only be opened if the last close is below the same average.

The long trades will be opened if a day closes with the faster moving average that crosses over the slower moving average; vice versa, the short trades will be opened when the same averages cross in the opposite way. The positions will be closed when the averages cross in the opposite way or when the trend phase changes (in other words, long positions will be closed if the faster moving average drops below the 200 period average and short positions will be closed if the faster moving average rises above the 200 period average on an uptrend).

The code for this strategy follows, with the option to choose between percent volatility and trading a percentage of the equity.

```
Input: Slow(20), fast(45), percvol(2), eqperc(10);

var: myshares(1000), MyATR(1);

myshares = intportion(Portfolio_Equity*(eqperc/100))/close;
```

```
MyAtr = averagetruerange(slow);

if percvol > 0 then myshares = intportion((Portfolio_Equity*percvol/
    100)/MyAtr);

if average(c, fast) crosses above average(c, slow) and c > aver-
    age(c, 200) then buy myshares shares next bar at market;

if average(c, fast) crosses below average(c, slow) and c < aver-
    age(c, 200) then sellshort myshares shares next bar at market;

if average(c, fast) crosses above minlist(average(c, slow), aver-
    age(c, 200)) then buytocover next bar at market;

if average(c, fast) crosses below maxlist(average(c, slow), aver-
    age(c, 200)) then sell next bar at market;
```

With reference to Chapter 9, we'll study the results complete with a commission of €10, as used since 2001 (beginning of 2018).

We'll trade with an initial capital of €1,000,000 euro and a portfolio of 10 stocks listed on the Italian market:

A2A

ENEL

ENI

ERG

G

MB

MS

TIT

AGL

STM

Figure 10.1 shows the result when entering the trade with 10% of the total equity for each position.

Performance Summary

	All Trades	Long Trades	Short Trades
Net Profit	€644,894.76	€490,608.64	€154,286.12
Gross Profit	€2,261,122.17	€1,126,722.99	€1,134,399.18
Gross Loss	(€1,616,227.41)	(€636,114.35)	(€980,113.06)
Account Size Required	€593,083.42	€300,840.95	€502,248.50
Return on Account	108.74%	163.08%	30.72%
Return on Initial Capital	64.49%	49.06%	15.43%
Profit Factor	1.4	1.77	1.16
Slippage Paid	€0.00	€0.00	€0.00
Commission Paid	€9,510.00	€4,658.86	€4,851.14
Open Position P/L	(€7,846.99)	(€7,846.99)	€0.00
Select Net Profit	€372,457.44		
Adjusted Net Profit	€392,470.80		
Max Portfolio Drawdown	(€268,118.13)		
Max Portfolio Drawdown (%)	(24.48%)		
Max Portfolio Close To Close Drawdown	(€208,492.84)		
Max Portfolio Close To Close Drawdown (%)	(17.25%)		
Return on Max Portfolio Drawdown	2.41		

FIGURE 10.1 Performance report always allocating 10% of the total equity per position.

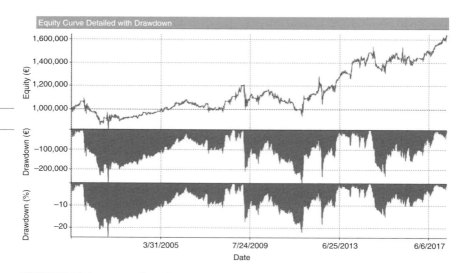

FIGURE 10.2 Equity line always allocating 10% of the total equity per position.

Figure 10.2 shows the corresponding equity line and Figure 10.3 shows the distribution of profits between the various stocks. Finally, Figure 10.4 shows the annual distribution of profits.

Overview

Market	Start Date	End Date	Net Profit	# Trades
A2a	4/18/2001	3/19/2018	€157,970.96	48
ENEL	9/2/2002	3/19/2018	(€26,772.53)	46
ENI	10/24/2001	3/19/2018	(€39,389.27)	40
ERG	7/3/2001	3/19/2018	€56,915.18	45
G	6/29/2001	3/19/2018	€131,477.50	49
MB	7/2/2001	3/19/2018	€176,813.53	53
MS	4/25/2001	3/19/2018	€59,062.97	51
TIT	4/19/2001	3/19/2018	€172,221.80	44
AGL	4/24/2001	3/19/2018	(€2,281.68)	51
STM	4/18/2001	3/19/2018	(€41,123.71)	50

FIGURE 10.3 Distribution of profits between the stocks, always allocating 10% of the total equity per position.

The final result is a profit of approximately €650,000 with a maximum percentage drawdown of around 24.5%.

If we wanted to compare similar profits, we'd have to use a percent volatility model that aims to limit daily fluctuations to within 0.3 (as can be seen in the code, we used the same faster-moving average period to calculate the ATR).

The results are shown in Figures 10.5–10.8.

As can be seen, there's not much difference, although there is a slight advantage with the percent volatility model. This, in fact, makes slightly more profit while suffering a few percentage points less drawdown. The drawdown curve also appears better in Figure 10.6 than in 10.2, while there aren't any substantial changes in the distribution of profits, both in terms of stocks and over the years.

Personally, I prefer the percent volatility model, but as it's harder to calculate the data to enter the trade, others might be more prone to choose the simpler percentage allocation model. If everything is automated, then of course the choice would be percent volatility.

Annual Period Analysis

Period	Net Profit	% Gain	Profit Factor	# Trades	Percent Profitable
2018	€50,825.72	3.2%	2.94	11	72.73%
2017	€145,156.91	10.07%	4.32	33	75.76%
2016	(€42,641.45)	(2.87%)	(0.76)	31	54.84%
2015	€26,001.46	1.78%	1.18	32	68.75%
2014	€120,102.13	8.98%	2.19	34	61.76%
2013	€144,782.81	12.14%	3.23	30	83.33%
2012	€97,268.07	8.88%	1.92	34	58.82%
2011	€21,940.62	2.04%	1.18	29	51.72%
2010	(€46,831.85)	(4.18%)	(0.66)	35	42.86%
2009	(€1,341.71)	(0.12%)	(0.99)	33	54.55%
2008	€111,080.57	10.99%	2.85	27	74.07%
2007	(€14,854.81)	(1.45%)	(0.78)	15	53.33%
2006	(€29,965.95)	(2.84%)	(0.71)	33	48.48%
2005	€80,663.03	8.27%	3.23	34	79.41%
2004	€45,747.63	4.92%	2.4	31	77.42%
2003	(€12,718.01)	(1.35%)	(0.84)	32	46.88%
2002	(€72,850.67)	(7.18%)	(0.56)	36	58.33%
2001	€14,683.28	1.47%	1.25	21	57.14%

FIGURE 10.4   Annual distribution of profits, always allocating 10% of the total equity per position.

Performance Summary

	All Trades	Long Trades	Short Trades
Net Profit	€683,150.71	€560,942.08	€122,208.63
Gross Profit	€2,660,343.64	€1,440,765.45	€1,219,578.19
Gross Loss	(€1,977,192.93)	(€879,823.37)	(€1,097,369.56)
Account Size Required	€786,166.85	€430,466.51	€574,975.76
Return on Account	86.9%	130.31%	21.25%
Return on Initial Capital	68.32%	56.09%	12.22%
Profit Factor	1.35	1.64	1.11
Slippage Paid	€0.00	€0.00	€0.00
Commission Paid	€9,510.00	€4,659.54	€4,850.46
Open Position P/L	(€12,653.75)	(€12,653.75)	€0.00
Select Net Profit	€507,897.20		
Adjusted Net Profit	€380,427.35		
Max Portfolio Drawdown	(€278,336.84)		
Max Portfolio Drawdown (%)	(22.01%)		
Max Portfolio Close To Close Drawdown	(€227,454.97)		
Max Portfolio Close To Close Drawdown (%)	(18.04%)		
Return on Max Portfolio Drawdown	2.45		

FIGURE 10.5   Performance report with a percent volatility model of 0.3%.

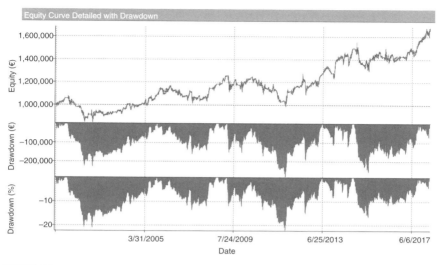

FIGURE 10.6 Equity line with a percent volatility model of 0.3%.

Overview

Market	Start Date	End Date	Net Profit	# Trades
A2a	4/18/2001	3/19/2018	€153,070.78	48
ENEL	9/2/2002	3/19/2018	(€79,864.64)	46
ENI	10/24/2001	3/19/2018	(€50,250.84)	40
ERG	7/3/2001	3/19/2018	€78,547.87	45
G	6/29/2001	3/19/2018	€187,438.91	49
MB	7/2/2001	3/19/2018	€202,627.59	53
MS	4/25/2001	3/19/2018	€79,874.86	51
TIT	4/19/2001	3/19/2018	€157,311.67	44
AGL	4/24/2001	3/19/2018	€35,919.34	51
STM	4/18/2001	3/19/2018	(€81,524.83)	50

FIGURE 10.7 Distribution of profits between the stocks with a percent volatility model of 0.3%.

Annual Period Analysis					
Period	Net Profit	% Gain	Profit Factor	# Trades	Percent Profitable
2018	€49,017.97	3.02%	2.08	11	72.73%
2017	€193,507.39	13.55%	3.51	33	75.76%
2016	(€41,739.77)	(2.84%)	(0.77)	31	54.84%
2015	€1,111.88	0.08%	1.01	32	68.75%
2014	€152,172.78	11.56%	2.33	34	61.76%
2013	€115,303.89	9.6%	2.13	30	83.33%
2012	€81,911.70	7.32%	1.78	34	58.82%
2011	(€27,722.80)	(2.42%)	(0.85)	29	51.72%
2010	(€52,681.62)	(4.39%)	(0.7)	35	42.86%
2009	€11,479.86	0.97%	1.07	33	54.55%
2008	€117,767.58	11%	2.94	27	74.07%
2007	(€5,400.15)	(0.5%)	(0.94)	15	53.33%
2006	(€67,358.30)	(5.89%)	(0.66)	33	48.48%
2005	€144,888.79	14.51%	3.4	34	79.41%
2004	€67,565.26	7.26%	1.99	31	77.42%
2003	€734.16	0.08%	1.01	32	46.88%
2002	(€94,519.59)	(9.23%)	(0.47)	36	58.33%
2001	€24,457.92	2.45%	1.64	21	57.14%

FIGURE 10.8   Annual distribution of profits with a percent volatility model of 0.3%.

■ 10.2 Some Improvements to the System

For a moment let's leave position sizing concepts aside and add some simple filters to the entry points to make them cleaner and avoid the false signals that can always be found in this type of strategy.

With this type of strategy the impulse that derives from the setup related to the moving average crossover is very important. In this case, there are a variety of different dynamics between long and short moves as they are related to the very nature of the stock market, which moves in a very different way depending on whether it's on an uptrend or downtrend. Even in terms of acceleration of the movements, they often behave in opposite ways.

So, on the basis of these considerations, it may be expedient to filter long entry points only when the prices show a certain propensity for acceleration, while short entry points should be filtered when the price is excessively dynamic.

We can measure acceleration using a well-known indicator in technical analysis: the ADX. For our purpose, we can use its value over a period of 5 days and filter long entries only if it is above 35 and short entries only if under 55.

These values were chosen as a result of some tests not here included to avoid departing from the main subject of discussion of the book, but they are in any case indicative values, and similar effects can be obtained with values other than those mentioned: such as, for example, a threshold of 30 for long entry points and 45–50 for short entry points.

The code of the system complete with filters, follows.

```
Input: Slow(20), fast(45), percvol(2), eqperc(10);

var: myshares(1000), MyATR(1), myEntries(0);

myshares = intportion(Portfolio_Equity*(eqperc/100))/close;

MyEntries = intportion(100/eqperc);

MyAtr = averagetruerange(slow);

if percvol > 0 then myshares = intportion((Portfolio_Equity*percvol/
    100)/MyAtr);

if average(c, fast) crosses above average(c, slow) and c > aver-
    age(c,200) and adx(5) > 35 then buy myshares shares next bar
    at market;

if average(c, fast) crosses below average(c, slow) and c < aver-
    age(c,200) and adx(5) < 55 then sellshort myshares shares next
    bar at market;

if average(c, fast) crosses above minlist(average(c, slow), aver-
    age(c,200)) then buytocover next bar at market;

if average(c, fast) crosses below maxlist(average(c, slow), aver-
    age(c,200)) then sell next bar at market;
```

Let's take a look at the results after applying the filters, also to see whether they're useful or not. Figure 10.9 shows the performance report of the system with the filters using 10% position sizing on the equity followed by the equity line in Figure 10.10, the distribution of stocks in Figure 10.11, and the annual distribution in Figure 10.12.

There's a notable improvement on all fronts, not only has the net profit increased, the drawdown has also decreased considerably. The trend of the

Performance Summary

	All Trades	Long Trades	Short Trades
Net Profit	€877,773.58	€545,460.59	€332,312.99
Gross Profit	€2,004,784.16	€830,350.58	€1,174,433.58
Gross Loss	(€1,127,010.58)	(€284,889.99)	(€842,120.59)
Account Size Required	€483,988.95	€174,870.80	€487,491.25
Return on Account	181.36%	311.92%	68.17%
Return on Initial Capital	87.78%	54.55%	33.23%
Profit Factor	1.78	2.91	1.39
Slippage Paid	€0.00	€0.00	€0.00
Commission Paid	€6,910.00	€2,664.68	€4,245.32
Open Position P/L	(€7,520.67)	(€7,520.67)	€0.00
Select Net Profit	€551,530.62		
Adjusted Net Profit	€642,012.74		
Max Portfolio Drawdown	(€228,262.70)		
Max Portfolio Drawdown (%)	(16.31%)		
Max Portfolio Close To Close Drawdown	(€133,946.68)		
Max Portfolio Close To Close Drawdown (%)	(7.89%)		
Return on Max Portfolio Drawdown	3.85		

FIGURE 10.9 Performance report with ADX filter and 10% exposure per position.

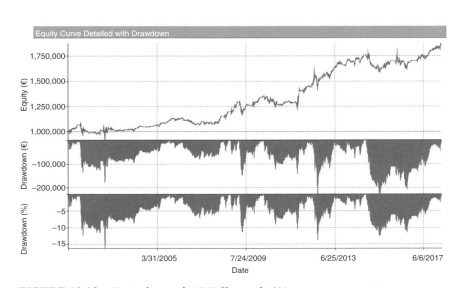

FIGURE 10.10 Equity line with ADX filter and 10% exposure per position.

Overview

Market	Start Date	End Date	Net Profit	# Trades
A2a	4/18/2001	3/19/2018	€157,446.04	35
ENEL	9/2/2002	3/19/2018	(€6,689.73)	33
ENI	10/24/2001	3/19/2018	(€50,627.22)	31
ERG	7/3/2001	3/19/2018	€117,887.63	29
G	6/29/2001	3/19/2018	€105,383.91	40
MB	7/2/2001	3/19/2018	€194,639.11	34
MS	4/25/2001	3/19/2018	€25,539.32	36
TIT	4/19/2001	3/19/2018	€183,791.72	36
AGL	4/24/2001	3/19/2018	€107,169.29	39
STM	4/18/2001	3/19/2018	€43,233.52	33

FIGURE 10.11 Distribution of profits between the stocks with ADX filter and 10% exposure per position.

Annual Period Analysis

Period	Net Profit	% Gain	Profit Factor	# Trades	Percent Profitable
2018	€29,804.86	1.62%	2.04	8	75%
2017	€135,446.25	7.94%	4.3	24	75%
2016	€2,310.46	0.14%	1.02	22	59.09%
2015	(€29,840.25)	(1.72%)	(0.78)	19	52.63%
2014	€52,465.10	3.12%	1.76	21	57.14%
2013	€111,623.74	7.12%	2.47	20	80%
2012	€161,059.99	11.44%	3.12	29	62.07%
2011	€140,147.45	11.06%	3.88	18	66.67%
2010	(€29,931.80)	(2.31%)	(0.77)	29	41.38%
2009	€90,592.42	7.51%	1.91	23	65.22%
2008	€116,613.28	10.7%	3.09	24	75%
2007	€15,447.11	1.44%	1.53	11	54.55%
2006	(€54,389.93)	(4.82%)	(0.48)	27	40.74%
2005	€78,093.32	7.43%	4.49	25	80%
2004	€35,635.86	3.51%	2.35	19	78.95%
2003	(€16,652.53)	(1.61%)	(0.72)	19	31.58%
2002	€18,098.90	1.79%	1.26	27	66.67%
2001	€13,728.69	1.37%	1.24	20	55%

FIGURE 10.12 Annual distribution of profits with ADX filter and 10% exposure per position.

equity line is better and the number of losing stocks has decreased as has the number of years that ended with a loss. This is without a doubt an appreciable result. Let's see what sort of figures we'd have obtained using the 0.3% percent volatility model (Figures 10.13–10.16).

Also in this case the results are quite similar, with a slight improvement in drawdown compared to the equal weighting of positions in percentage terms.

Performance Summary			
	All Trades	Long Trades	Short Trades
Net Profit	€876,633.01	€583,043.06	€293,589.95
Gross Profit	€2,259,885.94	€1,030,929.90	€1,228,956.04
Gross Loss	(€1,383,252.93)	(€447,886.84)	(€935,366.09)
Account Size Required	€634,821.18	€293,381.05	€556,629.48
Return on Account	138.09%	198.73%	52.74%
Return on Initial Capital	87.66%	58.3%	29.36%
Profit Factor	1.63	2.3	1.31
Slippage Paid	€0.00	€0.00	€0.00
Commission Paid	€6,910.00	€2,665.05	€4,244.95
Open Position P/L	(€11,787.36)	(€11,787.36)	€0.00
Select Net Profit	€580,625.81		
Adjusted Net Profit	€600,739.61		
Max Portfolio Drawdown	(€249,822.06)		
Max Portfolio Drawdown (%)	(14.29%)		
Max Portfolio Close To Close Drawdown	(€154,256.68)		
Max Portfolio Close To Close Drawdown (%)	(10.99%)		
Return on Max Portfolio Drawdown	3.51		

FIGURE 10.13 Performance report with ADX filter and 0.3% percent volatility.

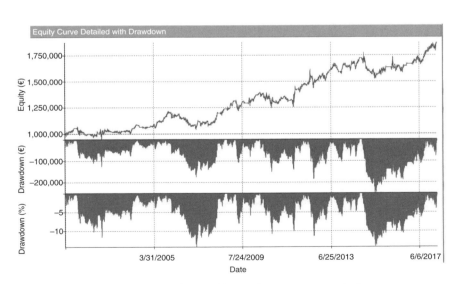

FIGURE 10.14 Equity line with ADX filter and 0.3% percent volatility.

Overview

Market	Start Date	End Date	Net Profit	# Trades
A2a	4/18/2001	3/19/2018	€148,923.59	35
ENEL	9/2/2002	3/19/2018	(€49,930.78)	33
ENI	10/24/2001	3/19/2018	(€64,056.86)	31
ERG	7/3/2001	3/19/2018	€153,192.07	29
G	6/29/2001	3/19/2018	€141,401.95	40
MB	7/2/2001	3/19/2018	€184,933.32	34
MS	4/25/2001	3/19/2018	€24,444.34	36
TIT	4/19/2001	3/19/2018	€167,279.54	36
AGL	4/24/2001	3/19/2018	€160,979.71	39
STM	4/18/2001	3/19/2018	€9,466.13	33

FIGURE 10.15 Distribution of profits between the stocks with ADX filter and 0.3% percent volatility.

Annual Period Analysis

Period	Net Profit	% Gain	Profit Factor	# Trades	Percent Profitable
2018	€21,433.90	1.16%	1.44	8	75%
2017	€178,103.86	10.69%	3.4	24	75%
2016	€29,702.23	1.82%	1.34	22	59.09%
2015	(€56,585.79)	(3.34%)	(0.63)	19	52.63%
2014	€75,825.04	4.69%	1.99	21	57.14%
2013	€66,467.93	4.29%	1.55	20	80%
2012	€125,528.28	8.81%	2.54	29	62.07%
2011	€122,776.02	9.43%	2.74	18	66.67%
2010	(€25,503.03)	(1.92%)	(0.84)	29	41.38%
2009	€85,780.75	6.91%	2.06	23	65.22%
2008	€125,795.26	11.28%	3.57	24	75%
2007	€34,112.46	3.15%	1.88	11	54.55%
2006	(€124,959.96)	(10.36%)	(0.37)	27	40.74%
2005	€140,573.75	13.19%	4.41	25	80%
2004	€44,046.15	4.31%	1.8	19	78.95%
2003	(€6,457.88)	(0.63%)	(0.87)	19	31.58%
2002	€5,034.43	0.49%	1.07	27	66.67%
2001	€23,172.24	2.32%	1.61	20	55%

FIGURE 10.16 Annual distribution of profits with ADX filter and 0.3% percent volatility.

TABLE 10.1	Summary of results.		
System	Net Profit	Max. % Drawdown
10% Equity no filters	644,894.76	24.48%
0.3% Perc Vol no filters	683,150.71	22.01%
10% Equity with ADX filter	877,773.58	16.31%
0.3% Perc Vol with ADX filter	876,633.01	14.29%

Table 10.1 is a summary of the results to give you a complete picture of the situation.

■ 10.3 Conclusions

In Chapter 8 we saw how using several instruments simultaneously made it possible to multiply the effects of money management strategies, above all with the aim of increasing the initial capital. If we start trading with several instruments and try to make the equity line softer, the techniques we've studied remain valid even when applied with lower risk percentages. It's always important to look for the ideal compromise between an increase in profits and surviving negative periods unscathed. If you're accountable to others who'll also be watching the trend of the capital, you should try to make this trend as stable as possible, to leave less room to doubt your work in the minds of those who know less about these sorts of transactions.

The systems used, as always, aim to limit fluctuations in the capital, both after closing a trade, and therefore when calculating entry points in terms of the maximum possible loss, or with the open trade, when calculating entry points on the basis of the volatility at that particular time.

For every system you intend to use, you should find the money management technique that's best suited for your own particular disposition to risk and how thick-skinned you are in terms of withstanding the ups and downs of the market.

Sometimes, as well as the by-now well-known money management techniques, it can be expedient to consider the type of signals used and try filters that can improve the quality of the trades, which, with position sizing models, can produce notable improvements in the final scenario.

CHAPTER 11

Discretionary Trading

■ 11.1 Trading Criteria and Definition

After reading the previous chapter, you'll probably be thinking the money management techniques in it must be combined with a trading system. Certainly, in order to plan things in an effective way, you should simulate the strategy you're thinking of using to see how it behaves, so it's always a good idea to draw up a trading system before you start trading on the market. But it isn't absolutely necessary to have one to apply the rules of money management. The only thing that is necessary to do a good job is to have a clear idea of what you want to do.

Unfortunately, people often start out without knowing what to do to begin working seriously, and start improvising as if this is the normal way to go about things. So, what does having a clear idea mean? And what does it mean if you don't have a clear idea?

First and foremost, let's define discretionary trading as it will be considered in this chapter: discretionary trading is taken to mean trades that aren't made on the basis of signals from a trading system but as a result of observing the market, either on chart or even on the order book. We won't consider scalping as, with this type of trading, which is quite fast and frenetic, the application of money management principles tends to be 'lost' in consideration of the potential absorption of the amounts traded on the market. Only a meticulous and honest study of your scalping can rationalise the amounts traded in an attempt to apply the rules of money management.

We will consider longer trades, however, which may be intraday trades with a profit target or trades closed end of day, or long-term multiday trades based on observations of daily charts, or trades made based on accumulation seen on the order book.

All too often, unfortunately, one studies potential market entry points meticulously, while leaving exit points to chance. The typical behaviour of a discretionary trader (if the reader is a discretionary trader but can't identify with this profile, all the better) is to look for 'good' entry levels, choosing a proper size (in other words, the number of shares to be traded) and the actual trade to enter the market. It's only after the trade has been opened that the trader starts to think about how and where to exit; it's in this phase that most of the troubles arise. If the stock falls, people often exit too soon on the basis of the 'cut your losses and run' rule, or stop levels are set further and further away, studying charts with a wide variety of time frames in order to find a good reason (or good excuse) for not closing a losing trade.

Appraisals of this kind, influenced by feelings based on an idea of how the trade is going, are often detrimental and can destroy all the good work done up to that point. The only justification for continuously following a trade is if the trade was opened on the basis of the meticulous observation of buy and sell movements, in order to be able to exit if things start going in the opposite direction to what was planned when it was opened. Trades of this kind, however, require talent and exceptional skill and, while some may think they have such things, those who trade like this don't last long on the markets.

To manage your trading properly, all your considerations should be made beforehand. Entry levels are definitely important, but exit levels are just as important, whether to take a profit or when a stop-loss is triggered. So the whole trade should be planned before it's opened and when entering the market you must already have a clear idea of the levels you'll exit at.

Above all, the exit level if things go wrong must be established right from the start, in this way you have a clear idea of the risk involved when opening the trade.

If you have a clear idea of the entry and exit levels, you can apply money management principles with due consideration.

In the previous chapters we saw many times how simulations based on the past can be used to establish which money management model is best suited to the trading system used. But now, in the case of discretionary trading there's no historical data from any trading system to base decisions on. Even if a particularly well-organised trader kept note of past trades, it would be quite difficult to have a sufficiently vast archive to base valid appraisals on.

So, decisions must be taken on the basis of more generic appraisals, which have an absolute value, however.

First, it can be said that, if a trader is trading stocks (with or without leverage) rather than futures, I wouldn't recommend using the fixed ratio method. As we saw, this method is difficult (or rather, complicated) to apply to trading on the stock market, and if it's complicated when you can base your decisions on a sufficiently high number of historical trades, it will be even more so without historical data to base decisions on.

So, when trading stocks and shares, the best thing is to choose between the fixed fractional method and the percent volatility model.

The choice between these two methods should be made on the basis of the types of trade you're going to open, and the characteristics of the type of exit to use for the same.

In previous chapters I explained that the percent volatility model is better for a very tight stop-loss, and in fact using the fixed fractional method in these cases meant the risk of trading large positions with numerous consecutive losses. The fixed fractional method, as you'll recall, considered the potential loss and on the basis of the same calculated the number of contracts (or shares) in order to limit the total percentage impact on the capital. When using a very tight stop-loss, the loss will be quite limited and, for the same percentage impact, you can enter the trade with more contracts. For example, if you have €100,000 and enter a trade using a stop-loss at 1 percentage point from the entry point and decided you didn't want to risk more than 0.5% of the total capital on each trade, you can open the position at €50,000. If the stop of the position is tighter, and let's make a hypothesis that it's the same 0.5%, you can open the position using the entire capital of €100,000. Actually, if you wanted to use an extremely tight stop-loss of 0.25% (which might occur when buying on a support level and deciding to use a stop just below the value of said support) you could even enter the market with €200,000 (which would obviously only be possible if you were using leverage).

The percent volatility model on the other hand doesn't consider the potential loss, but measures the movements of the stock and calibrates the entry based on the Average True Range of the last period.

If you want to use this method, you will have to have already calculated the average at *n* days of the true range for the stock. As this value is calculated on the basis of daily charts, you could calculate it the previous evening and therefore also know how many shares you want to trade with.

■ 11.2 An Example: Mediaset

Let's take a look at an example to see what might happen in practice.

We'll trade Mediaset stock using the daily chart. In the beginning of November we have a setup to place a trade. After a long down trend the stock rebounds and settles at 9.275 to then fall again but without breaking through the lows of the long down trend. A congestion channel follows. One hypothesis for the trade might be to enter long when there is a breakout at 9.275, with a 8.78 stop-loss below the lows of the long down trend.

A hypothesis for the target could be 9.90, which was a significant level in the month of August.

As this is expected to a be a long-term trade we'll use precise levels but decide to enter at 9.30 with a 8.75 stop, while still using 9.90 as a target.

Figure 11.1 shows the chart with details of the above.

There's a long wait for the trade. In general, this is a good sign: the stock will stay in the congestion channel longer. In any case the trade would have been entered on 5 January 2006 and the target would have been reached on 6 February. As the stock reached exactly the target high of 9.90 that day it is not certain the sell order would have been executed, but on 7 February it passed 9.90 and the trade can be considered closed.

The point we want to make, however, isn't the description of the trade, but rather how to calculate the number of contracts we would have bought on 5 January.

We're not using a very tight stop and we can consider using a fixed fractional method without qualms. Let's assume we don't want to risk more than 2% of our capital, which is €100,000.

The first thing to do is evaluate the stop-loss in percentage terms. As mentioned above, the stop was set at 8.75 and the entry at 9.30, so:

$$stop\ percentage = \frac{9.30 - 8.75}{9.30} * 100 = \frac{0.55}{9.30} * 100 = 5.91\%$$

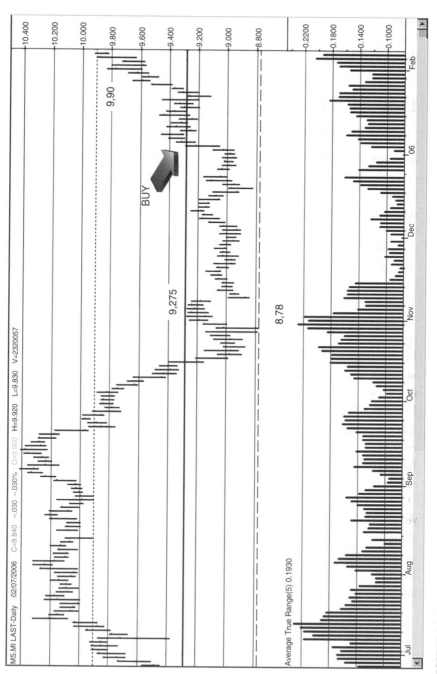

FIGURE 11.1 An example of a discretionary trade with Mediaset stock.

Now let's calculate the amount we're willing to risk. As mentioned above our percentage risk is 2%, so:

$$\text{amount risked} = 100{,}000 * 2/100 = €2{,}000.$$

With these two parameters, we can now calculate the amount to invest in the trade. The capital used for the trade must be equal to an amount 5.91% of which is €2,000 because, if the stop is triggered, losing 5.91%, we don't want to lose more than €2,000.

$$\frac{investedcapital * 5.91}{100} = 2{,}000$$

$$investedcapital = \frac{2{,}000 * 100}{5.91} = 33{,}841.$$

This means we can enter a Mediaset trade with €33,841 because, if we lose 5.91% of the same, it won't be more than a 2% loss of the total available capital (€100,000).

Let's suppose we enter the trade at 9.30, which means:

$$\text{number of contracts} = 33{,}841/9.30 = 3{,}638.$$

To check the calculations, let's see what would happen if the stop is triggered for those 3,638 contracts, we'd lose:

$$(9.30 - 8.75) * 3{,}638 = 0.55 * 3{,}638 = 2{,}000.9.$$

The figures add up!

Here's a formula you can use to directly calculate the number of contracts on the basis of the entry price and stop if used, as well as obviously the risk chosen and available capital:

$$\text{number of contracts} = \frac{investedcapital * risk\%}{(entrylevel - stoplevel) * 100};$$

in our case:

$$\text{number of contracts} = \frac{100{,}000 * 2}{(9.30 - 8.75) * 100} = 3{,}636.$$

Note that the difference between the two calculations (3,638 compared to 3,636) is only due to the subsequent rounding off in the first case; this obviously doesn't have a significant effect on the final result.

This formula is valid for stocks but not for futures. For the latter, you should consider the value of the ticks for a precise appraisal, but this isn't what we're looking at in this case.

The trade would have closed with the following result (trading 3,636 contracts as in the direct formula):

$$gain = (9.90 - 9.30) * 3,636 = €2,181.6.$$

Someone might say it wasn't a very good trade because, as shown by the calculations, it produced a profit that was quite similar to the potential loss. These kind of objections, however, should be considered more in terms of risk management as, it must be said again, money management establishes *how much* to trade, but not how. Anyway, if we want to make a case for this choice, note that although the risk/benefit ratio is more or less equal in monetary terms, for this type of entry there's a higher probability of closing with a profit than at a loss due to the congestion in the period before the breakout.

How might we have used the percent volatility model?

The chart also shows the five-day ATR. The five-day range was chosen as this represents a good compromise for medium-term trades like the one we're going to open using this discretionary approach (this average is calculated on the basis of the distance of the target prices from the entry price, and obviously no one knows in advance for how long the position will be open).

Remember that in Chapter 4, and in other examples, we saw that the percent volatility model limits fluctuations in the total capital, and the percentages used in this model were also generally lower than those of the reduced percentage method. So let's make a hypothesis that we want to trade limiting fluctuations in the capital to 0.5% of the total.

Every morning we'll check the value of the ATR indicator and on 4 January (obviously we'd have the figure of the previous day on the morning of 5 January, and use this) it was 0.1230, so now let's take a look at how we'd proceed:

First, we'd calculate the admissible range:

$$range = 100,000 * 0.5/100 = 500.$$

On the basis of our observation we know that the volatility of 1 MS share is €0.1230; so, in order to remain within the limit of a max. range of €500 we could buy:

$$number\ of\ contracts = 500/0.1230 = 4,065.$$

As you can see, the number is quite close to that calculated using the procedure that limited the risk if the stop-loss was triggered.

Also in this case, there's a formula that can be used:

$$number\ of\ contracts = \frac{totalcapital * extension\%}{Average\,Truerange(n) * 100}$$

where n is the number of days for which the ATR is calculated.

In this case, the trade would have made:

$$gain = (9.90 - 9.30) * 4{,}065 = €2{,}439.$$

I'll repeat a concept I already expressed in the previous chapter: the fixed fractional method is used to limit the effect on the capital if the trade is stopped out, so when closing the trade: in fact, you calculate and limit the effect if a stop-loss is triggered. The percent volatility model, however, limits the effect during the trade. In other words, you calculate the volatility of the stock in the previous days to see what effect it might have on the equity line while you have an open position.

Note that the percent volatility model doesn't in fact consider the strategic levels of the trade you are going to open. The formula doesn't consider the entry level (the number of contracts is calculated without even considering the entry price) or where the stop-loss is positioned, and it only considers how much the stock moved in the latest period, so how much it could move while we have a position open.

If the stop is a lot tighter, the percent volatility model calculation would produce exactly the same result (if applied to the same day obviously), while the fixed fractional method calculation would change, a lot.

For example, if instead of choosing the low of the long down trend we chose the low of the previous bar as the stop-loss level, the figure to monitor would be 9.06 (low of 4 January 2006), and in this case we would have entered the trade with:

$$number\ of\ contracts = \frac{100{,}000 * 2}{(9.30 - 9.06) * 100} = 8{,}333.$$

This is a very different result, which would, in this case, have produced more profit, as the stop was never triggered in the following bars.

This doesn't mean a choice of this kind is better, but goes to prove the intrinsic difference between the two methods. What's more, we applied the percent volatility model using 0.5%, which on the stock market may be suitable, but if we're trading futures with this percentage, we'd run the risk of not being able to make many trades (we'll go into this in greater detail later), and it would be better to use higher percentages better suited to the characteristics of the futures' market with the relevant leverage.

Once the trade has been opened, you follow its evolution as planned. If you want to open a second trade, you'd do so on the basis of the same considerations you made for the first, with the only difference being that the capital you'd base your calculations on wouldn't be the same. The rules presented for the core equity model, total equity model, and the reduced total equity model apply when considering the capital.

With the core equity model the capital to be considered for the following trade would be €98,000 when using percent risk (in fact, you deduct the stop-loss for the open position equal to €2,000 from the available capital), or approximately €97,764 when using percent volatility (with 4,065 contracts the loss with an 8.75 exit would be approximately €2,236).

The total equity model, each time, considers the value of the open position and adds this to the liquidity held.

If, for example, we bought 4,065 contracts (as we did with the percent volatility model), we'd have used:

$$4,065 * 9.3 = €37,804.5.$$

So we'd have a liquidity of:

$$100,000 - 37,804.5 = €62,195.5.$$

(We're not considering the cost of the commissions in order to simplify things, but you should always bear in mind that the value of your liquidity is usually clearly shown on the platform you're trading with so you don't have to calculate it.)

If the new position was opened on 26 January, we could refer to the existing position by calculating the value with a 25 January close. On this date, the MS stock closed at 9.37 so the value of the open position is:

$$4,065 * 9.37 = 38,089.05,$$

and our total equity would be:

$$62,195.5 + 38,089.05 = 100,284.55.$$

This is the capital to use in the total equity model calculations.

With the reduced total equity model, once again we'd consider 98,000 (or 97,764) as the capital, but supposing that once the MS stock passed €9.47, it would be expedient to move the stop to 9.11. See Figure 11.2.

At this point, if the stop is triggered, we'd risk losing:

$$4,065 * (9.3 - 9.11) = €772.35.$$

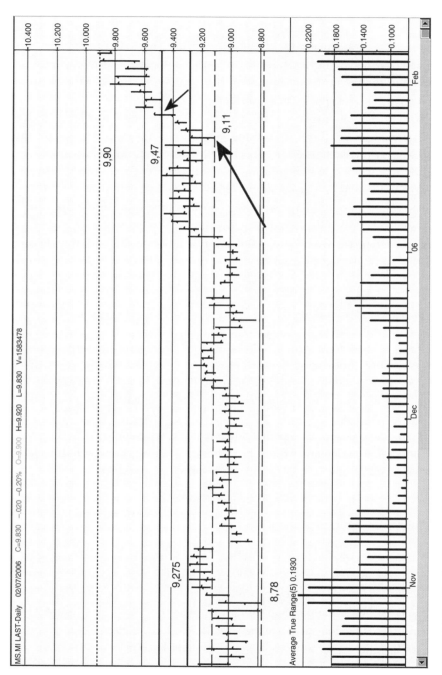

FIGURE 11.2 Moving the stop of the position to 9.11 after the high of 9.47.

The new capital of reference would therefore be:

$$100,000 - 772.35 = 99,227.65.$$

After closing the position, whatever the method used, the capital of reference would be (if there are no other open positions):

$$100,000 + (9.90 - 9.30) * 4,065 = 102,439.$$

■ 11.3 Adjusting Volatility During the Trade

Using the percent volatility model from the start the idea is to limit fluctuations in the capital with an open trade. On this basis, we can calculate a certain number of shares (or Futures' contracts) to buy when opening the trade, in terms of the volatility in the previous period.

But if the trade remains open for some time, the volatility can change considerably, and the movements of the equity line may no longer be within the preset limits.

If the volatility decreases, this isn't a problem, but if it increases, this could cause some difficulties.

On the basis of the above line of reasoning one might periodically review the number of contracts in order to keep the fluctuations in the equity line more or less constant. In theory this could be done every day, but doing so would be very time consuming. We could make a hypothesis of checking things every five trading days (once a week) and adjust the situation to the new volatility parameters.

In practice, every five days you note the new ATR and check how many contracts you should have on the basis of this figure. Then decide whether to adjust your portfolio.

Let's take a look at the ATR figures during the MS trade, starting 4 January and checking every week (Table 11.1).

We'll proceed week by week. As mentioned above, on 5 January we enter a trade with a position of 4,065 contracts. At the day's close on 11 January, using the total equity model our capital of reference would be:

$$\textit{capital of reference}_{11\ \text{Jan}} = 100,000 - 4,065 * 9.3 + 4,065 * 9.355$$
$$= 100,223.575.$$

The number of contracts that could be used for said capital of reference, with a maximum expansion limited to 0.5% as in our case and an ATR of

TABLE 11.1

date	ATR(5)	Close of day	Open next day
4/1/2006	0.1230	9.22	9.25
11/1/2006	0.1320	9	9.36
18/1/06	0.1540	9.3	9.33
25/1/06	0.1500	9.37	9
1/2/2006	0.1540	10	9.78

0.1320 (the value on 11 January) would be:

$$number\ of\ contracts = \frac{100,223.575 * 0.5}{0.1320 * 100} = 3,796.$$

It's clear that, at this particular time, we're overexposed: we have more contracts that the recommended number. So we decide to sell the excess contracts when trading opens that day, and will sell:

$$4,065 - 3,796 = 269\ contracts.$$

In its own way, this method made us save part of the profit made; but it could also have made us sell at a loss if the market prices were lower than our entry level and the volatility just increased.

On the evening of 18 January the sums required to calculate the capital of reference become a little more complicated as some of the contracts were sold (in practice, it's a lot simpler as the trading platform shows both the value of the open position and the liquidity of the account).

$$capital\ of\ reference_{18\ Jan} = 100,000 - 4,065 * 9.3 + 3,796 * 9.30$$
$$+ 269 * 9.36 = 100,016.14.$$

Remember the calculation is based on the initial capital – the initial amount bought (initial number of contracts multiplied by the entry price) + the current value of the portfolio (current contracts in the portfolio multiplied by the close price on 18 January) + contracts sold for the sale price (opening price on 12 January).

Using these figures and an ATR of 0.1540, we obtain:

$$number\ of\ contracts = \frac{100,016.14 * 0.5}{0.1540 * 100} = 3,247.$$

Once again (if we want to use this approach), we need to sell part of the contracts in the portfolio. This time:

$$3{,}796 - 3{,}247 = 549 \text{ contracts.}$$

These 549 contracts will be sold when trading opens next day at 9.33.

Let's take a look at next week, first calculating the capital of reference:

$$\textit{capital of reference}_{25 \text{ Jan}} = 100{,}000 - 4{,}065 * 9.3 + 3{,}247 * 9.37$$
$$+ 269 * 9.36 + 549 * 9.33 = 100{,}259.9.$$

The ATR is 0.1500, so:

$$\textit{number of contracts} = \frac{100{,}259.9 * 0.5}{0.1500 * 100} = 3{,}341.$$

This time the system tells us we can increase the number of contracts. We could also not increase the number of contracts, simply limiting ourselves to stay within the set range, but to complete the analysis, let's say when trading opened next day (at 9.405) we bought:

$$3{,}341 - 3{,}247 = 94 \text{ contracts.}$$

At the beginning of February, we repeat the procedure and calculate the capital of reference:

$$\textit{capital of reference}_{1 \text{ Feb}} = 100{,}000 - 4{,}065 * 9.3 + 3{,}341 * 9.775$$
$$+ 269 * 9.36 + 549 * 9.33 - 94 * 9.405$$
$$= 101{,}609.72.$$

Once again remember that, of this figure, the open position amounts to $3{,}341 * 9.775$, while all the other figures are part of the liquidity calculation as they are closed trades.

The ATR on 1 February is 0.1540, so we calculate:

$$\textit{number of contracts} = \frac{101{,}609.72 * 0.5}{0.1540 * 100} = 3{,}299.$$

Therefore, we have 42 contracts too many, which we sell when trading opens on 2 February at a price of 9.78.

No further adjustments are necessary, as the trade will be closed at the target of 9.90 before another week has passed.

The final calculation of the result is:

$$\text{gain} = (-4{,}065 * 9.3 + 269 * 9.36 + 549 * 9.33 - 94 * 9.405$$
$$+ 42 * 9.78) + 3{,}299 * 9.90 = \text{€}2{,}022.3.$$

Note that this result is lower than the result without the adjustments 'in time,' allowing for the fact that said adjustments would have added additional costs in terms of commissions, so it can be deduced that an approach of this kind isn't always the best; at least, not as shown here (with limited adjustments).

The above procedure may have seemed somewhat convoluted and complicated; but remember that, what the reader might have had most difficulty with is calculating the capital of reference; and it's unlikely this needs to be calculated, as the value of the portfolio at the end of the day is shown on the trading platform, along with the available liquidity, so all you have to do is add the two figures to know how much money you should use in your calculations. The above is used merely as an example.

The entire procedure could have been performed using the core equity model or the reduced total equity model, but we won't complicate things with other calculations as the intention was just to show how you can constantly check the volatility of the open position (or open positions).

An approach of this kind is also applicable, for all purposes, with portfolios that follow the rules of a trading system.

■ 11.4 Trading Futures

If you're considering trading futures instead of shares, there are other possibilities for applying money management techniques.

Using the fixed ratio method is very practical with futures as this method doesn't consider the parameters of the trade you're thinking of opening but just the value of your available capital compared to the initial capital.

The only difficulty is establishing the delta to use.

Initially, you could consider the stop-loss of the first trade and use a delta that's three times the stop-loss as long as it's acceptable (a stop-loss of €100 would mean a delta of 300, which is clearly low, and you should always be at least 2 percentage points from the initial capital).

Now let's consider a discretionary trade with DAX futures and see how to manage the trade on the basis of the chosen money management method.

Figure 11.3 shows the entry of the trade. On an uptrend, there was a nasty reversal bar, a bar that opened with a gap up, reached a high of 5,249 then reversed its trend and took the market to new lows, reaching a low of 5,153 and closing very near to the same. A signal of this kind should start

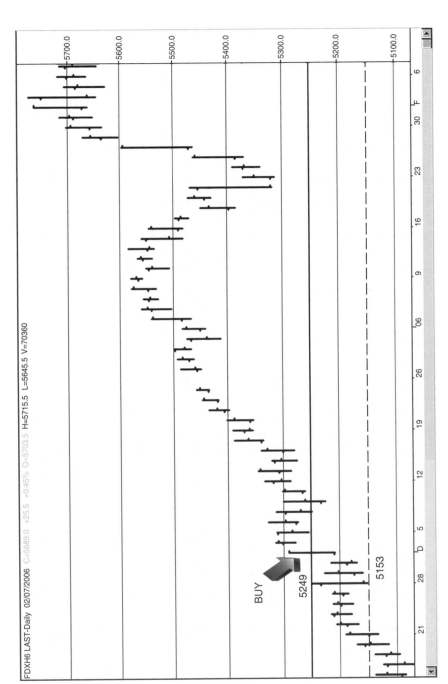

FIGURE 11.3 An example of a discretionary trade with DAX futures.

alarm bells ringing loudly for a probable reversal of the trend. The next day, however, the market showed signs of uncertainty. The next bar, an up movement, is in any case an inside bar (high smaller than previous high and low greater than previous low). There is even a second inside bar again next day, proving the considerable uncertainty of the market. At this point, we decide to enter in the direction the market decides to take. We'll enter long if the price breaks the high of 5,249, or short if it breaks the low of 5,153, and these levels would also be used as stop-loss levels when entering the trade. Immediately next day there's a bar with a strong up movement, and we enter the trade. At this point, we only know the level at which we will be long (5,249) and the level at which we'll exit if the market changes direction (5,153).

In the previous period, the market didn't show signs of a situation that let us identify a target, so we decide to exit only in the case of a probable reversal. We also decide to raise the exit point a little higher every now and then to make the most of any profits.

This is what we'll do a few days later, as shown in Figure 11.4.

Note that there's a relative high, after which there are two down bars, the second of which hits a low of 5,225.5 but then the market moves up again, and as soon as the new relative high is broken we decide to raise the exit level to 5,225.5.

The same principle will be applied in the future if there are other similar cases, as in fact occurs as shown in Figure 11.5.

A new high is registered, and in the next bar the market reaches a relative low of 5,276. The second bar after this one breaks the new high and we decide to raise the exit level to the intermediate low of 5,276. At this point, we're in a situation in which the trade will make a profit in any case as we've raised the exit level to be past the level we entered the trade at.

We continue as above, and soon there's a new case, as shown in Figure 11.6.

There's a new high with a relative low at the very next bar. This low is 5,414. The market recovers, moving up again, and 2 bars later the low breaks the old high. It's time to raise the exit level to 5,414.

The same phenomenon occurs again, but this time the exit level that was just set is reached, and the trade is closed, as shown in Figure 11.7.

Therefore, this is a new high, and with the next bar that has a relative low of 5,509, the market recovers and two bars later breaks (by just a little) the high recorded. So the exit level is raised to 5,509, a level that is broken when the next bar drops.

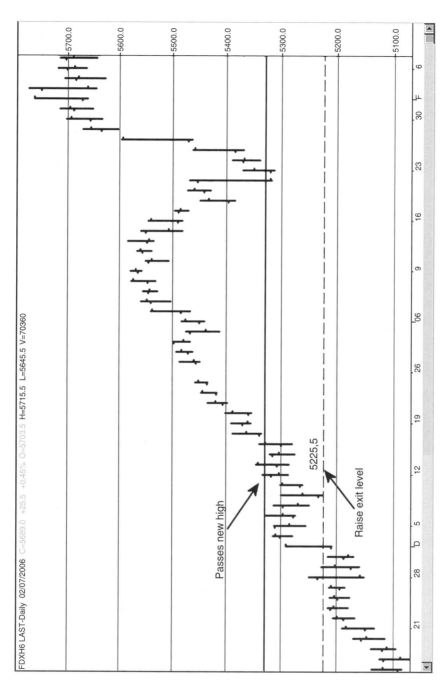

FIGURE 11.4 A broken relative high makes us raise the exit point to the intermediate relative low.

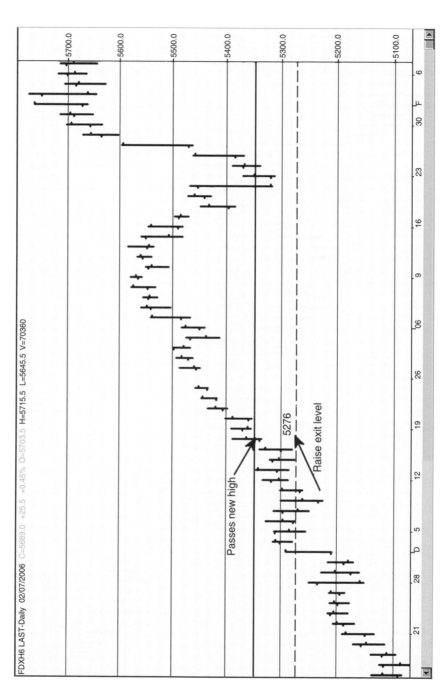

FIGURE 11.5 Another breakout of the relative high with the exit point raised to the intermediate relative low.

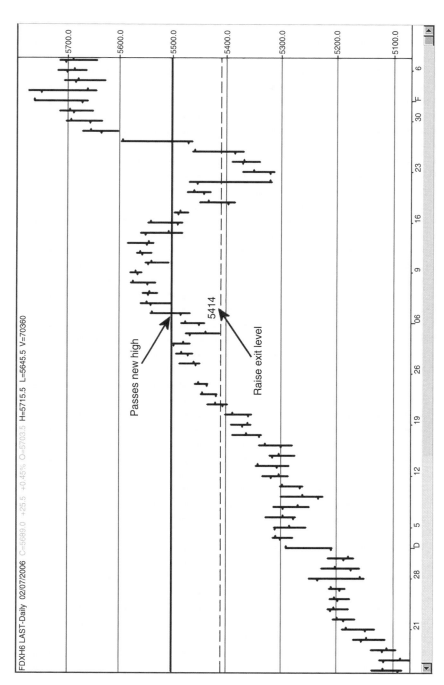

FIGURE 11.6 Raising the exit level again.

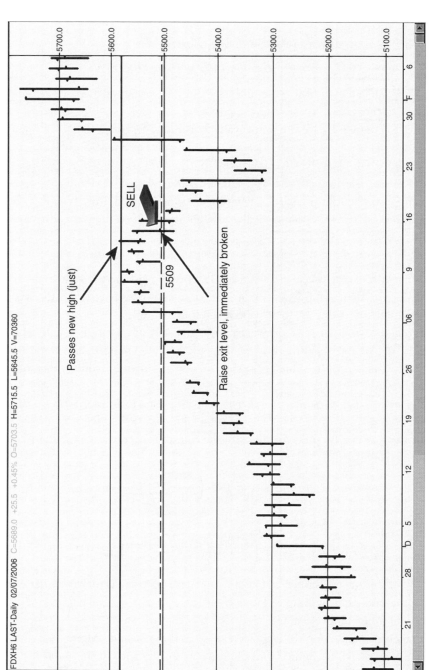

FIGURE 11.7 The new exit level is broken immediately.

Note that after closing the trade, there are other down bars, but then the market recovers.

The trade produces a profit with one contract of:

$$Gain = (5,509 - 5,249) * 25 = €6,500.$$

Now let's analyse how we could have applied money management techniques to this trade.

Let's assume we have the same available capital of €100,000 before opening the trade.

First we'll look at the fixed fractional method and ask ourselves how much we want to risk on the trade we're thinking of opening.

The entry would be at 5,249 with the stop-loss at 5,153, which is the equivalent of 96 DAX points. Each DAX point is €25, so the risk in this case is:

$$risk = 96 * 25 = €2,400.$$

This means that, for every DAX contract we're risking €2,400.

Now, to calculate how many contracts we can buy we have to decide what risk percentage we want to adopt for the total capital.

In the previous case we opted for 2% (note that this figure is usually chosen before deciding on the potential trade. It's not linked to the trade but rather the risk profile, which is set before you sit down in front of the computer to look for ideas for trades).

So, let's take the same trader as in the previous example, who doesn't want to risk more than 2% on each trade. In Chapter 4, we introduced a formula that can be used to calculate the number of contracts for the fixed fractional method:

$$ff\,contracts = INT\left(\frac{(C * f)}{Maxloss}\right).$$

Therefore, in our case:

$$ff\,contracts = INT\left(\frac{(100,000 * 2/100)}{2,400}\right) = 0!!!$$

What this means is the trade in question isn't feasible, as the risk is greater than the one we're willing to take.

Remember that rejecting a trade for this sort of reason is part of money management and shouldn't be seen as something stupid. Money management protects your capital from undesirable events and, in this case, losing €2,400 instead of 2,000 is considered undesirable.

At this point there are four possible scenarios:

1. Ignore the trade and wait for a more suitable occasion for our risk profile.

2. Increase the risk percentage from 2% to 2.5% to 'cover' the potential loss.

3. Increase the level of the stop-loss to a point at which we wouldn't lose more than €2,000.

4. Wait for a retracement to enter at a level at which we wouldn't lose more than €2,000 with the chosen chart stop.

Let's consider the various options.

The first scenario is certainly the simplest, as you won't have to think about the trade anymore so you can calmly look at something else, but if the market was favourable to the trade you were considering, this could lead to regretting the decision taken, and for the next trades you might be tempted to leave prudent money management aside.

The second choice, despite how logical and intelligent it may seem is, in my opinion, the most imprudent course of action you could take. If you decide to use a money management model you should always follow its indications. You can't make changes once you've started just because you don't want to miss a trade. A 0.5% adjustment today could (in the case of a successful trade) encourage you to make bigger adjustments tomorrow, meaning all the good planning had been done in vain. This is definitely a choice I'd strongly advise against.

The third option is a possibility, and if we enter the trade at 5,249 we should set a stop at 5,169; in fact:

$$(5,249 - 5,169) * 25 = €2,000.$$

But would this new level be in line with the considerations we made? Let's see in Figure 11.8.

The level would be just below the low of the second inside bar (its low is 5,171). We could consider this level to be acceptable in chart terms for this reason, but it would be pushing things for the reasons mentioned above. The trend we entered the trade for would be invalidated when the opposite end of the bar, with a low of 5,153, broke out; the fact that the new level is just under the inside low is purely coincidental. What's more, the low of the first inside bar is lower than the potential new stop and could act as a support in a fall. All the above would shake things up in terms of

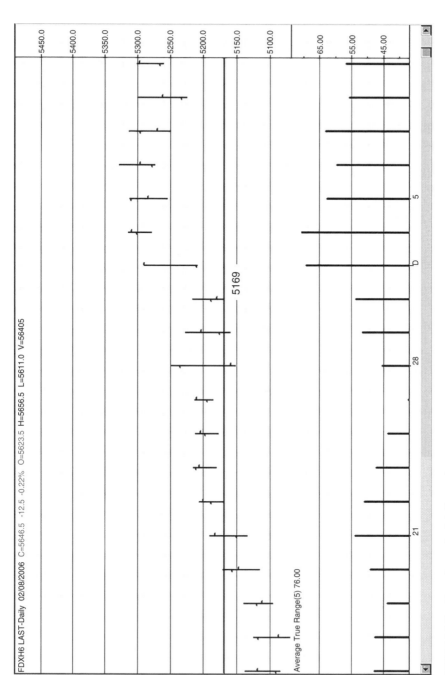

FIGURE 11.8 Hypothesis of a 5,169 stop-loss.

our discretionary decision undermining the basis on which the decision was made, altering the concept of the trade. So, in my opinion, this isn't a good choice. There will certainly be some who might object, saying that if we take option 1 we ignore this trade and look into others, and this solution could be one of the other trades we find, but in the end there are many ways to convince oneself a decision is right and this could also be one of them, and in principle I wouldn't recommend this route.

Last but not least, the fourth option. With a stop-loss of 5,153, in order to set things up so that if this stop is triggered we don't lose more than €2,000, we have to use a maximum limit at which to enter the trade, this limit is:

$$limitebuy = (5,153 + 2,000/25) = 5,153 + 80 = 5,233.$$

In practice, we calculated how many DAX points are equal to €2,000, dividing this amount by the value of each point (€25), then added this result to the stop-loss exit level.

Those choosing this option would in effect place an order in the trading book at 5,233 and wait for a market retracement to bring the price to this level.

This is definitely the most advisable choice; although, there will be some psychological repercussions. Entering on a retracement level that's below the set chart entry point isn't easy because the chosen trend could appear to be weakened. It can also be quite nerve-racking because there's nothing to guarantee the prices will reach that level and the wait could be in vain.

This is, however, the best solution in conceptual terms, and it's the one I'd recommend using, if possible.

What would happen in the case described? Let's see in Figure 11.9. The trade is entered a few days later.

At this point the fixed fractional method has no further effect and the trade proceeds under its own steam with 1 DAX contract until the close, which, as we saw above, is at 5,509.

In this case, the total result of the trade is:

$$Gain = (5,509 - 5,233) * 25 = €6,900.$$

Even without the direct effect of money management (increasing the number of contracts on the basis of the capital) it's obvious we would have made more than with the normal trade that made €6,500.

Now let's take a look at what would have happened if we applied the percent volatility model as the money management technique.

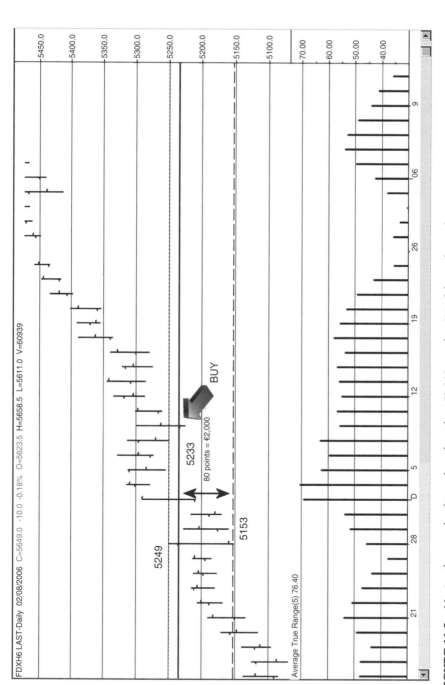

FIGURE 11.9 Moving the entry level to reduce the risk to €2,000, equal to 2% of the total capital.

When we discussed the case of the MS trade, I emphasised how a percentage of 0.5% could be unsuitable for futures, at least with a capital of €100,000.

Before we consider variations, let's see what we would have obtained using this percentage. First, let's take a look at the ATR when the trade was entered. Here's the data in Figure 11.10.

The day before we entered, the trade the ATR was 53.60 points, equal to:

$$53.60 * 25 = 1,340.$$

With futures, you have to multiply the ATR by the value in euros of one future's point in order to obtain the volatility in euros. With the stock in our list this wasn't necessary simply because 1 point, in that case, was exactly €1.

Now, if we take this path with the percentage we considered at the time of 0.5% we'd have a maximum limit range of:

$$range = 100,000 * 0.5/100 = €500.$$

Obviously, we're already in difficulty limiting movements to €500 while using an instrument in the portfolio with which we could move by as much as €1,340.

If we wanted to trade in these conditions we could only do so if the ATR was less than 20; in fact, with an ATR of 20 the volatility of the Future is exactly €500 per contract (20 * 25 = 500).

This condition never arises in the period after the theoretical entry and this goes to show that it would be fruitless to wait for volatility to drop before entering. The chart also shows that it's very rare to see an ATR of 20 with DAX futures so, if you want to use it with this money management model, you'd need a much bigger capital than the €100,000 we're considering in this case. We can say that the percent volatility model with a percentage of 0.5% is telling us DAX futures are not an option with a limited capital of €100,000.

In any case, in order to study how the method would behave, we won't change the risk profile of the money management model, but will consider we have an available capital of €500,000 and see how to make the trade.

As mentioned above, the volatility in euros of the future is €1,340 the day before entry, so we calculate:

$$number\ of\ contracts = ENT\left(\frac{500,000 * 0.5}{1,340 * 100}\right) = 1.$$

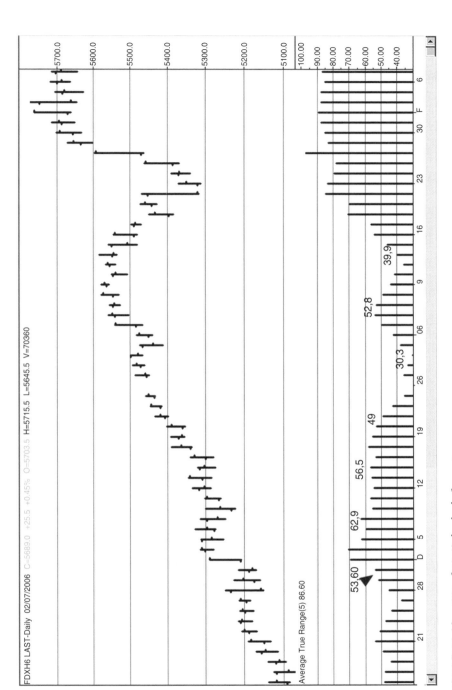

FIGURE 11.10 ATR of 53.60 the day before entry.

TABLE 11.2

date	ATR(5)	Close of day	Open next day
7/12/2005	62.9	5269.5	5233
14/12/05	56.5	5303.5	5300
21/12/05	49.0	5419	5418.5
29/12/05	30.3	5479.5	5467
5/1/2006	52.8	5543.5	5547
12/1/06	39.9	5544.6	5550.5

So we can buy just one contract.

If we don't make any subsequent adjustments, this contract will be the only one we have until closing the trade and nothing would change compared to the initial example with one contract.

If, however, we want to apply what we did in the MS example and monitor the trend of the volatility during the trade, we'd proceed as follows. First, let's see what data we need. The trade opens on 1 December 2005, then we'll monitor it every five trading days (Tables 11.2 and 11.3).

Let's take things step by step:

The trade will in any case be closed on 13 January with two contracts, the second one bought on market open, but in this case the trade is unfavourable. The exit, as mentioned above, is at 5,509, with a total result of:

$$Gain = 505{,}212.5 + (5{,}509 - 5{,}249) * 25 + (5{,}509 - 5{,}550.5) * 25$$
$$- 500{,}000 = €10{,}675.$$

In this case, the diversified management of the contracts during the trade, monitoring the volatility every week, produced decisively more profit!

To tell the truth, it must be stressed that adjusting the exposure on the basis of the weekly volatility produced more profit than the case without adjustments. We can't, however, make a comparison with the fixed fractional method shown above because in that case we were trading with an initial capital of €100,000. If we want to make a comparison with the same initial capital, we can calculate the number of contracts that could be used with the fixed fractional method and a capital of €500,000:

$$ff\,contracts = INT\left(\frac{(500{,}000 * 2/100)}{2{,}400}\right) = 4.$$

TABLE 11.3

7 Dec   *capital of reference* $_{7dec}$ = $500,000 + 1 * (5,269.5 - 5,249) * 25 =$ **500,512.5**

         volatility of Future in euros = $62.90 * 25 =$ **1,572.5**

         number of contracts = $INT \left(\dfrac{500.512, 5 * 0.5}{1.572, 5 * 100} \right) = 1$

14 Dec   *capital of reference* $_{14dec}$ = $500,000 + 1 * (5,303.5 - 5,249) * 25 =$ **501,362.5**

         volatility of Future in euros = $56.5 * 25 =$ **1,412.5**

         number of contracts = $INT \left(\dfrac{501.362, 5 * 0, 5}{1.412, 5 * 100} \right) = 1$

21 Dec   *capital of reference* $_{21dec}$ = $500,000 + 1 * (5,419 - 5,249) * 25 =$ **504,250**

         volatility of Future in euros = $49 * 25 =$ **1,225**

         number of contracts = $INT \left(\dfrac{504.250 * 0, 5}{1.225 * 100} \right) = 2$

Now we can purchase a second contract when trading opens next day, in other words at 5,418.5!

29 Dec   *capital of reference* $_{29dec}$ = $500,000 + 1 * (5,479.5 - 5,249) * 25 + 1 * (5,479.5 - 5,418.5) * 25 =$ **507,287.5**

         volatility of Future in euros = $30.3 * 25 =$ **757.5**

         number of contracts = $INT \left(\dfrac{507.287, 5 * 0, 5}{757, 5 * 100} \right) = 3$

A third contract is purchased when trading opens next morning at 5,467

5 Jan   *capital of reference* $_{5jan}$ = $500,000 + 1 * (5,543.5 - 5,249) * 25 + 1 * (5,543.5 - 5,418.5) * 25 + 1 * (5,543.5 - 5,467) * 25 =$ **512,400**

         volatility of Future in euros = $52.8 * 25 =$ **1320**

         number of contracts = $INT \left(\dfrac{512.400 * 0, 5}{1320 * 100} \right) = 1$

We have to sell 2 contracts, which are sold when trading opens next day at 5,547. Supposing they are the 2 purchased subsequently, this adds liquidity amounting to:

$[(5,547 - 5,418.5) + (5,547 - 5,467)] * 25 = 5,212.5$

12 Jan   *capital of reference* $_{12jan}$ = $505,212.5 + 1 * (5,544.5 - 5,249) * 25 =$ **512,600**

         volatility of Future in euros = $39.9 * 25 =$ **997.5**

         number of contracts = $INT \left(\dfrac{512.600 * 0, 5}{997, 5 * 100} \right) = 2$

Another contract is purchased when trading opens next morning at 5,550.5

With four contracts, the entry would have been on level breakout and not a retracement, and would have produced a final profit of:

$$Gain = 4 * (5,509 - 5,249) * 25 = €26,000.$$

As can be seen, we would have made a lot more profit in this case if we used the fixed fractional method.

I mentioned above that with futures you can also use the fixed ratio method, and it can also be a practical option.

As explained earlier in the book, the fixed ratio method starts with one contract until sufficient profit has been accumulated to use two (this profit is a quantity called *delta* and is set by the trader). In this specific case, therefore, there are no limits in terms of initial capital, as you can start using the system anyway. This could be a practical choice for those who don't want to miss out on any trades, but can be risky in the case of negative results (or worse if there is a series of consecutive negative results).

In any case, there's still the question of setting the delta, which, as we don't have any historical data available, is quite difficult to do. In this case, the estimated loss was €2,400 (we calculated it in the case the stop-loss was triggered), and as mentioned above, we could use this figure multiplied by 3, so €7,200, which we can round off to 7,000.

So the trade would be made in any case with one contract; as we've seen, with one contract the trade produces a gain of €6,500, which means a following DAX trade would still have been made with one single contract, as we haven't increased the initial capital by the €7,000 necessary to start using a second contract.

The fixed ratio method is particularly simple to apply because, in practice, it just considers the levels reached by the equity and doesn't consider the inherent risk of the trade you want to open, or the consequences of the same on the trend of the equity while the trade is open. Obviously, the flip side of the coin with management that's simplified in this way is there's no real control of the entity of the risk, which, in certain cases, could be detrimental.

It's plain to see that, for those who don't want to get into complicated calculations with futures, the fixed ratio method is definitely the way to go. Those who want to have more control over the evolution of the trade, however, should adopt the fixed fractional method or even the percent volatility model, periodically checking the volatility.

■ 11.5 Conclusions

Money management principles can also be applied to discretionary trading, as long as you plan things well. Carefully planning the trade you want to open isn't only necessary in order to decide which money management method to use; it's also necessary to avoid unpleasant surprises or finding yourself in situations in which there's very little time to decide what to do about something you missed.

The money management models we've discussed until now are applied in the same conceptual way. The only difference lies in choosing the parameters, which can't be based on exhaustive historical data and must be chosen by the trader in line with his or her feelings and disposition to risk.

If you use the percent volatility model, while the trade is open you can monitor the level of exposure on the basis of the current volatility and, by using suitable calculations, adjust the number of contracts used. This procedure can involve some difficulties but also be very effective to make the most of market trends. This type of method can, of course, be used both for automatic systems and a series of trades chosen personally by the trader.

CHAPTER 12

Questions
and Answers

Does money management study the trades to place, and provide for the strict application of a stop-loss and a set profit target?

No, money management only tells you *how much* to invest. It doesn't tell you where and how to exit a trade. Trade management and studying trades is part of 'risk management.'

But in some cases money management tells me not to open a trade. Isn't this the same as specifying entry and exit levels?

No! If the chosen money management model advises you against opening a certain trade, it does so because it finds the risk of that trade excessive for the risk you are willing to take. In this case 'how much' is equal to 0.

The strategies in the book produce astonishing results. Can they be used?

The strategies in the book are basic models used to show how to apply the rules of money management. They are trend-following strategies that worked in the past and might work again in the future; however, I wouldn't recommend them to anyone as they're very basic, and there could be long periods in which they don't produce profits. It would be better to concentrates one's efforts on developing something more solid.

Can you really obtain these kinds of results using money management?

Yes you can, the correct application of money management techniques produces notable results; but everything takes time, and you shouldn't expect to emulate Larry Williams and increase your capital a hundredfold in just one year. Throughout the book, medium to long-term investments have been taken into consideration, and in these periods there were highs and lows. It can be hard to get through the bad times without changing everything and starting from scratch again.

When you refer to the 'risk' of a position, do you mean the capital invested in that position?

No, the risk is how much you could lose on the current trade, unless you're considering losing the whole investment (this could occur if you're working with options), the risk is just the part that would be lost if a stop is triggered.

A strategy with a 5% risk is called aggressive. 5% doesn't seem like much to me, so why is it called aggressive?

5% could be considered a medium–low figure; but if this is the percentage you're risking on every trade, a sequence of bad trades could produce a drawdown that would be difficult for most traders to withstand. A lower risk percentage certainly makes it easier to get through bad periods without losing sleep.

I heard that Ryan Jones, who invented the fixed ratio method, entered the Robbins contest and ended up with a 95% drawdown. Is this true?

The results of the World Cup Trading Championship can be surprising — surprisingly good or surprisingly bad. A money management technique can be considered extremely important but it won't stop a trading strategy going bad. The Fixed Ratio money management method, for example, doesn't stop a strategy due to insufficient funds but continues with one contract for as long as there's capital to trade with. If you're competing in a championship, you need to use an aggressive approach, whatever the technique you're using. The Fixed Ratio method helps limit drawdowns when you've accumulated capital but it's more aggressive at the start, and this can produce extremely negative results.

Can you write the codes directly in EasyLanguage with the formulas to calculate the number of contracts, so you don't have to do so before each trade?

If you want to do so you can, but I wouldn't recommend it. If you're back-testing you could, but in real time there are limits. It's nice to have a signal from TradeStation with the number of contracts to use; but you need to remember that TradeStation considers you're following the strategy to the letter. Its calculations are based on the capital that's grown with all the registered trades. If, for any reason (an error, a holiday, or bad mood) you miss a trade, your available capital won't be the same as that in the list used for the calculations, and this could change the results considerably.

If I started with a strategy and things are going well but I have to withdraw funds from the capital to cover personal costs, what should I do?

This isn't a problem. If you have to withdraw funds you simply adjust the available capital. If you're using a fixed fractional method you do your calculations for the next trade with the remaining capital. The same goes for the percent volatility and fixed ratio methods. In other words, it's as if you lost the amount of money you've withdrawn in a losing trade.

If I find myself with additional liquidity and add it to the capital I'm trading with, do I have to start from scratch?

No, the same reasoning applies as in the previous question. A new source of capital can be considered in the same way as a winning trade and you continue to trade with the new capital as if you made the profit trading.

Just one thing to watch out for, both in this case and the above. If you're using filters for the trades based on the position of the equity line in relation to its average, you should adjust the calculations as if the amount added (or withdrawn) was added or subtracted from the start, so this amount doesn't affect the 30-day average, or that of any other period.

In the book you say someone recommended using the Kelly formula and using 50% of the resulting figure to calculate how much to invest. Isn't it simpler to do just that?

Often, even 50% of the Kelly percentage can be too aggressive, depending on the system to which the method is applied. Kelly referred to systems that weren't used for trading. The application of this formula on the stock market is something of a strained interpretation, and it's much better to use other, more suitable, methods.

But Larry Williams made sparks fly with the Kelly formula, so if it worked for him, why shouldn't I use it, too?

Larry Williams is a brilliant trader, but the year he won the championship with over 10,000% was a particularly favourable year for him. Let's just say that, as well as using excellent techniques and the Kelly formula, Larry Williams also had a good deal of luck on his side when he reached that result.

You must remember that, in the same year, he passed the $2 million mark and then his funds quickly fell to 700,000 USD, which was the only bad period that year. If this had happened in the first month, he wouldn't have finished the championship. In the following years, the Kelly formula revealed its true nature and Larry Williams stopped using it in favour of the fixed fractional method, taking the maximum historical loss of the system as the loss of reference.

I like the fixed ratio method. Why does no one talk about it in the trading world?

The fixed ratio method isn't used much as a technique in the professional trading world because, at first when using the strategy it can be too aggressive. Many professional traders prefer to take things easy at the start; but it must be said that they usually have more than enough capital from the start, so have no qualms about starting with a fixed fractional method set up in a conservative way.

The fact that the number of contracts is obtained from the square root of the capital is considered a sort of mathematical 'alchemy' that makes this method somewhat more mysterious, that's all. In reality, as in all things, it has its advantages and if you like it there's no reason not to use it.

You mention the drawdown a lot, but how important is it really? If I can increase my capital tenfold what do I care if it's a rollercoaster ride to get there?

Whenever one mentions increasing their capital tenfold or any other incredible performance, they're always talking about the past. If a system is good, it will probably also be good in the future, but no one can guarantee that for sure. If we knew that after a certain period of time the capital would increase by a certain amount, of course we wouldn't worry how much it fluctuated to get there, but no one knows what will happen and the final result is just hypothetical even with what we might consider to be a high probability of success. Too big a drawdown will inevitably result in a period of sufferance, raising doubts about the validity of the system you're using to make trades.

I want to stop taking trades from the strategy if the equity drops below its average. Do you always have to use a 30-period average?

The 30-period average is just one of the many solutions adopted – 30 periods provides a good response and considers a sufficient period of trades. A lot depends on the number of trades the strategy usually makes in a year. If, to take an absurd example, the strategy shows less than 30 trades/year, it would be better to use a lower period. In any case, this type of stop is chiefly used as a precautionary measure against the 'death' of the system. It's not really used to improve performance, and other methods could be used such as the breakout of a low after 30 (or another number) of periods.

If I really want to use 30 periods, should I consider the theoretical trades of the strategy or those I've actually made. I missed a few. Should I consider them or not?

As the stop is used to block the basic strategy and not specific trading, all the calculations should be made on the basis of theoretical trades, the ones in the report in other words. These are the result of the unconditional application of the rules. If you miss some trades, that's another problem and nothing to do with the strategy.

Why in the book do you say you don't really believe much in trade dependency and using the z-score?

These studies enter into a realm that's overly 'statistical.' If you apply mathematics to trading too much, you run the risk of turning it into some sort of scientific monster that loses its foundations. It's always better to keep things simple, and there are already more than enough possible complications with standard money management solutions, so including these kinds of studies in my opinion is excessive.

I've got a great strategy with an 80% success rate thanks to some special filters. Can I use the Monte Carlo simulation to prepare a good plan of action?

It's certainly possible but, in general, if you're using a heavily filtered strategy, it's a good idea to study the trend without the filters and apply the Monte Carlo simulation to the results of this approach. The results will definitely be worse, but closer to the real situation. In principle, having cleaned the strategy of losing trades with filters that make sense, you run the risk of distorting the studies by making the results too good. Let's say the filters should be applied later, to improve a strategy that's already basically a good one.

In the work plan is it more important to plan profits or drawdown limits?

Profits should definitely be an objective, but the range of potential variations of the same is often very wide. Let's say that, if after the period considered the profits are below the limit of two standard deviations from the mean, then the strategy isn't working very well. The same could be said though if profits were over the limit of two standard deviations from the mean. Such a good performance should start alarm bells ringing, because it could mean you're trading too aggressively on the market.

Drawdowns, on the other hand, are more important, and the range of the variation is narrower. Therefore, it's easier to see whether the point you're at is within acceptable limits.

If I want to use a portfolio of stocks and futures, is it best to use the same strategy for everything?

The best solution would be to use different strategies that diversify not only the instrument but also the logic. For example, with some instruments you could trade using trend following strategies such as the channel breakout or (as often mentioned in the book) a moving average crossover. With other instruments, you could adopt strategies in which trading is based on a price pattern or study countertrend strategies. In this way, you'll have the greatest diversification and optimal synergy with the instruments.

Is it very important to limit global exposure?

Yes, it is, and it's a good idea to dedicate the time required to it. In the same way as you limit risk for a single position, it's just as important to limit total risk. If you open too many positions you'll go from risk control to a strategy of diversification but lose the importance of the exposure. Limiting the number of positions, on the other hand, maintains the initial money management basis intact to avoid overexposure on the market.

Can trading give you a constant monthly income?

Alas, you'll often see the promise of a monthly income in adverts the aim of which is to sell you a certain type of service or a certain product. Profits made from trading don't guarantee such a level of stability for them to be comparable to a monthly wage. There could be months, or even years, that close at a loss and you need to cover your back to be prepared for such things.

I.1 The Impact of a Trading System on Planning

The classic approach described in this book involves applying a money management model to a system, or portfolio of systems or instruments, to maximize their effectiveness.

As mentioned in the book, money management won't transform a losing system into a winning one, or eliminate particularly critical points inherent to the same system; however, creating a winning model after developing the basic system may not always be the most effective way to exploit the profit amplification effect.

If we know the intervention dynamics of the money management algorithm, it may be possible to reconsider some aspects that marked the stages of development of the operating rules, considering not the single trading system as the final product but rather, the whole system + position sizing package.

In order to better understand this aspect, let's take a specific example to see how a change made to the classic approach can produce indubitable benefits.

■ I.2 The Trading System

For the first stage, we'll develop a banal automatic trading system and take a look at the considerations that resulted in the final product.

For our example, we'll use Euro Stoxx 50 futures traded on EUREX. This market is one of the most liquid in the world, so it's a good example of an underlying that can be traded with a growing number of contracts.

Every tick of the instrument is equal to one point of the same, with a value of 10 euros.

We'll create a system to be used only for intraday trading based on Toby Crabel's well-known Opening Range Breakout principle. This principle attempts to follow a trend that sets in during the day and is based on the principle of entering a trade at the market price when it has already moved in one direction by a certain amount, generally greater than the last movements.

In general, this approach involves studying daily bar charts, and entry points are defined in various ways, by measuring a movement from the open of the day, hence the name Opening Range Breakout, which refers to the breaking of a range starting from the open value. These entries though may need monitoring for more than one day and this isn't what we're aiming for in this example; so, in line with the proposed intraday logic, we'll take a detailed look at each single day in order to study the entries. To do this, we'll use a 60-minute chart.

Using the intraday bar chart, we can check whether it's a good idea to trade only within a certain period of time rather than generically trading any time the market is open; to do this, in the code, we enter the 'StartTime' and 'EndTime' as inputs for the time limits within which you want to consider any breakouts.

The breakout levels can be defined on the basis of the previous day's range, multiplying it by a value we can arbitrarily call 'MyPerc,' which will be subject to study, as well as the above-mentioned times.

The EasyLanguage code follows:

```
Input: MyPerc(0.5, MyStopLoss(0), StartTime(0), EndTime(2200);
var: MaxSetup(0), minSetup(9999), MyRange(0), Mycontracts(1);
if date<> date[1] then begin

    MyRange = highd(1)-lowd(1);
    MaxSetup = opend(0) + MyRange*MyPerc;
    minSetup = opend(0) – MyRange*MyPerc

End;
if Time > StartTime and Time < EndTime then begin

    if close < MaxSetup then buy MyContracts contracts next bar at MaxSetup stop;
    if close > minSetup then sellshort MyContracts contracts next bar at minSetup stop;

end;
setstopcontract;
if MyStopLoss > 0 then setstoploss(MyStopLoss);
setexitonclose;
```

FIGURE AI.1   Initial strategy EasyLanguage code.

The above code buys over a certain level, calculated by adding a portion of the previous day's range to the opening price; or sells if there's a loss equal to the same portion of the previous day's range in relation to the opening price.

As entries can be triggered only after a certain time (further on we'll study the optimal time, called StartTime), there's an additional condition tied to the fact we still need to be below the buy long entry level (close < MaxSetup) or above the sell short entry level (close > MinSetup) in order to take the trades into consideration (this prevents entering the market after a breakout that occurred outside the set times).

The system closes the positions at the end of the day (setexitonclose) and has a monetary stop for each contract that's only used if the relevant input (MyStopLoss) is other than 0. (Note that currently the system is tested with one single contract as each Money Management algorithm will only be considered subsequently.)

Until December 2018, the market in question had been trading continuously from 8:00 to 22:00. Yet before June 2006 it traded at different times, with the market opening at 9.00 and closing at 20.00. Extended times were first adopted on 1 June 2006; therefore, we'll focus our studies starting from that date to simplify the analysis. These studies also include 15 euros in trading costs per side (the hypothesis is for one tick of slippage and a commission of 5 euros per contract).

For the first study, let's make a hypothesis of working for the whole day, so with a StartTime = 800 and an EndTime = 2200, checking which portion of the previous day's range produces the best results. In Figure AI.2 we can see that the entry points that are 25% higher than yesterday's range are those that produce the most profit, so we'll use a MyPerc value = 1.25 for the subsequent analyses.

Note that the chosen value does represent the absolute optimal value, but the net profit chart in Figure AI.2 shows we're not dealing with an unstable value as the results on either side (1.2 and 1.3) are in any case similar. Therefore, this is a case in which choosing the best value deriving from the optimisation isn't necessarily a risk.

Now, with a joint optimisation of StartTime and EndTime, changing these values every hour, we can see how the best results can only be obtained with a start time after 10.00 and an end time before 18.00. The results are shown in order of decreasing net profit, and Figure AI.3 shows the most interesting results.

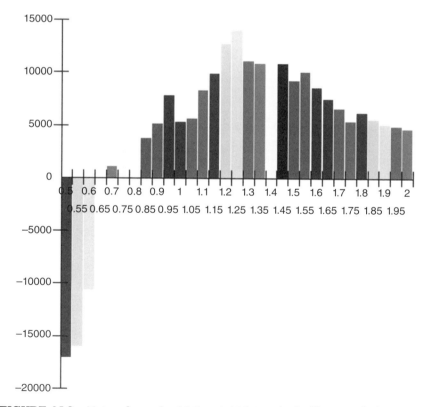

FIGURE AI.2 Net profit trend as MyPerc (which is multiplied by yesterday's range) changes.

#	StartTime: Input	EndTime: Input	All: Net Profit	All: Total Trades	All: % Profitable	All: Max Winning Trade	All: Max Losing Trade	All: Avg Winning Trade	All: Avg Losing Trade	All: Win/Loss Ratio	All: Avg Trade	All: Max Intraday Drawdown	All: ProfitFactor
1	1,000	1,800	16,000.00	233	54.51	1,820.00	-630.00	265.51	-173.73	1.53	68.67	-1,875.00	1.90
2	1,000	1,900	15,900.00	250	52.40	1,820.00	-630.00	267.48	-166.43	1.61	63.60	-1,925.00	1.83
3	1,000	2,100	15,190.00	288	50.00	1,820.00	-630.00	260.28	-160.36	1.62	52.74	-2,455.00	1.68
4	1,000	1,700	15,090.00	197	54.82	1,820.00	-630.00	288.43	-186.74	1.54	76.60	-1,835.00	1.94
5	1,100	1,800	15,030.00	230	54.35	1,820.00	-630.00	262.00	-173.73	1.51	65.35	-1,875.00	1.85
6	1,100	1,900	14,930.00	247	52.23	1,820.00	-630.00	264.11	-166.43	1.59	60.45	-1,925.00	1.78
7	1,000	2,000	14,870.00	270	50.00	1,820.00	-630.00	264.22	-160.00	1.65	55.07	-2,345.00	1.71
8	900	1,800	14,790.00	243	53.91	1,820.00	-1,010.00	265.57	-185.19	1.43	60.86	-2,175.00	1.74
9	900	1,900	14,690.00	260	51.92	1,820.00	-1,010.00	267.48	-177.02	1.51	56.50	-2,225.00	1.69
10	1,100	2,100	14,220.00	286	49.65	1,820.00	-630.00	257.11	-160.36	1.60	49.72	-2,455.00	1.64
11	1,100	1,700	14,120.00	194	54.64	1,820.00	-630.00	284.72	-186.74	1.52	72.78	-1,835.00	1.88
12	900	2,100	14,050.00	296	49.66	1,820.00	-1,010.00	262.04	-169.93	1.54	47.47	-2,905.00	1.57
13	1,100	2,000	13,900.00	267	49.81	1,820.00	-630.00	260.90	-160.00	1.63	52.06	-2,345.00	1.67
14	900	1,700	13,880.00	207	54.11	1,820.00	-1,010.00	287.68	-199.35	1.44	67.05	-2,055.00	1.76
15	900	2,000	13,730.00	278	49.64	1,820.00	-1,010.00	266.01	-170.22	1.56	49.39	-2,795.00	1.60
16	1,200	1,800	13,480.00	223	54.71	1,550.00	-630.00	249.51	-173.06	1.44	60.45	-2,885.00	1.79
17	1,200	1,900	13,380.00	240	52.50	1,550.00	-630.00	252.06	-165.59	1.52	55.75	-3,150.00	1.73
18	1,200	1,700	12,610.00	185	55.14	1,550.00	-630.00	272.75	-187.78	1.45	68.16	-2,805.00	1.83
19	1,200	2,100	12,590.00	280	49.64	1,550.00	-630.00	246.04	-158.90	1.55	44.96	-3,515.00	1.58
20	1,200	2,000	12,350.00	260	50.00	1,550.00	-630.00	249.15	-159.05	1.57	47.50	-3,355.00	1.62
21	1,000	1,600	11,960.00	135	57.04	1,820.00	-630.00	311.69	-215.00	1.45	88.59	-1,965.00	1.99
22	1,300	1,900	11,940.00	228	51.75	1,550.00	-630.00	248.39	-162.34	1.53	52.37	-3,350.00	1.69
23	1,300	1,800	11,830.00	210	53.81	1,550.00	-630.00	245.84	-169.68	1.45	56.33	-3,085.00	1.74
24	1,400	1,900	11,490.00	205	51.71	1,550.00	-630.00	242.36	-147.92	1.64	56.05	-3,125.00	1.81
25	1,400	1,800	11,440.00	185	54.05	1,550.00	-630.00	241.10	-154.51	1.56	61.84	-2,815.00	1.90
26	900	1,600	11,290.00	147	56.46	1,820.00	-1,010.00	308.55	-230.97	1.34	76.80	-2,755.00	1.79
27	1,100	1,600	11,050.00	129	56.59	1,820.00	-630.00	313.70	-215.45	1.46	85.66	-1,865.00	1.93
28	1,300	1,700	11,000.00	170	54.12	1,550.00	-630.00	272.50	-185.13	1.47	64.71	-3,005.00	1.78
29	1,300	2,100	10,950.00	269	48.70	1,550.00	-630.00	242.37	-156.39	1.55	40.71	-3,715.00	1.53

FIGURE AI.3 Profit trend on the basis of the chosen trading time windows.

```
Input: MyPerc(0.5, MyStopLoss(0), StartTime(0), EndTime(2200);
var: MaxSetup(0), minSetup(9999), MyRange(0), Mycontracts(1);
Input: MyLongDay(0), MyShortDay(0);
if date<> date[1] then begin

    MyRange = highd(1)-lowd(1);
     MaxSetup = opend(0) + MyRange*MyPerc;
  minSetup = opend(0) – MyRange*MyPerc
End;
if Time > StartTime and Time < EndTime then begin

     if close < MaxSetup and dayofweek(date) <> MyLongDay then buy MyContracts contracts next
     bar at MaxSetup stop;

     if close > minSetup and dayofweek(date)<>MyShortDay then sellshort MyContracts contracts next
     bar at minSetup stop;

end;
setstopcontract;
if MyStopLoss > 0 then setstoploss(MyStopLoss);
setexitonclose;
```

FIGURE AI.4   New EasyLanguage code excluding some days of the week

The work we're doing is entirely closed by the end of the day with all the open positions closed. Therefore, it may be a good idea to conduct another study to find out whether there are any days in the week that aren't very well suited to long positions and others that aren't good for short positions. Figure AI.4 shows the EasyLanguage code changes.

The optimisation of each datum from 0 (trading every day) to five shows whether it's advisable to exclude some days. The results are shown in Figure AI.5.

Figure AI.5, in fact, shows how, as regards situation '0.0,' there are various combinations that give better results. As we're performing more of a clean-up operation rather than looking for the most consistent profits, it's important to make a choice on the basis of the quality of the remaining trades. The results are therefore ordered starting from those with a higher average trade and excluding Friday long trades and Wednesday short trades, which improves not only net profit (from 16,000 to 16,580) but, above all, the average trade (from 68.67 to 85.91).

The last thing to do at this point is to check whether using a stop-loss will produce further improvements.

An optimisation from 0 to 1,000 (0 equal to no stop-loss) produces the results in Figure AI.6.

Figure AI.6 shows the best result is obtained without a stop-loss, and it's also evident that very tight stop values produce quite disappointing results.

	MyLong-Day: Input	MyShort-Day: Input	All: Net Profit	All: Total Trades	All: % Profitable	All: Max Winning Trade	All: Max Losing Trade	All: Avg Winning Trade	All: Avg Losing Trade	All: Win/Loss Ratio	All: Avg Trade	All: Max Intraday Drawdown	All: ProfitFactor
1	5	3	16,580.00	193	56.99	1,820.00	-630.00	278.00	-177.22	1.57	85.91	-1,625.00	2.18
2	4	3	16,130.00	189	55.03	1,820.00	-630.00	288.17	-170.86	1.69	85.34	-1,630.00	2.17
3	4	4	14,470.00	182	53.85	1,820.00	-480.00	278.88	-156.83	1.78	79.51	-1,275.00	2.13
4	5	4	14,410.00	186	55.91	1,820.00	-1,100.00	268.65	-169.13	1.59	77.47	-1,405.00	2.07
5	3	3	14,560.00	188	54.26	1,820.00	-630.00	284.71	-176.59	1.61	77.45	-2,375.00	2.01
6	5	1	14,980.00	195	56.92	1,820.00	-630.00	262.25	-176.63	1.48	76.82	-1,305.00	2.06
7	5	0	16,590.00	216	56.02	1,820.00	-630.00	270.17	-176.92	1.53	76.81	-1,535.00	2.03
8	0	3	15,990.00	210	55.24	1,820.00	-630.00	272.50	-173.56	1.57	76.14	-1,995.00	2.02
9	4	0	16,140.00	212	54.25	1,820.00	-630.00	278.96	-171.40	1.63	76.13	-1,625.00	2.01
10	4	1	14,530.00	191	54.97	1,820.00	-630.00	271.43	-170.37	1.59	76.07	-1,425.00	2.04
11	5	5	13,660.00	185	56.76	1,820.00	-630.00	268.19	-188.31	1.42	73.84	-1,575.00	1.94
12	4	5	13,210.00	181	54.70	1,820.00	-630.00	278.28	-181.52	1.53	72.98	-1,635.00	1.92
13	1	1	14,390.00	198	55.05	1,820.00	-630.00	269.91	-176.82	1.53	72.68	-1,995.00	1.96
14	2	3	13,090.00	187	54.55	1,820.00	-630.00	270.78	-177.20	1.53	70.00	-1,945.00	1.90
15	3	0	14,570.00	211	53.55	1,820.00	-630.00	275.66	-176.38	1.56	69.05	-2,255.00	1.88
16	0	0	16,000.00	233	54.51	1,820.00	-630.00	265.51	-173.73	1.53	68.67	-1,875.00	1.90
17	3	4	12,390.00	181	53.04	1,820.00	-1,100.00	275.00	-168.80	1.63	68.45	-1,865.00	1.88
18	3	1	12,960.00	190	54.21	1,820.00	-630.00	267.67	-176.02	1.52	68.21	-1,975.00	1.89
19	0	4	13,820.00	203	54.19	1,820.00	-1,100.00	263.36	-166.48	1.58	68.08	-1,485.00	1.91
20	0	1	14,390.00	212	55.19	1,820.00	-630.00	257.61	-173.08	1.49	67.88	-1,665.00	1.91
21	5	2	12,010.00	183	55.19	1,550.00	-630.00	251.09	-171.15	1.47	65.63	-2,435.00	1.90
22	1	0	14,400.00	221	54.30	1,820.00	-630.00	262.75	-176.60	1.49	65.16	-1,875.00	1.84
23	0	5	13,070.00	202	54.95	1,820.00	-630.00	262.97	-183.18	1.44	64.70	-1,885.00	1.81
24	3	5	11,640.00	180	53.89	1,820.00	-630.00	274.43	-187.25	1.47	64.67	-2,265.00	1.78
25	4	2	11,560.00	179	53.07	1,550.00	-630.00	260.53	-164.88	1.58	64.58	-2,355.00	1.88
26	1	4	12,220.00	191	53.93	1,820.00	-1,100.00	260.00	-169.30	1.54	63.98	-1,485.00	1.84
27	1	1	12,790.00	200	55.00	1,820.00	-630.00	254.09	-176.28	1.44	63.95	-1,665.00	1.84
28	2	0	13,100.00	210	53.81	1,820.00	-630.00	263.10	-176.91	1.49	62.38	-1,825.00	1.79

FIGURE AI.5 Excluding Friday from long trades and Wednesday from short trades improves the results in average trade terms, and also net profit.

StopLoss: Input	All: Net Profit	All: Total Trades	All: % Profitable	All: Max Winning Trade	All: Max Losing Trade	All: Avg Winning Trade	All: Avg Losing Trade	All: Win/Loss Ratio	All: Avg Trade	All: Max Intraday Drawdown	All: ProfitFactor
0	16,580.00	193	56.99	1,820.00	-630.00	278.00	-177.22	1.57	85.91	-1,625.00	2.18
50	1,460.00	288	23.61	1,820.00	-80.00	277.79	-79.23	3.51	5.07	-3,905.00	1.08
100	5,750.00	252	35.32	1,820.00	-130.00	291.01	-123.62	2.35	22.82	-3,580.00	1.29
150	11,530.00	219	46.12	1,820.00	-180.00	293.37	-156.03	1.88	52.65	-2,645.00	1.64
200	12,020.00	208	50.00	1,820.00	-230.00	287.02	-174.80	1.64	57.79	-2,735.00	1.67
250	12,750.00	202	52.48	1,820.00	-280.00	282.45	-186.85	1.51	63.12	-2,210.00	1.74
300	12,690.00	197	53.81	1,820.00	-330.00	282.45	-198.28	1.42	64.42	-2,075.00	1.74
350	12,730.00	195	54.36	1,820.00	-380.00	282.45	-202.47	1.40	65.28	-2,325.00	1.74
400	12,750.00	195	54.36	1,820.00	-430.00	282.45	-202.24	1.40	65.38	-2,015.00	1.74
450	13,790.00	193	55.44	1,820.00	-480.00	279.91	-197.07	1.42	71.45	-1,625.00	1.85
500	14,250.00	193	55.96	1,820.00	-530.00	278.70	-195.68	1.42	73.83	-1,625.00	1.90
550	14,700.00	193	56.48	1,820.00	-580.00	278.62	-195.88	1.42	76.17	-1,625.00	1.94
600	15,060.00	193	56.48	1,820.00	-630.00	278.62	-191.38	1.46	78.03	-1,625.00	1.98
650	14,860.00	193	56.48	1,820.00	-680.00	278.62	-193.88	1.44	76.99	-1,635.00	1.96
700	14,660.00	193	56.48	1,820.00	-730.00	278.62	-196.38	1.42	75.96	-1,685.00	1.93
750	14,460.00	193	56.48	1,820.00	-780.00	278.62	-198.88	1.40	74.92	-1,735.00	1.91
800	15,340.00	193	56.48	1,820.00	-830.00	278.62	-187.88	1.48	79.48	-1,735.00	2.02
850	15,490.00	193	56.48	1,820.00	-880.00	278.62	-186.00	1.50	80.26	-1,625.00	2.04
900	15,440.00	193	56.48	1,820.00	-930.00	278.62	-186.63	1.49	80.00	-1,625.00	2.03
950	15,390.00	193	56.48	1,820.00	-980.00	278.62	-187.25	1.49	79.74	-1,625.00	2.03
1,000	15,340.00	193	56.48	1,820.00	-1,030.00	278.62	-187.88	1.48	79.48	-1,625.00	2.02

FIGURE AI.6 Trend in profits as the stop-loss changes.

The above shouldn't give us the wrong idea though that it's better to trade without a stop-loss. In fact, the above strategy has a time stop and positions are closed by the end of the day. Therefore, there are no cases in which losing positions remain open in the hope they'll recover. This, in fact, is the cause of more than a few disasters, and almost always locks up trading. There must always be a stop, in other words an action that closes both winning and losing trades. It may be a monetary stop (which in this case proves less effective), a time stop (as used in this example) or a condition of stop and reverse (typically found in some trend following strategies always in the market). Hope should never be a reason for keeping a position open.

The basic strategy can be considered to be completed, and Figures AI.7 and AI.8 respectively show the performance report and the equity line.

This certainly isn't a strategy that'll make us millionaires, but there's no doubt that, even using an extremely simple approach, we were able to make a profit.

As mentioned above though, the chosen market is well suited to trading also with a significant number of contracts, so we'll proceed by applying one

TradeStation Performance Summary			Collapse ⌃
	All Trades	**Long Trades**	**Short Trades**
Total Net Profit	€16,580.00	€5,790.00	€10,790.00
Gross Profit	€30,580.00	€10,390.00	€20,190.00
Gross Loss	(€14,000.00)	(€4,600.00)	(€9,400.00)
Profit Factor	2.18	2.26	2.15
Roll Over Credit	€0.00	€0.00	€0.00
Open Position P/L	€0.00	€0.00	€0.00
Select Total Net Profit	€13,840.00	€5,790.00	€8,050.00
Select Gross Profit	€27,210.00	€10,390.00	€16,820.00
Select Gross Loss	(€13,370.00)	(€4,600.00)	(€8,770.00)
Select Profit Factor	2.04	2.26	1.92
Adjusted Total Net Profit	€12,089.19	€3,434.62	€6,903.44
Adjusted Gross Profit	€27,664.31	€8,874.46	€17,646.30
Adjusted Gross Loss	(€15,575.12)	(€5,439.84)	(€10,742.86)
Adjusted Profit Factor	1.78	1.63	1.64
Total Number of Trades	193	78	115
Percent Profitable	56.99%	60.26%	54.78%
Winning Trades	110	47	63
Losing Trades	79	30	49
Even Trades	4	1	3
Avg. Trade Net Profit	€85.91	€74.23	€93.83
Avg. Winning Trade	€278.00	€221.06	€320.48
Avg. Losing Trade	(€177.22)	(€153.33)	(€191.84)
Ratio Avg. Win:Avg. Loss	1.57	1.44	1.67
Largest Winning Trade	€1,820.00	€950.00	€1,820.00
Largest Losing Trade	(€630.00)	(€590.00)	(€630.00)

FIGURE AI.7 Performance report of the strategy developed.

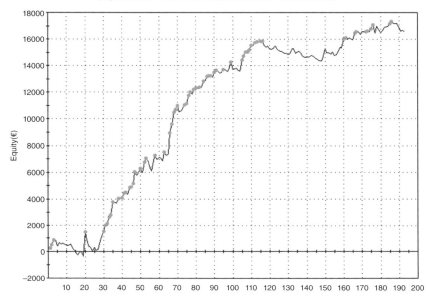

FIGURE AI.8   Equity line of the strategy developed.

of the money management models described in the book, using the classic percent f, and assuming we start with a capital of 100,000 euros (with the available data we could decide to use much less capital with this threshold, but in this appendix the idea isn't to verify the trading limits of the strategy we've just developed).

Entering the set of instructions necessary to calculate exposure in the EasyLanguage code shown in Figure AI.9, we add the data on risk and capital as well as the 'MaxLosing' input, which is simply the max. loss ever recorded. In our case, as can be seen in Figure AI.7, this value is 630 euros.

Applying this set of rules to the above system changes the results, as shown in Figures AI.10 and AI.11.

On the basis of whether the scenarios in Figures AI.10 and AI.11 are acceptable, we'll have finished the 'classic' development.

However, if we consider how contracts are calculated using the percent f method, a lot depends on the entity of the maximum loss. So, returning to the table in Figure AI.6 we'll see that, by adopting a monetary stop value of 350 euros (35 ticks of the instrument), it's true that net profit drops by about 23% (12,730 euros compared to 16,580 euros) but the max. loss is 380 euros (350 stop-loss + 30 trade costs), which could open interesting opportunities when calculating contracts using percent f.

```
Input: MyPerc(0.5, MyStopLoss(0), StartTime(0), EndTime(2200);
var: MaxSetup(0), minSetup(9999), MyRange(0), Mycontracts(1);
Input: MyLongDay(0), MyShortDay(0);
    Input: MyPercRisk(2), MyStartCapital(100000), MaxLosing(630);
var: MyEquity(0);
if date<> date[1] then begin
    MyRange = highd(1)-lowd(1);

    MaxSetup = opend(0) + MyRange*MyPerc;
    minSetup = opend(0) – MyRange*MyPerc
    MyEquity = MyStartCapital + netprofit;
    If MaxLosing >0 then MyContracts = intportion(MyEquity*MyParcRisk/100)/MaxLosing);
End;
if Time > StartTime and Time < EndTime then begin
    if close < MaxSetup and dayofweek(date) <> MyLongDay then buy MyContracts contracts next
    bar at MaxSetup stop;
    if close > minSetup and dayofweek(date)<>MyShortDay then sellshort MyContracts contracts next
    bar at minSetup stop;
end;
setstopcontract;
if MyStopLoss > 0 then setstoploss(MyStopLoss);
setexitonclose;
```

FIGURE AI.9   New EasyLanguage code with the instructions for calculating the contracts with percent f.

Therefore, in the hypothesis of using a fixed stop of 350 euros per contract we'll recalculate the profits deriving from the application of the percent f model with a 2% risk (this time the MaxLosing parameter will be set at 380). Figure AI.12 shows the performance report and Figure AI.13 the equity line.

It's immediately obvious that, in this case, the version with the stop-loss produces much better results than that with a simple time stop. The lowest ever loss, in fact, permits a greater exposure for the same risk, and the impact on the final results is all but negligible.

Trading with a 2% risk may be reasonable but, in order to highlight the above phenomenon let's conduct some tests also with a risk of 5% per trade.

In Figure AI.14 the performance report has no stop-loss and therefore the max. system loss is 630 euros per contract. Figure AI.15 shows the relevant equity line.

Now let's perform the same operation with a 350 euros stop-loss per contract. Figure AI.16 shows the performance report, and Figure AI.17 the equity line.

	All Trades	Long Trades	Short Trades
Total Net Profit	€56,790.00	€20,410.00	€36,380.00
Gross Profit	€108,560.00	€38,000.00	€70,560.00
Gross Loss	(€51,770.00)	(€17,590.00)	(€34,180.00)
Profit Factor	2.10	2.16	2.06
Roll Over Credit	€0.00	€0.00	€0.00
Open Position P/L	€0.00	€0.00	€0.00
Select Total Net Profit	€49,630.00	€23,360.00	€26,270.00
Select Gross Profit	€98,450.00	€38,000.00	€60,450.00
Select Gross Loss	(€48,820.00)	(€14,640.00)	(€34,180.00)
Select Profit Factor	2.02	2.60	1.77
Adjusted Total Net Profit	€40,614.63	€11,655.65	€22,607.42
Adjusted Gross Profit	€98,209.21	€32,457.13	€61,670.28
Adjusted Gross Loss	(€57,594.58)	(€20,801.48)	(€39,062.86)
Adjusted Profit Factor	1.71	1.56	1.58
Total Number of Trades	193	78	115
Percent Profitable	56.99%	60.26%	54.78%
Winning Trades	110	47	63
Losing Trades	79	30	49
Even Trades	4	1	3
Avg. Trade Net Profit	€294.25	€261.67	€316.35
Avg. Winning Trade	€986.91	€808.51	€1,120.00
Avg. Losing Trade	(€655.32)	(€586.33)	(€697.55)
Ratio Avg. Win:Avg. Loss	1.51	1.38	1.61
Largest Winning Trade	€5,460.00	€2,850.00	€5,460.00
Largest Losing Trade	(€2,950.00)	(€2,950.00)	(€2,240.00)

FIGURE AI.10   Results with percent f equal to 2%.

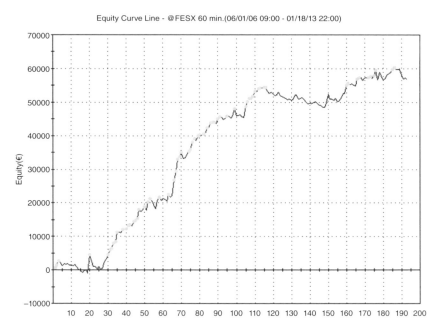

FIGURE AI.11   Equity line with percent f equal to 2%.

	All Trades	Long Trades	Short Trades
Total Net Profit	€82,080.00	€29,430.00	€52,650.00
Gross Profit	€208,010.00	€72,280.00	€135,730.00
Gross Loss	(€125,930.00)	(€42,850.00)	(€83,080.00)
Profit Factor	1.65	1.69	1.63
Roll Over Credit	€0.00	€0.00	€0.00
Open Position P/L	€0.00	€0.00	€0.00
Select Total Net Profit	€63,680.00	€29,430.00	€34,250.00
Select Gross Profit	€189,610.00	€72,280.00	€117,330.00
Select Gross Loss	(€125,930.00)	(€42,850.00)	(€83,080.00)
Select Profit Factor	1.51	1.69	1.41
Adjusted Total Net Profit	€48,217.26	€11,198.01	€23,715.42
Adjusted Gross Profit	€187,806.28	€61,622.90	€118,207.33
Adjusted Gross Loss	(€139,589.03)	(€50,424.88)	(€94,491.92)
Adjusted Profit Factor	1.35	1.22	1.25
Total Number of Trades	195	79	116
Percent Profitable	54.36%	58.23%	51.72%
Winning Trades	106	46	60
Losing Trades	85	32	53
Even Trades	4	1	3
Avg. Trade Net Profit	€420.92	€372.53	€453.88
Avg. Winning Trade	€1,962.36	€1,571.30	€2,262.17
Avg. Losing Trade	(€1,481.53)	(€1,339.06)	(€1,567.55)
Ratio Avg. Win:Avg. Loss	1.32	1.17	1.44
Largest Winning Trade	€9,300.00	€4,960.00	€9,300.00
Largest Losing Trade	(€3,420.00)	(€3,420.00)	(€3,420.00)

FIGURE AI.12 Performance report with a 350 euros stop-loss per contract and a percent f model set at 2%.

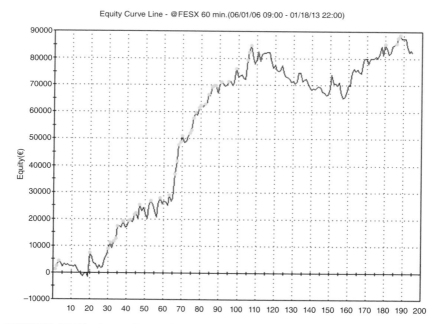

Equity Curve Line - @FESX 60 min.(06/01/06 09:00 - 01/18/13 22:00)

FIGURE AI.13 Equity line with a 350 euros stop-loss per contract and a percent f model set at 2%.

	All Trades	Long Trades	Short Trades
Total Net Profit	€232,580.00	€87,740.00	€144,840.00
Gross Profit	€476,760.00	€172,360.00	€304,400.00
Gross Loss	(€244,180.00)	(€84,620.00)	(€159,560.00)
Profit Factor	1.95	2.04	1.91
Roll Over Credit	€0.00	€0.00	€0.00
Open Position P/L	€0.00	€0.00	€0.00
Select Total Net Profit	€223,250.00	€103,670.00	€119,580.00
Select Gross Profit	€439,180.00	€172,360.00	€266,820.00
Select Gross Loss	(€215,930.00)	(€68,690.00)	(€147,240.00)
Select Profit Factor	2.03	2.51	1.81
Adjusted Total Net Profit	€159,650.32	€47,149.28	€83,694.92
Adjusted Gross Profit	€431,302.72	€147,218.71	€266,049.20
Adjusted Gross Loss	(€271,652.40)	(€100,069.43)	(€182,354.29)
Adjusted Profit Factor	1.59	1.47	1.46
Total Number of Trades	193	78	115
Percent Profitable	56.99%	60.26%	54.78%
Winning Trades	110	47	63
Losing Trades	79	30	49
Even Trades	4	1	3
Avg. Trade Net Profit	€1,205.08	€1,124.87	€1,259.48
Avg. Winning Trade	€4,334.18	€3,667.23	€4,831.75
Avg. Losing Trade	(€3,090.89)	(€2,820.67)	(€3,256.33)
Ratio Avg. Win:Avg. Loss	1.40	1.30	1.48
Largest Winning Trade	€20,150.00	€14,880.00	€20,150.00
Largest Losing Trade	(€15,930.00)	(€15,930.00)	(€12,320.00)

FIGURE AI.14   Performance report with a percent *f* model set at 5% and a simple time stop.

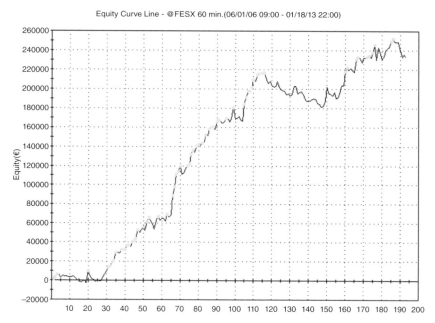

Equity Curve Line - @FESX 60 min.(06/01/06 09:00 - 01/18/13 22:00)

FIGURE AI.15   Equity line with a percent *f* model set at 5% and a simple time stop.

	All Trades	Long Trades	Short Trades
Total Net Profit	€330,330.00	€125,890.00	€204,440.00
Gross Profit	€964,120.00	€345,010.00	€619,110.00
Gross Loss	(€633,790.00)	(€219,120.00)	(€414,670.00)
Profit Factor	1.52	1.57	1.49
Roll Over Credit	€0.00	€0.00	€0.00
Open Position P/L	€0.00	€0.00	€0.00
Select Total Net Profit	€254,010.00	€125,890.00	€128,120.00
Select Gross Profit	€887,800.00	€345,010.00	€542,790.00
Select Gross Loss	(€633,790.00)	(€219,120.00)	(€414,670.00)
Select Profit Factor	1.40	1.57	1.31
Adjusted Total Net Profit	€167,942.21	€36,285.74	€67,553.94
Adjusted Gross Profit	€870,476.39	€294,141.05	€539,183.24
Adjusted Gross Loss	(€702,534.18)	(€257,855.31)	(€471,629.31)
Adjusted Profit Factor	1.24	1.14	1.14
Total Number of Trades	195	79	116
Percent Profitable	54.36%	58.23%	51.72%
Winning Trades	106	46	60
Losing Trades	85	32	53
Even Trades	4	1	3
Avg. Trade Net Profit	€1,694.00	€1,593.54	€1,762.41
Avg. Winning Trade	€9,095.47	€7,500.22	€10,318.50
Avg. Losing Trade	(€7,456.35)	(€6,847.50)	(€7,823.96)
Ratio Avg. Win:Avg. Loss	1.22	1.10	1.32
Largest Winning Trade	€40,670.00	€29,140.00	€40,670.00
Largest Losing Trade	(€22,420.00)	(€22,040.00)	(€22,420.00)

FIGURE AI.16 Performance report with a 350 euros stop-loss per contract and a percent *f* model set at 5%.

FIGURE AI.17 Equity line with a 350 euros stop-loss per contract and a percent *f* model set at 5%.

The differences are obvious and, even though the trend of the equity line isn't very stable, it's evident that greater exposure for the same risk can produce a notable increase in final profit.

The above derives from considerations based on the experience of the individual developer. The choice of one money management model over another, whether you need to change the basic settings of the strategy, remains entirely in the operator's hands. In fact, it's very hard to suggest a correct development path that's valid for any approach, and only deep-rooted knowledge of money management dynamics will give you the right intuition for one particular strategy being developed.

■ II.1 Understanding the Type of Strategy

The money management approach linked to a portfolio of systems has shown how different models can produce significantly different results. The simple possibility of adopting a different model for the portfolio of systems each time, has also been considered.

While this was logical in the case of a 'common engine' system applied to several instruments, it can be a weaker approach if systems with significantly different features are combined.

As usual, a specific example is the best way to illustrate the possible options to handle situations of this kind in a more effective way.

In the previous appendix we traded Eurostox50 futures using an intraday strategy. The conclusions we reached show that, the combination of strategy and position sizing model may even raise doubts about the validity of the basic strategy structure. In the end, we also found that a strategy with a monetary stop-loss was preferable as, although less effective than a version with just a time stop, it does prove to be more effective once the percent f model is applied.

We'll use this version of the strategy in this appendix, in the hypothesis of using it with another, quite different, strategy.

Despite being applied to Eurostox50 futures, the new strategy won't be based on 60-minute bar charts but rather 240-minute charts, and will simply open countertrend trades when a min. or max. period is reached.

The basic code is that shown in Figure AII.1.

```
If marketposition <= 0 then Buy mycontracts contracts next bar at lowest(low, 15) limit;
If marketposition >= 0 then sellshort mycontracts contracts next bar at highest(high, 25) limit;
```

FIGURE AII.1   Countertrend strategy code.

This strategy, in the period that goes from 1 June 2006 to January 2013, produced approximately 40,000 euros in 266 trades (also in this case 15 euros in trading costs were considered). Figure AII.2 shows the performance report.

Now, in the hypothesis of combining the two systems and using them with an initial capital of 100,000 euros, it's immediately obvious that a percent f based on the max. system loss won't produce great benefits for the combined forces, as the max. loss of the new system is 5,240 euros, which requires a notable amount of available capital or a particularly high percentage of risk per trade.

TradeStation Performance Summary			Collapse ☆
	All Trades	**Long Trades**	**Short Trades**
Total Net Profit	€40,270.00	€17,910.00	€22,360.00
Gross Profit	€108,690.00	€60,730.00	€47,960.00
Gross Loss	(€68,420.00)	(€42,820.00)	(€25,600.00)
Profit Factor	1.59	1.42	1.87
Roll Over Credit	€0.00	€0.00	€0.00
Open Position P/L	(€255.00)	€0.00	(€255.00)
Select Total Net Profit	€49,960.00	€31,380.00	€18,580.00
Select Gross Profit	€104,910.00	€60,730.00	€44,180.00
Select Gross Loss	(€54,950.00)	(€29,350.00)	(€25,600.00)
Select Profit Factor	1.91	2.07	1.73
Adjusted Total Net Profit	€24,790.81	€4,672.21	€13,469.99
Adjusted Gross Profit	€100,588.73	€54,531.77	€42,727.13
Adjusted Gross Loss	(€75,797.92)	(€49,859.56)	(€29,257.14)
Adjusted Profit Factor	1.33	1.09	1.46
Total Number of Trades	266	133	133
Percent Profitable	67.67%	72.18%	63.16%
Winning Trades	180	96	84
Losing Trades	86	37	49
Even Trades	0	0	0
Avg. Trade Net Profit	€151.39	€134.66	€168.12
Avg. Winning Trade	€603.83	€632.60	€570.95
Avg. Losing Trade	(€795.58)	(€1,157.30)	(€522.45)
Ratio Avg. Win:Avg. Loss	0.76	0.55	1.09
Largest Winning Trade	€1,920.00	€1,370.00	€1,920.00
Largest Losing Trade	(€5,240.00)	(€5,240.00)	(€2,690.00)

FIGURE AII.2   Countertrend strategy performance report.

In order to make a comparison with values considered 'reasonable' until now, we'll analyze the results with a 2% risk.

On the basis of what we've learned so far, we can see that in order to use the new system with a 2% risk per trade, we need a capital of at least:

$$\left(\frac{5,240}{2}\right) * 100 = 262,000 \text{ euros.}$$

Therefore, with 100,000 euros we can only start to trade using the second system if the equity produced by adding the profits of the first one is over the threshold, we've just calculated.

Figure AII.3 shows the portfolio equity line chart and the relevant draw-down data.

As can be seen from the trend of the line, the level required to start trading with the second system is never reached. In fact, the result obtained doesn't allow for the combination of the two systems at all, and is a mere exercise in applying a position sizing model to the trading system shown in the previous appendix.

Increasing the risk produces two effects. The first is a faster and more noticeable increase in terms of capital from the first trading system, while the second is the need for a lower level of liquidity in the second system to start trading.

With a percent f model set at 2.5%, for example, this level is equal to:

$$\left(\frac{5,240}{2}\right) * 100 = 209,600 \text{ euros}$$

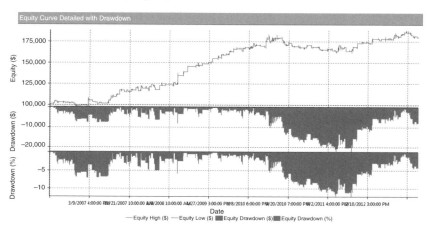

FIGURE AII.3 Portfolio equity line of the two systems with a percent f model set at 2%.

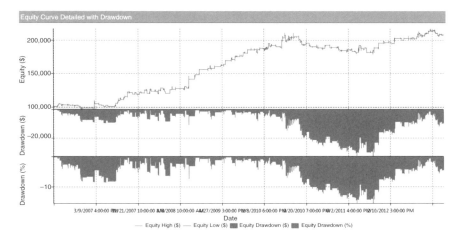

FIGURE AII.4   Portfolio of the two systems with a percent *f* model set at 2.5%.

Figure AII.4 shows how said level is (just) exceeded several times.

However, if we measure the contribution of the two systems to the line in Figure AII.4 we'll see that of the 107,840 euros in profit (the line ends at 207,840 euros), only 2,720 were produced by the countertrend trading system, and in particular in 20 trades. Therefore, its contribution is still negligible, and it's difficult to consider this as a portfolio also in this case.

It's only with a risk percentage of 5.24% that the second system can trade from the start (5.24% of 100,000 covers the entire max. loss of the system, equal to 5,240 euros). In reality, we need to check which system starts trading first and, if it's the first, the level the equity line reached when the second could start trading, in order to evaluate the exact percentage (the initial capital of 100,000 euros may have increased or decreased in the meantime); but even this isn't enough as, while trading with the two systems, there may have been losses that reduced the available capital to below the 100,000 euros mark. Therefore, we'll take the 5.24% risk as a purely mathematical exercise and evaluate the results of the portfolio of systems shown in Figure AII.5.

Figure AII.6 shows the equity line, and in Table II.1 we see the contribution of each system.

As can be seen, the second system managed to make all the 266 trades planned and its contribution was just over 20% of total profits.

Performance Summary

	All Trades	Long Trades	Short Trades
Net Profit	$522490	$304370	$349490
Gross Profit	$1536190	$671910	$943680
Gross Loss	($1013700)	($367540)	($594190)
Account Size Required	$170890	$70490	$154430
Return on Account	305.75%	431.79%	226.31%
Return on Initial Capital	522.49%	304.37%	349.49%
Profit Factor	1.52	1.83	1.59
Slippage Paid	$0	$0	$0
Commission Paid	$324060	$135600	$188460
Open Position P/L	($1530)	$0	($1500)
Max Portfolio Drawdown	($167270)		
Max Portfolio Drawdown (%)	(28.11%)		
Max Portfolio Close To Close Drawdown	($136540)		
Max Portfolio Close To Close Drawdown (%)	(23.9%)		
Return on Max Portfolio Drawdown	3.12		

FIGURE AII.5 Result of the portfolio of the two systems with a percent *f* model set at 5.24%.

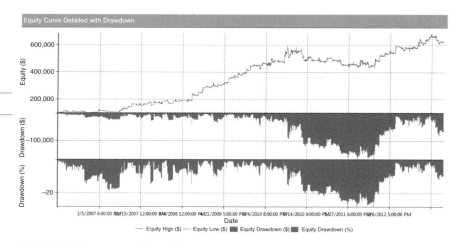

— Equity High ($) — Equity Low ($) ■ Equity Drawdown ($) ■ Equity Drawdown (%)

FIGURE AII.6 Equity line of the portfolio of the two systems with a percent *f* model set at 5.24%.

TABLE AII.1	Results of the two systems with a percent *f* model set at 5.24%.

	Net Profit	Number of Trades
System 1	399.85	196
System 2	122.64	266

Performance Summary			
	All Trades	Long Trades	Short Trades
Net Profit	$519490	$291610	$332250
Gross Profit	$1497720	$720860	$839930
Gross Loss	($978230)	($429250)	($507680)
Account Size Required	$140100	$81290	$113730
Return on Account	370.8%	358.73%	292.14%
Return on Initial Capital	519.49%	291.61%	332.25%
Profit Factor	1.53	1.68	1.65
Slippage Paid	$0	$0	$0
Commission Paid	$255105	$109500	$145605
Open Position P/L	($3315)	$0	($3240)
Max Portfolio Drawdown	($90075)		
Max Portfolio Drawdown (%)	(19.86%)		
Max Portfolio Close To Close Drawdown	($77750)		
Max Portfolio Close To Close Drawdown (%)	(15.82%)		
Return on Max Portfolio Drawdown	5.77		

FIGURE AII.7   Results of the portfolio with a 7% 'daily' risk.

If we want to compare the effect of each single system on the portfolio, we could consider the concept of max. loss in a different way and, in particular, not in terms of a single trade but a period of time.

For example, we might consider how much, in the available history, is the max. daily loss of each single system. The 'daily' reports can be found in the reports of each single system, and in these reports it's easy to see which was the worst day for the system.

The 'weight' of a single day makes sense, particularly if your trading results are measured on a daily basis. In this case, it's very important to parametrize everything for the effect of each single day. If weekly or monthly measurements are made, we can take these time slots as a sampling period.

Analyzing the performance report, we can see that system 1 had its worst day with a loss of –700 euros, while system 2 had its worst day with a loss of –3,310 euros. (These values cannot be deduced from the data reported in the book figures shown so far, and were obtained directly by the author from detailed trading system reports.)

In order to know whether the data will be useful to create a somewhat better scenario, it's necessary to push the risk per single day toward values that are able to produce similar results to the best case yet in terms of net profit. In particular, trading with a 7% risk produces the results in Figures AII.7 and AII.8.

A comparison of the percentage drawdown values of the two approaches clearly shows the improvement obtained when taking the worst day as the parameter of reference as far as risk is concerned. Also, a simple glance at the two equity lines confirms the better trend of the one in Figure AII.8.

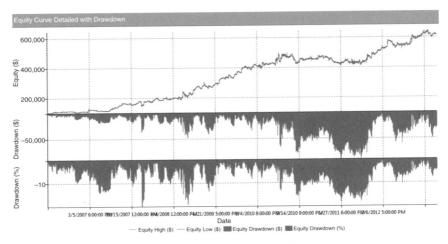

FIGURE AII.8 Equity line of the portfolio with a 7% 'daily' risk.

In both cases, the levels used for the risk percentages are obviously merely indicative and only useful for the purpose of this mathematical exercise. Trading with levels over 5% for each single loss or 7% for each single day is, without a doubt, an ill-advised approach. Although the drawdown levels shown in this analysis might be considered tolerable by many readers, risk levels of this type represent a real hazard for potential future scenarios.

It becomes more logical to accept higher risk percentages if we analyze the max loss over a longer period of time. Therefore, we'll run a monthly analysis, and for strategy 1 this will show a max. loss of 880 euros, while for strategy 2 the max. monthly loss is 5,500 euros. (N.B.: The max. losses can be found in the detailed trading system reports of each single contract.)

Therefore, applying a max. monthly loss limit produces results similar to those in Figures AII.5 and AII.7. Trading with a 10% risk percentage, in Figures AII.9 and AII.10, produces the results shown.

Once again, the results based on time slots show more acceptable drawdown levels, and a more regular equity line trend than those based on single trade max. system losses.

In this case, there would be a scenario that could also be used, as a 10% per month risk might be considered acceptable, and in any case, it's definitely more logical than 7% per day or 5.24% per single trade.

Lastly, we should also give due consideration to the type of strategies. The first is an intraday strategy and it could be a good idea to measure the monthly

Performance Summary

	All Trades	Long Trades	Short Trades
Net Profit	$531120	$302670	$347160
Gross Profit	$1550230	$727320	$894570
Gross Loss	($1019110)	($424650)	($547410)
Account Size Required	$154650	$82150	$129120
Return on Account	343.43%	368.44%	268.87%
Return on Initial Capital	531.12%	302.67%	347.16%
Profit Factor	1.52	1.71	1.63
Slippage Paid	$0	$0	$0
Commission Paid	$283515	$120690	$162825
Open Position P/L	($2805)	$0	($2745)
Max Portfolio Drawdown	($114945)		
Max Portfolio Drawdown (%)	(21.36%)		
Max Portfolio Close To Close Drawdown	($96140)		
Max Portfolio Close To Close Drawdown (%)	(18.43%)		
Return on Max Portfolio Drawdown	4.62		

FIGURE AII.9   Performance report of the portfolio with a 10% 'monthly' risk.

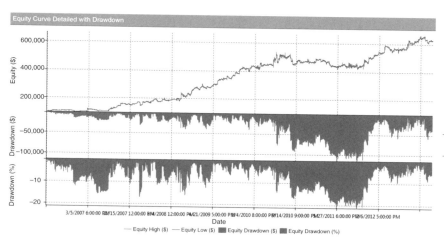

FIGURE AII.10   Equity line of the portfolio with a 10% 'monthly' risk.

performance, as this 'averages' out the daily results over a more reliable period of time. The second strategy however is always in the market; the positions are simply reversed with opposing entry points. Risk on a monthly basis can certainly make sense, but it has less impact compared to what each individual position could consistently have on the equity line. As mentioned in the previous chapters, one way to measure the effect of system positions on equity is to size exposure using the percent volatility method.

Therefore, we'll consider the case in which the first strategy is weighed on a monthly basis (as in the previous example) with a 10% risk (which we found reasonable), while the second strategy is applied counting the contracts in

Performance Summary			
	All Trades	Long Trades	Short Trades
Net Profit	$555470	$347350	$336100
Gross Profit	$1695630	$856710	$916830
Gross Loss	($1140160)	($509360)	($580730)
Account Size Required	$172530	$105570	$130410
Return on Account	321.96%	329.02%	257.73%
Return on Initial Capital	555.47%	347.35%	336.1%
Profit Factor	1.49	1.68	1.58
Slippage Paid	$0	$0	$0
Commission Paid	$300900	$131250	$169650
Open Position P/L	($7650)	$0	($7305)
Max Portfolio Drawdown	($109955)		
Max Portfolio Drawdown (%)	(21.26%)		
Max Portfolio Close To Close Drawdown	($93840)		
Max Portfolio Close To Close Drawdown (%)	(18.54%)		
Return on Max Portfolio Drawdown	5.05		

FIGURE AII.11 Results of a mixed approach based on types of strategy.

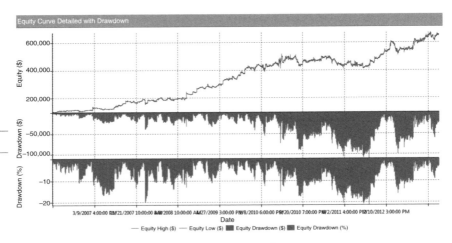

FIGURE AII.12 Equity line with a mixed approach.

order to prevent the equity line fluctuating by more than 0.125% per day (the average range of potential fluctuation was calculated as the average true range for the last five days), and 0.125% was chosen as it's the value that produces results similar to those in the previous examples.

Figures AII.11 and AII.12 show the results of this approach.

As can be seen, for the same drawdown, the latter approach produces slightly better results, which confirms its validity.

If we wish to further refine this, we could use a 9% monthly risk for the first strategy and a percent volatility of 0.15% per day for the second on the average true range in five days. This approach would bring net profit to just over 600,000 euros with an increase in max. drawdown with the open position of around 25%. This however is an exercise for optimising past trades, which doesn't leave a great deal of opportunity for similar improvement in real-time future trades.

What we wished to illustrate in this appendix is how important it is to consider also a model that produces the best possible contribution to the basket from each single strategy. The example shown is limited to the combination of two strategies only to show the different results. If we apply this logic to a more numerous group of systems, there would be concrete benefit in terms of final results.

■ III.1 The Advantages of Forex

Today the online trading market is literally teeming with all kinds of ads promoting Forex trading.

Unfortunately, most of these ads give people the idea that there's some sort of 'wonderland' where you can get rich quick, often after simply reading a few explanatory notes on how the market in question works. In many years of trading, one thing I've learned is that nothing comes easy in trading, and if people approach this profession with the idea of getting rich their results will often be a letdown, if not totally disastrous.

Often in this book I've emphasised the importance of limiting losses and conserving capital, and profits will be an almost natural consequence of a job well done.

But I don't want to demonize Forex because, if used with due caution, it can also offer some considerable advantages.

Strictly in terms of trading, it's undeniable that the variety of the offer on the Forex market means notable diversification, not only in terms of instruments but also in terms of actual approaches. Various currency pairs are well-suited to trend trading, while others tend to revert to the mean value, which makes opening countertrend positions preferable. It's important to note that while trend positions could in theory have an infinite duration (once a trend has started it could, at least in theory, last forever), it doesn't make sense to consider countertrend positions the same way, because if a position opened in countertrend was intended to last for too long, it would by definition become a trend position, as the market would be moving in a new direction.

The concept of countertrend in this case denotes finding the mean value of the prices and the departure from that mean. The trader will attempt to enter the market when the price moves away from the average established, expecting it will return to the same. This, to a certain extent, is the same as following an uptrend, buying as the trend falls towards the low retracement line and selling as it nears the high part of the channel (or selling short).

To end this brief digression, we could recap by saying that trend trading provides for breakout entry points with stop orders, while countertrend trading attempts to enter the market with limit orders placed on retracements. EUR/USD, GBP/USD, and EUR/JPY are usually valid trend trading currency pairs, while USD/JPY, GBP/CAD, and EUR/NZD are better suited to countertrend trading to name but a few, without wishing to influence the reader's trading, but, rather, simply summing up the author's experience in terms of the studies conducted so far.

Setting aside the advantages associated with diversification, let's look at the advantages strictly in terms of the subject of this book, money management.

In the previous pages, we described the effects of applying a position-sizing algorithm to various strategies, and it's evident that this can emphasize the effects of a winning strategy considerably.

I must once again underline, to avoid any misunderstandings, that money management will not turn an approach that's basically a loser into a winner. To trade on the markets, you need winning strategies, and a suitable money management algorithm can maximize the benefits. A losing strategy will remain such, with the exception of some isolated cases.

Whatever the model applied, the basic principle is to scale the position on the basis of the level of capital reached. As already mentioned, the number of trades helps make position sizing more effective, as one can act more frequently and therefore follow the evolution of the capital 'from closer at hand.'

Let's suppose we're trading EuroFX futures; obviously changing exposure means a move of one contract at a time, and for every new contract we add (or subtract) we should wait for the relevant change in terms of capital.

Perhaps, the change from the first contract to the second and then the third will take quite a long time as it may be necessary to accumulate a considerable amount of revenue. Before adding the second contract, all the trades will be made using the same 'multiplier' equal in fact to 1, as only 1 contract can be used. So, let's suppose we're using a winning strategy. The effect of the trades between one step and the next will therefore be limited in terms of the possibility to be amplified as this is linked to the step-by-step increment to which market exposure is subject. This is the same practical obstacle that emphasised the purely theoretical aspects of optimal f calculated in a continuous environment in which we were able to use infinitesimal fractions of a contract, while in reality obviously this cannot be done.

Now considering the Forex market, we have to be aware that one EuroFX futures contract is the equivalent, in dollar move terms, to an exposure of 125,000 USD in EURUSD. This amount doesn't correspond to the standard lot, which is €100,000, but it can in any case be used due to the fact that most brokers offer the option of trading not only with standard lots but also with mini lots (€10,000) or micro lots (€1,000).

At this point, it's evident that, whereas before we had to wait for a certain increment in order to add a new futures' contract, in this case we can use a variety of intermediate lots to follow the equity trend much more closely.

To better analyze this characteristic, a series of random trades on Excel has been created, corresponding to a hypothetical series of results for a EuroFX futures trading system. The equivalent result on Forex was then calculated, in the hypothesis of trading with one standard lot (for example, a result of 250 USD in the first case would produce 200 USD in the second, while 150 USD in futures would be the equivalent of 120 USD in Forex).

This series was used as a reference to which a position sizing algorithm was applied, in particular percent f model set at 0.5% on an initial capital of 100,000 USD. If we make a hypothesis of various possibilities in terms of scalability of the lots in Figure AIII.1 we can compare the final results after 100 trades depending on whether we want to trade EuroFX futures with standard lots of €100,000, mini lots of €10,000 or even micro lots of €1,000.

It's immediately clear that even using €100,000 lots produces advantages over futures' contracts (which would be the equivalent of a €125,000 Forex exposure). The real game-changer, though, is the possibility of scaling the positions in multiples of €10,000, and there's another minor improvement if micro lots are used.

The action described in this appendix is very similar to what we said about the number of trades, which explained how money management models

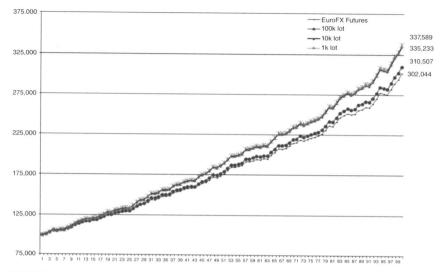

FIGURE AIII.1 Numerical results of the application of the same position sizing model to different trading scenarios in terms of lots.

become more effective the greater the number of changes made to the number of contracts. Also in this case, using smaller lots is the same as making a greater number of changes. In fact, you don't change from 1 to 2 in 1 go, keeping the first contract going for many trades; rather, there's an almost-continuous change, trade after trade, made possible by the infinitesimal steps we can now have.

Considered in these terms, the Forex market is certainly interesting. An extremely dynamic management of the position maximizes the results of our efforts to apply an effective money management model. In this case, the Forex market is the market par excellence.

The same reasoning goes naturally also for CFDs, which, depending on the instrument they're replicating, offer various scalability options. It's advisable, when dealing with these instruments, to consider the impact of the spread in the calculations, as often it's significant (not by chance this is where the brokers offering the instrument make a profit) and this may have a huge effect on final results.

Online Trading

■ IV.1 The Trader

We've discussed the risks associated with trading, how to try to avoid the worst-case scenarios, and concentrated on various techniques that can be used to effectively size a position. All of the above are made up of a certain dose of science, while attempting to juggle the figures to avoid being overwhelmed.

But the risks don't end there. Learning the notions in this book isn't enough to trade lightheartedly on the markets; there are other perils to watch out for.

Figure AIV.1 shows an example of the risks in the trading world.

First and foremost, one might ask, what is trading really? Someone who's new to this world will often have the wrong idea after watching a film, reading an article, or perhaps end up falling prey to misleading advertising.

In terms of films, I must say the characters portrayed, while it's true they may certainly exist, are nothing like this trader or many others I know.

The greedy, unscrupulous banker, always wearing braces and chewing on a huge cigar, belongs to a different world than the reality we live in on a daily basis. Anyone who starts trading on the stock exchange with the idea of one day becoming that sort of character, perhaps looking for the same sort of power to wield, would do better to choose another career. They'd probably get as far as buying a pair of red braces to hold up their pants.

So, all intentions of becoming the next Gordon Gekko aside, the aspiring trader does, however, have to take moral scruples into account; some people might offer the reproach that traders don't actually produce anything, others might accuse them of exploiting the gullible. One might make the first

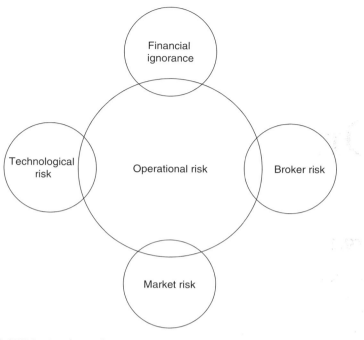

FIGURE AIV.1 Trading risks.

objection about many other professions too, but apart from this, it's just not true that traders are 'of no use' to society. A trader's role on the markets, as much as it may be just a drop in the ocean compared to the overall dimensions of the same, is still one piece of the puzzle, and if various pieces are lost, the puzzle will never be complete. No matter how small, an individual trader's contracts put on the market contribute to the market's liquidity. This brings us to the second objection. Speculation is seen as something bad, and it would be if the trader effectively manipulated the prices for personal gain, but what traders actually do is enter market movements, to become part of the same, and as a part of these movements they also limit the range due to the greater added weight, as a result making it more difficult for the market to be manipulated by anyone who might actually try to do so. Obviously, one trader's contribution is but a grain of sand, but a beach is formed of many grains of sand, and removing them one by one will eventually change that beach forever.

Liquidity is fundamental for a market and lies at its very heart. On commodities' markets it's essential to offer to those that produce physical goods, at a fair price, the opportunity to buy instruments to cover the risk. If the markets didn't offer a full range of said opportunities, it wouldn't be the trader who suffered, but the manufacturer first and foremost.

To put it simply, one might imagine the trader represents an obstacle to the buyer who wants to speculate on the price of soya, or the seller who wants to do so with gold futures.

These are perhaps somewhat extreme concepts, but they do represent the real situation. We shouldn't forget that those who criticize often do so out of envy rather than to be constructive towards society.

■ IV.2 Trading Profits

This might be a sore point for some; unfortunately, trading for 'the masses' is no longer driven by the markets, it's driven by the trading market. This market has everything more or less anyone might need to start trading online.

One starts with education and then brokerage, and it's all absolutely legitimate. I opened the Unger Academy to pass on what I know about automatic trading. The problem is with the messages related to the services offered.

In order to tempt the interested party (or arouse their interest), most appeal to one of the most common traits found in humans: greed. Some also play on fear but, in general, this is less harmful; it can often produce results but it's not as effective as dangling the prospect of riches in front of someone's nose.

If you look at the ads for online trading, they all play on the concept of making money, and a lot of it! Most ads promise you'll earn mind-boggling figures with very little effort, very quickly, and above all with a ridiculously low capital.

Is it really possible? Yes it is, in the same way you can buy a lottery ticket, but if I told you to buy a lottery ticket because I once won the jackpot years ago, not many people would do so, would they? Obviously not, because it's perfectly obvious how improbable that win is, and that luck is the only real reason for such success. In trading, this doesn't happen. The world of trading has always appeared different, so people believe the dodges proposed by the cat and the fox, and throw themselves into the fray. I use that term because it's what most people do, but believe me when I say, at least if you've bought a lottery ticket you know how much you'll likely lose – the price of the ticket, no more.

The fairytale of the home trader who takes a break from his/her daily routine to grease the wheels of the trading account is nothing other than a fable. It's something that can't really exist, and it only does in the mind of people who want to keep believing in such fairytales.

Risk takes the stage, disguised as an opportunity; but it's a false opportunity because all it does is eliminate some unfortunate person who dabbled in trading blinded by a mirage called get-rich-quick. This person will never be a trader: first and foremost because they'll lose everything, but also because at the end of the day, they're not that interested anyway.

In the book there have also been cases of interesting performance, but always at considerable risk, and it's been said many times that these cases shouldn't be taken as examples of profit but only as far as the technicalities of money management are concerned. This is because any example made obviously refers to the past, and strategies that worked in the past may no longer work in the future, or in any case may no longer work sufficiently well to meet the requirements of a certain position sizing algorithm. We've seen how money management can also amplify the negative phases, and it's easy to imagine where that might lead.

So is it impossible to make money on the stock exchange? I wouldn't say that. I would dampen overenthusiasm that comes from believing in foolish advertising, but with serious hard work you can get a considerable amount of satisfaction from trading, and this is the sore point, serious hard work. In other words, you can't all of a sudden become a trader. You need more than the eager trader's manual on how to make money, you need to study with dedication and perseverance.

Then what? When will you get good at trading? I can't provide certain figures but, based on my experience over the years in direct contact with other 'real' professionals in the sector, I'd say a good trader using a trust-worthy trading system infrastructure could make something like 30% per year, and I'm talking about home traders, not the Goldman Sachs broker where the masses can represent a further obstacle.

Not much? Too much? My vote goes for the second, although many might think it's not much at all. For that matter, if we consider different initial capi-talisation situations, it's obvious you won't get rich from one day to the next.

In reality, the profits mentioned can't be considered a negligible per-formance and remain valid for a good trader. What's more, this kind of performance can be obtained with a moderate risk: in other words, not a percent f model set at 5%, but much less. Of course, everyone is free to choose their own exposure and raise that number as high as they want; but the risks increase greatly and often this leads to trouble and nothing else.

I also mentioned trading systems, yes, I'm a systematic trader. Here at the Unger Academy I teach people how to build trading systems, but in the book there's also an example of discretionary trading. So, do I know about that, too? Personally, I wouldn't say I'm great at discretionary trading. I would say, though, that if we compared the best systematic trader in the world with the best discretionary trader in the world, the second would come out on top. So why am I a systematic trader? Simply because I don't think I'll ever be the best discretionary trader in the world, or even come close, but I do know how to build trading systems.

■ IV.3 Systematic or Discretionary?

At this point, now that I've said I prefer systematic trading, it's only right I offer an explanation.

I prefer systematic trading first and foremost because it's repeatable and measurable; there are no hypotheses that aren't corroborated by figures. Once a trading system has been built, that's it, and there's no room to accuse the user of psychological failings or anything else when accumulated losses have him/her cornered. Discretionary trading is in reality too simple a field for real course crooks to be a big success. These people are often very good at using psychological tricks to play the student on the hook, and convince him/her the losses are caused by the approach adopted, and not by the self-proclaimed guru's teachings. It goes without saying that these 'gurus' never take the trouble to prove the worth of their techniques on the actual market.

I'm not saying this for the purpose of controversy, but simply to warn novices against this type of risk, which is treacherous to say the least.

I certainly don't want to insinuate that all those who teach discretionary trading are crooks; on the contrary, I know a few who are really good traders. What I can say though with conviction, is that while systematic trading, consisting of rules, can be taught, this isn't always true for discretionary techniques, which involve a human component that can't always be passed on to others.

Remaining within the scope of money management, you'll have seen how many simulations were run and how many calculations done to evaluate the various techniques. This was possible because we had the figures for the approaches in question. We would never have been able to make particularly detailed plans based on discretionary rules without a track record to give us at least an idea of how advantageous said technique was.

Systematic trading also gives the trader greater freedom. The fact that most systematic traders remain glued to the monitor studying charts of external data flows and develop systems put on the market in real time is another question; one should be able to dedicate one's time to something else once the systems are validated for use, simply guaranteeing valid supervision to make sure everything is functioning as it should. With discretionary trading, this is often impossible.

Creating a technologically valid infrastructure involves those technological risks shown in Figure AIV.1. If you don't have the right software or a computer that's up to the job, you run the risk of an unexpected interruption in trading which, in general, means unwelcome losses (imagine a missed stop-loss or reverse orders not executed on the market in highly volatile conditions).

■ IV.4 Choosing the Broker

When talking of risks, one must of course include the broker. It's not really a question of the risk the broker could go bankrupt and our accounts end up empty, although this can happen and sometimes can't really be avoided (it happened to me with PFGBest). It's more a question of staying away from real crooks who, enticing clients with extremely interesting conditions, end up draining the financial resources of the victim like a disease drains your energy.

Often, there'll be a consultant who tells you which trades to make, encouraging you to go too far in terms of exposure. Sometimes things will work out (purely by chance), but more often than not, things go from bad to worse. At this point, the consultant suggests (or openly asks) you to pay more money into your account to either make up for losses or unblock positions in difficulty. This continues until the client gives up (usually after heavy losses) or, if the client wants to close the account after making a profit, the consultant miraculously disappears, and this person who previously wouldn't leave you alone suddenly won't even answer your messages!

These swindles are set up by various brokers based abroad, and it's all but impossible to bring them to justice, so these organisations con people without really risking a great deal; once again, though, everything is based on exploiting greed or the belief you can make cash quick.

When you choose a broker, you will have usually already chosen which market you want to trade on. Many brokers only offer their services on OTC (over the counter) markets like Forex and CFDs in general. These aren't regulated markets though, and this can mean additional risks. I'm not saying you need to be particularly worried about them, but there may be a catch. In January 2015, the sudden movement, after the decision taken by the Swiss National Bank to remove its 1.20 CAP on the euro, caused quite a few problems also in relation to the possibility of brokers 'adjusting' contract prices. It wasn't exactly an illegal decision but, in some cases, was clearly not advantageous for traders.

Apart from this case, it's important to remember that many brokers also act as market makers with these instrument, so traders fight both against market movements and against the brokers. Once again, while I certainly don't want to insinuate that brokers are dishonest, it's evident that one can in some ways be considered to be at a disadvantage.

■ IV.5 Which Platform?

Which platform to use to build your trading systems (if this is the route you're taking) is important, both in terms of technological evaluation and the choice of the broker.

Without a doubt, the most widely used software is MetaTrader, which is extremely popular thanks to the fact that it's offered for free by almost all brokers you can trade Forex and CFDs through.

Opening an account with one of these brokers will give you immediate access to the platform where you can program your own systems. The broker also provides you with the real-time data flow to trade with. While all this might seem wonderful, it's important to stress there are some obstacles. The first is the programming language used in MT4 (the most widely used MetaTrader version), which can be confusing at first and isn't exactly easy to use. The other obstacle is that the available historical data are often too limited to check the validity of the system developed on the basis of past data.

While you can solve the first problem by taking a specific MQL course (which, however, still isn't that easy to pick up quickly), the historical data problem is slightly more complex. Online you can also find free databases, but they're not that easy to import and, if you do manage to do so, this data isn't the same as that of the broker. As these are OTC markets, the prices may change from one broker to the next – not by much, obviously, but what might work with one broker may not produce results with another.

If you decide to trade in futures (or on the stock exchange), you'll need another type of software such as MultiCharts or TradeStation, NinjaTrader, ProRealTime, AmiBroker, and others.

MultiCharts uses practically the same programming language as TradeStation (called PowerLanguage on MultiCharts and EasyLanguage on TradeStation), and it's quite easy to learn, but the data must be acquired from external suppliers, which means additional costs. The platform itself isn't the cheapest, but does offer a 30-day free trial. TradeStation is also a broker and, depending on the offer, may be advantageous to minimize costs in the case of a certain amount of trading costs per month with the platform. In any case, opening an account with a minimum capital of a few thousand euros may be the best solution for those who want to start investing just a small amount.

The same can be said for NinjaTrader, which is programmed using C#, a real programming language, and this can represent a significant obstacle.

ProRealTime offers various advantages such as simple language (similar to that used in MultiCharts) but also has various limits both in terms of the complexity of the systems that can be programmed and in terms of the available data limited to what's supplied (intraday for a fee) that can't be edited – for example, importing ASCII data (not supported).

AmiBroker is very versatile but limited to real time, and the initial learning curve can be steep.

Finally, I'd like to emphasise that you can become a trader, but it should never be considered a way out of a difficult economic situation. Trading isn't a solution for just about anyone who's unemployed, or a cure-all for all the economic problems a big family might run into. It's a good idea to bear this in mind to avoid turning your dream into a nightmare. Trading is a very demanding profession, which can be learned with study and self-sacrifice just like any other. No one would dream of opening a dental studio without knowing the first thing about it, just because dentists earn a lot, but many new traders approach trading with this idea.

losses, 61
money management study, 246
order, change, 116t
parametrization, 60
percentage drawdown trend,
fixed ratio method (usage),
148f
performance summary, 36f
profits trend, risk (impact),
149f
risk percentage, 75f
sequence, Monte Carlo
simulation, 115t
stake, establishment, 1–2
stop-loss, triggering (absence),
38f, 50, 52
theoretical trades, consideration,
250
usage, cessation, 250
volatility, adjustment, 225–228
TradeStation strategy
equity curve, 39f
performance, contract/Kelly
formula (contrast), 40, 41f
trades, example, 38f
TradeStation strategy performance
report
annual strategy results, 37f
strategy report, 36f
Trade Your Way to Financial Freedom
(Tharp), 82
Trading
5% risk strategy, 247
aggressive trading
strategy, 247
cessation, 70–71, 106, 109
continuation, minimum risk
percentage (usage), 78f

criteria/definition, 215–218
discretionary trading, 215
equity curve trading, 103–110
foreign exchange (Forex) trading,
advantages, 278–281
futures, trading, 228–244
impact, 154f–155f. *See also*
Constant monthly income.
online trading, 282
platform, selection, 288–289
preference, 286–287
profits, 284–286
risks, 283f
scenarios, position sizing model
(application results), 281f
steps, selection/results, 95t, 96f,
97t
techniques, refinement, 94
Trading Game, The (Jones), 68
Trading system, 33, 252–267, 286
analysis, moving average basis,
33–35
combination, usage, 157–168
dynamics, example, 34f
EasyLanguage code, 35, 254f
impact, 252
improvements, 208–214
Kelly formula, application,
37–52
strategy report, 36f
True range. *See* Average true range
usage, 199–200

V
Van Tharp, K., 82, 101, 170
Vince, Ralph, 60–61, 66
Volatility
adjustment, 225–228

Volatility *(Continued)*
 allowed volatility, usage, 88f
 limitation, results, 84f, 85f
 market volatility, decrease, 84
 maximum allowed percent
  volatility, change, 90f
 percent, impact, 165f
 period volatility, 82

W

Williams, Larry, 60, 66–67, 249
Win/loss alternation, 111

Winning, probability, 22–24, 27,
 29, 37
Work plan, 141
 method, contrasts, 251
 usage, 141–155
Worst-case scenario (WCS),
 61–63

Z

z-score (trade dependence),
 110–112, 144
 usage, 250